Dog Behavior and Training

Veterinary Advice for Owners

Compiled by Lowell Ackerman, DVM
Edited by Lowell Ackerman, DVM
Gary Landsberg, DVM
Wayne Hunthausen, DVM

TS-252

Overleaf: Dogs communicate with one another using their own language, as illustrated by this beautiful Boxer mama giving her young one a lesson in life. Photo courtesy of Jacquet Boxers by Isabelle Francais.

Distributed in the UNITED STATES to the Pet Trade by T.F.H. Publications, Inc., One T.F.H. Plaza, Neptune City, NJ 07753; distributed in the UNITED STATES to the Bookstore and Library Trade by National Book Network, Inc. 4720 Boston Way, Lanham MD 20706; in CANADA to the Pet Trade by H & L Pet Supplies Inc., 27 Kingston Crescent, Kitchener, Ontario N2B 2T6; Rolf C. Hagen Ltd., 3225 Sartelon Street, Montreal 382 Quebec; in CANADA to the Book Trade by Vanwell Publishing Ltd., 1 Northrup Crescent, St. Catharines, Ontario L2M 6P5 ; in ENGLAND by T.F.H. Publications, PO Box 15, Waterlooville PO7 6BQ; in AUSTRALIA AND THE SOUTH PACIFIC by T.F.H. (Australia), Pty. Ltd., Box 149, Brookvale 2100 N.S.W., Australia; in NEW ZEALAND by Brooklands Aquarium Ltd. 5 McGiven Drive, New Plymouth, RD1 New Zealand; in Japan by T.F.H. Publications, Japan—Jiro Tsuda, 10-12-3 Ohjidai, Sakura, Chiba 285, Japan; in SOUTH AFRICA by Lopis (Pty) Ltd., P.O. Box 39127, Booysens, 2016, Johannesburg, South Africa. Published by T.F.H. Publications, Inc.

MANUFACTURED IN THE UNITED STATES OF AMERICA
BY T.F.H. PUBLICATIONS, INC.

Contents

Many small breeds are naturally inclined to stand on their hind feet. The West Highland White Terrier, like most other terrier breeds, has great poise and balance. Photograph by Isabelle Francais.

About the Editors

Dr. Lowell Ackerman is a Diplomate of the American College of Veterinary Dermatology and a consultant in the fields of dermatology, nutrition and medicine. He is the author of 13 books and over 150 articles and book chapters dealing with pet health care and is the co-author of a veterinary textbook dealing with pet behavior problems. In addition, he has lectured extensively on these subjects on an international basis. Dr. Ackerman is a member of the American Veterinary Society of Animal Behavior.

Dr. Wayne Hunthausen is a pet behavior therapist who works with people, their pets and veterinarians throughout North America to help solve pet behavior problems. He writes for a variety of veterinary and pet publications and is co-author of two textbooks dealing with pet behavior. Dr. Hunthausen frequently lectures on pet behavior and currently serves on the behavior advisory board for several scientific journals. He is currently president of the American Veterinary Society of Animal Behavior.

Dr. Gary Landsberg is a companion-animal veterinarian at the Doncaster Animal Clinic in Thornhill, Ontario, Canada. He is also extremely active in the field of pet behavior and offers a referral consulting service for pets with behavior problems. He is the co-author of two veterinary textbooks dealing with pet behavior problems. Dr. Landsberg has lectured throughout North America and Europe and is the past president of the American Veterinary Society of Animal Behavior.

German Shepherd puppies at five weeks old just beginning to get acquainted with their young human companion. Photograph by Judith E. Strom.

Preface

Behavioral problems are the number-one killer of pets in the U.S. This might seem surprising. Surely behavioral problems can't be the number one killer of pets. It must be car accidents, or perhaps cancer. The sad truth is that as many as eight million pets are euthanized (killed) each year because of behavior problems. Veterinarians spend about 20% of their time discussing behavior concerns with clients. Between 50% and 70% of animals in shelters are there because their owners either couldn't or wouldn't deal with their behavior problems. If these behavior problems were caused by a virus, we would consider it an epidemic. Make no mistake about it—unacceptable behavior, not disease, is the number one killer of pets in this country.

What can we do about it? Knowledge is the key! Sound, timely and practical information is the best defense. Proper socialization and training are the best ways to prevent problems from occurring. Early intervention with behavior counseling results in fewer problems that progress to a point where the animal is abandoned or destroyed. This book bridges the gap between understanding the causes of behavior problems, preventing them, and managing them once they're evident. This information is relayed by some of the pre-eminent experts in this relatively new field.

Only a veterinarian is trained and legally permitted to diagnose and treat medical problems. Thus, the veterinarian is the first person to be consulted with a behavior problem. Before any condition is dismissed as a "training failure," it is critical to determine that there is not a medical reason for the problem. In addition, some problems are more amenable to pharmacological or surgical treatment than to behavioral modification and training. Should your veterinarian feel that a referral to a veterinary specialist or other behavior counselor is warranted, he or she can refer you to the most appropriate person in your area for your pet's problem. Listed in the following directory are some of the professional organizations that are involved in the training and advancement of this growing field.

As our knowledge of animal behavior grows, so does the way we train and shape our pet's behavior. Physical discipline and harsh punishment are seldom indicated and not only are inhumane but can lead to excessive fear and anxiety. Reward, motivational training, behavior modification techniques and a firm but fair approach to discipline are the order of the day.

This book provides a wealth of information for the pet-loving public. Written entirely by veterinarians, it provides insight into the effectiveness of various treatments for the most common behavioral problems and how those problems are best prevented.

Lowell Ackerman, DVM, PhD
Gary Landsberg, BSc, DVM
Wayne Hunthausen, DVM

The basics of training and behavior most often begin with SIT, as demonstrated by this handsome growing Boxer puppy. Photograph courtesy of Jacquet Boxers by Isabelle Francais.

International Directory of Behavior Organizations

American Veterinary Society of Animal Behavior
c/o Secretary-Treasurer
Dr. Debra Horwitz
Veterinary Behavior Consultations
253 S. Graeser Road,
St. Louis, MO 63141

American College of Veterinary Behaviorists
c/o Dr. Katherine Houpt, Secretary
Dept. Of Physiology
College of Veterinary Medicine
Cornell University
Ithaca, NY, 14853-6401

Companion Animal Behavior Therapy Study Group
Mr. D. Mills, Secretary
De Montford University, Lincoln
Caythorpe Court
Catythorpe
Nr Grantham, Lincs, NG32 3EP, UK

International Society for Animal Ethology
Dr. S.M. Rutter, ISAE Membership
Institue of Grassland and Environ-
mental Research
North Wyke, Okehampton, Devon,
EX20 2SB, UK

Animal Behavior Society
Dr. Janis Driscoll
Dept. Of Physiology,
Campus P.O. Box, 173364
Denver, CO, 80217-3364

European Society for Veterinary Clinical Ethology
Dr. J. Dehasse
129, Avenue de la Fauconnerie 92,
B-1170
Brussels, Belgium

Robert K. Anderson is a veterinarian who has nearly 70 years of experience in modifying the behavior of animals. He has been active in research, teaching and consulting for many years at the University of Minnesota and is Professor and Director Emeritus of the Animal Behavior Clinic for the College of Veterinary Medicine. He is also Professor and Director Emeritus of the Center to Study Human-Animal Relationships and Environments which offered the first college-level course in the nation for students to learn about relationships of animals and people. He is a Diplomate of the American College of Veterinary Behaviorists and the American College of Veterinary Preventive Medicine and has received many awards, such as the Veterinarian of the Year for the Minnesota Veterinary Medical Association and the Bustad Award as Companion Animal Veterinarian of the Year for the American Veterinary Medical Association. He now has a referral practice in Minneapolis/St. Paul, Minnesota and offers lectures and consulting services in the U.S. and other countries of the world.

Canine Development and Socialization

By Robert K. Anderson, DVM
Diplomate, American College of Veterinary Behaviorists
Professor and Director Emeritus, Center to Study Human-Animal Relationships, University of Minnesota

INTRODUCTION

Pam, Tim and the children were watching intently as their veterinarian conducted a health exam of their new puppy. As Dr. Chris finished the vaccinations, she turned to the daughter Jennifer and remarked, "This is a lovely little puppy and we are providing protection against diseases so you and your brother Gary can have a healthy dog to play with. In addition we want you as a family to learn how to care for and feed your puppy so he can grow into a strong healthy dog. And it is most important for you to learn how to manage natural behaviors of your puppy that may be unwanted and difficult for you to handle as a family.

"What do you mean, Doctor.", asked Pam, "I was told that we just need to love our puppy and he will become our best friend and companion."

"Not quite," said Dr. Chris, "we are now recognizing that love is great, but love is not enough. Just as we have learned that we need good nutrition and dental care, we have learned new things about managing the behavior of our puppies and dogs. In fact we offer a program here at this hospital for families with new puppies. We help children and adults understand the needs of their dogs for wellness programs. These needs include learning how to prevent behavior problems that may be more serious than disease."

"Wow", said the son Gary, "You mean barking, jumping and nipping can be that serious"? "Yes," said Dr. Chris, "it often is serious if we don't learn to manage and control behavior so people don't get hurt."

"Well," said the father, Tim, "give us the information on this new program, including the costs and the benefits, and we'll consider it." After consideration, the family decided to join the wellness program. The first thing offered was a seminar on puppy development and behavior. This was followed by four weeks of classes at the hospital to provide early learning experiences and socialize puppies, between eight and 12 weeks of age, to other puppies and to other families of children and adults.

Everyone in the family was delighted with the seminar. They became aware, for the first time, that dogs are really very much like their close relative, the wolf. But, of course, dogs are domesticated and have learned to coexist with people as companions and loyal workers/ guardians. Tim took his laptop computer to take notes during the seminar. The following paragraphs are excerpts from Tim's summaries, of many questions and answers, to help new owners understand and manage natural puppy behavior and increase the companionship and joy of having a dog.

QUESTIONS AND ANSWERS

What is the pattern of development of puppies for several weeks after birth?

From birth to about two weeks of age, puppies are pretty helpless with nearly all effort devoted to eating and sleeping. Their eyes and ears are not yet open and body temperature is maintained by the warmth of their mother, siblings and environment. This is often called the neonatal period. Even during this early period, careful handling by people will be beneficial to stimulate learning and development of the immune system.

The period from 14 to 21 days seems to be a transition period when pups begin to develop their motor skills as well as develop their vision and hearing. By about three weeks,

pups can respond with a startle reaction to a noise and many are able to drink milk. Their first teeth are just beginning to push through the gums, and in several weeks they can begin to eat solid food.

Why is understanding natural elimination behavior so important for housetraining?

During the first three weeks, puppies are unable to eliminate without help. Mother dog needs to lick the anogenital area of each puppy to stimulate elimination several times a day. When she licks the ano-genital area, she also ingests the puppies' feces and urine. This is a natural behavior that has the important function of keeping the nest clean until puppies can go outside the nest. By about three to four weeks of age, puppies begin to walk outside the whelping box and to eliminate away from their nest.

This desire to eliminate away from their sleeping place is a natural behavior that is very useful in housetraining. Using this natural behavior, puppies will quickly learn to eliminate away from their confinement area and can be taught to eliminate in one selected place as desired by the new owner. New owners need to understand the importance of using this natural behavior to quickly succeed with house-training by ten to 12 weeks of age.

How soon after birth can puppies learn?

Studies on many species of animals have shown that learning may occur in special ways very early in life during what some have called sensi-

Puppy talk. Photo by Anderson & Foster.

tive periods for learning. Some have compared the brain to a sponge that takes in and retains information quickly and easily in the first few hours to the first few weeks of life. Some animals, such as horses, that need to follow and recognize their mothers at a few hours after birth need to learn earlier than others who are sheltered the first several weeks of life.

When do puppies open their eyes and begin to hear well?

Because they are nearly help-less pups are sheltered during the first two weeks after birth. Vision and hearing don't develop until the third week of life. However, on the basis of scientific studies, it appears that a period for early learning and lifetime retention of early learning experiences does occur in puppies.

When is the most sensitive or optimum period of learning in puppies/dogs?

In puppies, it appears that the most sensitive period for early learn-ing occurs from three to 13 weeks of age. Since each individual is different, we often consider the sensitive period for early learning in puppies to range from the first day after birth to 16 weeks of age. Studies indicate that this is the best time for puppies to absorb information and learn from new experiences. It appears that these sensitive weeks are an optimum time for a puppy to become comfortable with exposure to all sizes and appearances of people, to other dogs and to many other sounds, sights and situations that may be encountered in later life without being fearful.

Why do breeders/new puppy owners need to understand the importance of early learning?

This period in the puppy's life becomes extremely important to a pup's development and is referred to as an optimum time for socialization. This means that the breeder during the first seven or eight weeks of life and the new owner after seven weeks have a joint responsibility for starting the pup off right in life with appropriate socialization experiences. If people care about a dog's development, they must take responsibility for exposing puppies to many experiences with people — children and adults. Puppies should become comfortable with people handling all parts of their body; should respond easily to control by people; should become comfortable interacting with other dogs, young and old; and should become comfortable with many sounds, sights and situations within and outside the home, in the yard and in the community. This learning is best during this sensitive early period of life from birth to 16 weeks of age.

Will socialization stimulate development of the brain and the immune system?

It has been suggested that the easiest way for a breeder to socialize puppies during the first seven weeks of life is to have the mother dog and her pups in the kitchen of the home with a family of several young children. The kitchen provides an environment for exposing the pups to many sounds, sights and situations they will encounter in later life. Careful handling each day, during the first several weeks, by children and adults in the family will expose the pups to handling and control by people as well as stimulate and improve the development of the brain and the immune system of the puppy.

How early do puppies show adult brain wave patterns by electroencephalograph?

An important reason for continuing socialization and early learning for puppies in their new homes is related to the development of a puppy's brain. Scientific, but non-invasive, EEG studies of the brains of puppies provide excellent evidence that puppies' brains develop so rapidly that they show mature adult brain wave patterns by the age of seven to eight weeks. This means that puppies' brains are ready by seven to eight weeks of age to learn control by people and socialization in the home as well as in socialization classes.

Good things coming! Photo by Anderson & Foster.

At what age should puppies start socialization classes?

To help people who purchase new puppies, experts recommend that veterinary clinics, dog trainers and animal shelters offer puppy socialization classes. Puppies should be enrolled in these classes at eight to nine weeks of age—after they have their first vaccination in the series of several vaccinations recommended by their veterinarian. These early learning experiences with people and other puppies, beginning at eight or nine weeks of age are more important to the life of the puppy than waiting until the whole series of vaccinations is completed. In our experience, the risk of behavior problems without early socialization is much greater than the risk of infection for an eight-week-old puppy that has had its first vaccination.

What is the best length of time for teaching/learning sessions for a dog's brain?

Not only do dogs learn best in the first weeks of life, but scientific evidence is available to show that dogs learn best in short two-minute teaching/learning sessions. Experiments show that dogs learn more and retain more in ten sessions of two minutes than in one session of twenty minutes. This means that dogs can learn easily to obey and please people using short two-minute training sessions in their own home. No need to have practice sessions of 15 to 30 minutes or longer. Puppies can be taught in short two-minute sessions, ten or more times a day, for effective learning.

Where — in what place —do puppies learn to obey best?

Puppies learn to obey best in locations where they are taught. Think about it. For years people have observed that dogs may obey very well in a training ring, but respond less well at home. So, if we want puppies to respond eagerly and obey wherever we are, we must teach puppies in every room in the house, in the yard, in the car, on walks and in any place we wish our dog to respond quickly to our requests. This place and situation training becomes easy if we practice in one to two minute sessions 10 to 20 times a day.

Who should teach the new puppy — mother or dad or the children?

Behavior is related or associated, in the puppy's brain, with the person or persons who teach and assume leadership. We all know families where the dog may obey mother or father best but does not obey well for the rest of the family. If we want the puppy to respond quickly to obey all persons in the family, then the puppy must receive instruction from all persons in the family over three years of age — children, teens, women and men. This encourages age, gender and size equality for leadership of people in the eyes of the puppy.

When — what time of day and how often during the day —should we teach the puppy?

We should teach at one or more unpredictable intervals during each hour when people are home — short

Keeping cool. Photo by Michelle Mero Riedel.

one to two minute sessions from time of waking in the morning to time of going to bed at night. Don't follow a schedule, just be unpredictable in asking puppy to respond in short one to two-minute sessions. This teaches puppy to be eager to respond at any time, any place. Too often we practice 30 minutes each day at a scheduled time. And puppies soon learn to obey quickly, only at the scheduled time of day during the formal training session. Instead of once a day, we want a puppy to learn to respond quickly and eagerly any time and any place — so we must teach at different unpredictable times of day and in many places.

Why do puppies need leadership and a strong pecking order (hierarchy) to live peacefully in a dog pack or as part of a family pack.

Puppies' brains and behavior develop in accord with survival skills. These patterns of behavior are very different from humans just as their physiology and anatomy are different. For example dogs in nature live in a pack and have a strong pecking order (hierarchy). Puppies may begin to growl at other puppies as early as three weeks of age if given a bone. They may also begin play fighting at three to four weeks of age to test other puppies and establish a pecking order in the litter.

Do dogs recognize or use human concepts of equality, fairness or sharing?

A puppy's genetic and species behavior does not include any human concept of fairness or equality. There is no equality and no fairness in "dogdom." We often want our dogs to be equal and we try to treat them with fairness. But this is contrary to the inherent behavior patterns in a puppy's brain. Puppies begin to play fight during the third and fourth weeks of life to establish a ranking within the litter.

This genetic behavior to establish a pecking order continues when puppies are taken from the litter and brought to a new home. Two dogs in a household cannot live together peacefully and comfortably until they have established a pecking order. Pecking orders often change when a new dog is introduced into the home or as a top dog's age or strength changes in relation to the other dog in the household.

How do puppies try to control their owners and become "top dog" in a family — at least part time?

When puppies are brought to a new home, they continue to use all their skills to be a leader in the family and get what they want when they want it. Puppies do this by jumping, play nipping, barking, growling, crying out as if in pain to avoid control, and demanding attention from people when and where the puppy wants it.

Most families change their lifestyle to accommodate and please the new puppy. As the puppy grows older, it continues to learn how to avoid people control and to please people only when the puppy wants to please. And this means puppy obeys quickly, only about 50-70 percent of the time. This lack of control and

Three in a basket. Photo by Michelle Mero Riedel.

leadership by the family can lead to unwanted behaviors and increasing frustration/anger by family members. Unfortunately this may also lead to the dog's being removed from the household.

What is the role and importance of eye contact for leadership by people?

Eyes of a puppy are closed at birth and they open at two to three weeks of age with individual and breed variations. Vision appears to be rather fully developed by four to five weeks of age. Canine eyes and vision are not the same as with people. Canine eyes have a greater range of sight from side to side, about 250 degrees. They also have more rods than cones in the eye. Cones are more suited to register fine detail from shorter distance. Rods increase the ability of the dog as a hunter/predator to see greater distances and detect movement of prey.

Eyes are also important in conveying signals and messages between puppies or between puppies and people. When two puppies approach each other in the park, they usually stare at each other to see which dog will move its eyes (blink) first. Moving the eyes is a very powerful signal that one puppy is willing to act in a subordinate manner in this relationship and accept the other dog as its leader. This important signal is so subtle that most people are not aware of what has happened.

Most people do not understand that staring into the eyes of a puppy/dog is a challenge to the dog and may trigger aggressive actions. People should avoid eye contact with strange puppies/dogs to reduce risk of threat and confrontation, unless the person is prepared to assert leadership and dominance. On the other hand, people must never let their own dog outstare them. Whenever people have eye contact with their own puppy, the dog must move its eyes first to signal that the puppy is accepting the leadership/dominance of the person — child or adult. This powerful form of communication through eye contact with your puppy should start at four to seven weeks of age and continue throughout the life of the dog. All members of the family must use this body language since the puppy should accept all people in the family, including children, as leaders for the dog.

How does "position" reinforce leadership of people over puppies/dogs?

Puppies' brains are programmed to require a pecking order. Although they are very comfortable with a strong leader, but they often challenge other dogs and people to be sure the leader is still a strong leader. Leaders reinforce their dominance by eating first, by seeking the best resting places, and by leading the way. In a dogs mind leaders always go through outside doors first.

To emphasize leadership by people, we have puppies sit and wait while people go through outside doors ahead of the puppy. Why? Because when two dogs wish to go through a door, the leader dog goes through the door first.

This is one way to tell which puppy/dog is subordinate and which is the leader by observing this very natural behavior. Owners should start developing this powerful form of body language with their puppy at an early age of seven to eight weeks. Remember, in the brain of the puppy, leaders always go first through outside doorways.

Can I establish leadership by petting/stroking puppies over the head and neck?

In establishing dominance, many dogs will come together, sniff front, sniff rear and then one will try to put their head and neck at right angles over the neck and shoulder of the other to indicate dominance. Or one dog may mount from the front over the head or from the rear to get above a subordinate dog. Dominance and leadership are also expressed naturally by people with the body language of petting/stroking a puppy firmly over the head, neck and shoulders.

Puppies immediately recognize the dominance or the attempt at dominance of a person who strokes them slowly and firmly over the head, neck and shoulders. Puppies

Mother and puppies. Photo by Michelle Mero Riedel.

often calm down and become comfortable when owners exercise leadership by making eye contact, staring them down, and stroking the puppy over the head and neck. Conversely, puppies who do not want to be subordinate will try to outstare people and resist the hands of people who try to control by holding or by petting/stroking over the head and neck of the puppy/dog.

People who want to be leaders should always win. If puppy wins 10 to 30 percent of the time, he will try harder because he now knows if he is persistent, he will win, just as slot machine players are motivated to keep pulling the handle by intermittent winning at the slot machine. Note when a puppy wins part time it often thinks of the owner as an adversary to beat, just as gamblers think of beating the machine.

How do collars or headcollars and leashes reinforce leadership and control?

As stated throughout this program, people are urged to use motivation as the primary way to gain leadership and control of their puppy. But, most people need some method of humane restraint to provide control when a puppy wants to be the leader and tries to do unwanted behavior. That's why many veterinarians and obedience instructors recommend using a nylon buckle collar or a nylon headcollar plus outdoor and indoor leashes to provide back-up control and leadership for people. Most people are familiar with the usual buckle collar and an outdoor leash. The headcollar is similar to a halter worn by other domestic animals such as horses. Headcollars use a dog's natural instincts to respond to leadership and control of another dog.

When people desire control and pull on the leash, the headcollar prevents pulling ahead or forging when walking, assists pups to sit and stay, and stops or prevents unwanted barking, jumping and nipping/mouthing. The indoor lead is a ten-foot lead that puppy wears in the house (drags on floor) to give people a line to grab and control a puppy from 1 to 10 feet away. It is also useful, like an umbilical cord, to keep a puppy in view, when it is out of confinement during the housetraining program.

Why do puppies respond to leaders who speak softly and in a praising voice?

Puppies' ears are closed at birth and do not open until the transition period of development at two or three weeks of age. Then, hearing develops rapidly as the brain matures. By seven to eight weeks, puppies' hearing is many times better than the hearing of people. That's why we like to have dogs who will bark to alert us about strange noises before we hear them. Stop and think about other examples of their sensitivity to sound. Many owners claim that their dogs will show "alert be-havior" to the sound of the motor of the owner's car before it reaches the driveway of their house.

If we recognize the ability of our dogs to hear so well, why do we shout and yell at our dogs? Do we need to use a loud command voice to help our dogs hear? No! ! Puppies learn quickly to respond eagerly to the soft, praising voice of a child as well as the soft, praising voice of an adult.

If we want dogs to respond quickly to all members of a family, all members should speak to the dog in a soft, praising voice that telegraphs to the dog that good things will happen if you obey quickly. Speaking softly and in a praising tone also gives gender and age and size equality for people in the brain of the dog, when the adults, particularly males with deep voices, speak in the same soft, praising (higher tone) voice.

Why are puppies so easily motivated to obey with rewards?

Puppies'/dogs' brains are programmed to evaluate the benefits and the costs of nearly all behaviors. Even as puppies, dogs are cost/benefit analysts. They do only those things which are beneficial (pay off in their mind). They also evaluate each situation to choose the behavior that may be of greatest benefit (pay off best for the effort expended). For these reasons, dogs quickly learn how to manipulate people to gain rewards for both wanted and unwanted behaviors. For example, many dogs will resist coming when owners call until the reward for doing what the owner wants is greater than the reward for

Puppy love. Photo by Michelle Mero Riedel.

doing what the dog wants. To have a dog that is eager to please people, we need to understand how a dog responds to body language, to humane restraint and to rewards of petting, praise, affection and sometimes food, as people learn in the puppy socialization class.

What are some of the rewards that motivate puppies?

Each puppy may show individual differences in the degree of motivation to different rewards. For most dogs, the best reward is attention by people. Eye contact is often the most powerful reward, followed by verbal praise, petting and affection. However, they need to be hungry enough for attention so they will work diligently for the reward of attention.

Dogs quickly recognize that, as Dr. Voith has stated it, "nothing in life is free." Therefore, in teaching puppies, we can quickly motivate them by withholding attention and then have them earn their rewards of eye contact, praise, petting and affection by quickly and eagerly obeying the leaders.

Dogs who work very hard for negative attention such as scolding, yelling, etc., will stop the unwanted behavior temporarily, only to try again when they want more attention. And we reinforce this unwanted behavior with scolding only part of the time, which is even stronger reinforcement on the variable ratio schedule — the most powerful schedule of reinforcement.

Food is also an excellent reward for most puppies. Most owners have observed who eagerly some dogs will obey to receive rewards of treats or rewards of regular food if it is fed by hand as part of a scientific learning program using a variable ratio schedule.

Why is the scientific use of rewards so helpful in managing behaviors of puppies?

Appropriate use of rewards motivates a puppy to be eager to please children as well as adults and lets us use positive commands to substitute desired behavior in place of unwanted behaviors, and we have no need to use negatives or punishment. We can avoid saying "no" which is usually ineffective because the pup soon learns to use it to stimulate attention getting rewards. We can also stop scolding and yelling if the dog is motivated by positive reinforcement to obey quickly and eagerly with desired behavior for all members of the family, even children three years and over.

By appropriate and scientific use of rewards and conditioned stimuli, puppies can be motivated to please us from eight weeks of age until old age hinders their physical ability to respond. These eager-to-please responses enhance the joy and companionship of having a dog and provide mutual benefits for improving health and quality of life.

Why does early teaching and socialization benefit development for a lifetime?

When puppies learn to please people early in life, we provide a foundation for lifetime reinforcement of learning more easily and better than learning to please at a later age. This early bonding improves companionship, promotes interactions with other dogs and people, and prevents behavior problems that too often result in removal from the household and ultimate euthanasia of the dog. The greatest cause of death among dogs is euthanasia related to unwanted behavior.

Understanding the social and behavioral development of your puppy can help new owners prevent problem behavior. Learning is a life-long endeavor. And even though early learning is the best time for development and socialization, dogs continue to learn throughout their lifetime for as long as they continue to use their brain. "Use it or lose it"——just as we do with our muscles. Yes — old dogs, as well as puppies, can also learn new tricks.

ADDITIONAL READING

Anderson, R. K., and Foster, R. E. *Promise Behavior Management System for Dogs,* 1994, Alpha-M Inc. 511 Eleventh Ave. So., Minneapolis, MN 55415.

Anderson, R.K., B.L. Hart, L.A. Hart, *The Pet Connection, Its Influence on Our Health and Quality of Life,* 1984, Center to Study Human-Animal Relation-ships and Environments, University of Minnesota, Box 734 Mayo Bldg., 420 Delaware St. S.E., Minneapolis, MN 55455.

Dunbar, Ian, *Dr Dunbar's Good Little Dog Book,* 1992 James and Kenneth Publishers, 2140 Shattuck Ave., Berkeley, CA 94704.

Hthausen, Wayne; Landsberg, G: *A Practitioner's Guide to Pet Behavior Problems,* 1995, American Animal Hospital Association, Denver, CO.

Neville, Peter, *Do Dogs Need Shrinks, What to Do When Man's Best Friend Misbehaves,* 1992, Carol Publishing Group, New York, N.Y. 10022.

Young puppies benefit from regular interaction with people. Unsocialized puppies will do notably less well as family pets. If your young puppy shies away from people, shows signs of fear and anxiety, it likely has not been properly socialized by its breeder. Photograph by Judith E. Strom.

Dr. Avery Gillick received his undergraduate degree (B.Sc.) in psychology from McGill University and later his veterinary medical degree, Diploma in Medicine and Master's degree (M.Sc.) from the Ontario Veterinary College in Guelph, Canada. He served on the faculty of the Ontario Veterinary College as an assistant professor before entering private veterinary practice in the Toronto area. Dr. Gillick works at the Morningside Animal Clinic where, in addition to his other duties, he accepts referral cases in medicine.

The Role of Dogs in Society

By Avery Gillick, DVM
Morningside Animal Clinic
4560 Kingston Road
Scarborough, Ontario
M1E 2P2

INTRODUCTION

The relationship that man has had with the canine species is an ancient one that dates back to our earliest development. Although our ancestors and the canine may have, in some circumstances, been competing for the same shelters (e.g., caves) and food sources, they were not natural enemies. The wild dogs (e.g., wolf, fox, coyote) were most likely "camp followers" of early man. Possessing superior senses of smell and hearing, the canine could alert man both to approaching danger and the presence of game. The social order of these early ancestors to our pet dogs was based on a hierarchical pack behavior. Their unique traits made the dog easily tamed, domesticated and trainable.

As time passed the canine moved beyond the role of a camp follower and became a hunter, guardian, beast of burden and companion. His endearing qualities made him man's "best friend".

In the wild, the canine is a loyal pack member. From its early development, the puppy shows a remarkable ability to imprint using sight, sound and smell. The pup is bold, inquisitive and playful. It will learn to recognize and copy a variety of vocal and behavioral mannerisms that will allow it to communicate with its siblings and pack members.

Dogs are welcomed visitors at many hospitals and nursing homes. Here, a resident looks forward to spending time with his canine friend. Photo by G. Gibbs.

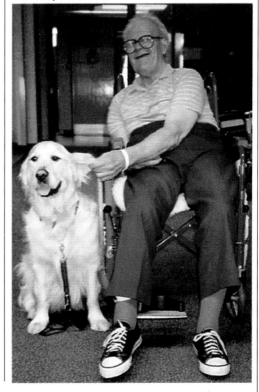

The pup (up to six weeks of age) has a high imprintability and a strong drive to follow and approach new objects (approach behavior). At six to twelve weeks of age, the pup begins to recognize foreign and potentially dangerous objects and will demonstrate approach-avoidance behavior. It will approach an object, person or pack member more cautiously and, if it senses anything different, may demonstrate a number of "avoidance" patterns ranging from barking to escape. Possessing a strong ability to mimic behavior of its senior members, within months it becomes an active part of the pack and begins to demonstrate a more mature adult behavior. Included in this behavior package are sexual, social and hunting traits and skills, with varying dominant and submissive characteristics that rank the maturing dog in the pack.

BREED DEVELOPMENT

Over time, man selected dogs for certain traits, properties and qualities that were felt to be important or endearing. The development of dogs with enhanced physical and behavioral properties led to the formation of myriad breeds. The traits we began to manipulate and select for included physical characteristics as well as a large number of social, sexual, herding, guarding, play and prey behaviors.

Considering the large number of breeds evident today, it is easy to see how successful we were in this manipulation. The development of all breeds such as sight hounds (e.g., Saluki), scent hounds (e.g., Beagle), working breeds (e.g., shepherds, collies) and hunting dogs (e.g., Vizsla, retrievers) reflects our search for a companion with some enhanced ideal, quality, trait or utility.

Some breeds have been developed mainly for their social or behavioral qualities. Included in this group are pets that I like to refer to as "infant" breeds (e.g., Shih Tzu, Lhasa Apso, Pomeranian, Pug, Pekingese, Maltese, etc.). Pups of these breeds all have large, domed foreheads and relatively large eyes that humans most identify with infants. There is also a tendency for these breeds to act as and behave as "puppies" well into adulthood. Have we created "perpetual" puppies, or are these dogs puppy-like because of the way people relate to them?

Dogs have many traits that we find desirable. They are variably described as loyal, dependable, loving, playful, friendly, protective and trustworthy. These characteristics are the basis of our fascination, bonding and love of dogs.

All breeds have these positive qualities, at least to some degree. However, we must also remember that they are dogs and follow a different set of guidelines than people. They also have drives to exhibit play, prey, sexual, marking and aggressive behaviors. In all likelihood, this is the source of most so-called "abnormal behaviors" that are reported in dogs. By observing and understanding canine behavior, we can take steps in carefully selecting a pet, properly training it, and preventing unwanted behaviors from ever occurring.

Well-disciplined dogs can be trained to assist the blind, deaf, and disabled. Photo by G. Gibbs.

THE ROLE OF DOGS IN THE HOME

One cannot doubt that the companion dog has reached a level of prominence in today's society. In fact, most dog owners consider their pets as "family members." The reason the canine has become so valuable is a complex one that largely is due to a smaller nuclear family and the pressures and demands of modern urban society.

The tendency in modern society to surround ourselves with plants and flowers in our homes, parks, and landscaping probably underscores man's basic need to surround himself with "nature." Man is happiest when he is in harmony and in contact with nature. Our relationship in urban societies with the dog (or other pet) is often the only contact with another species that is afforded us. We marvel at our pets' growth, take comfort in their well being, treasure their antics and are jealous of their joy in play. Our

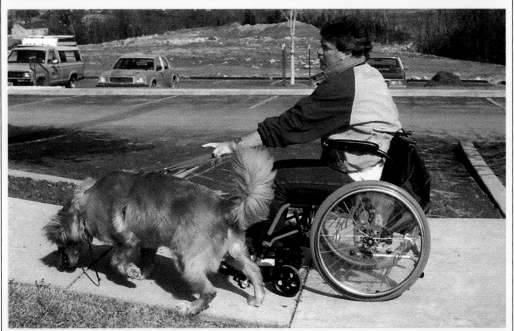

"Finnigan," a service dog from Support Dogs of St. Louis, Inc., practices pulling uphill in a team training session. Photo courtesy of Nona Kilgore Bauer.

concerns about our pets' diets and health underscore our own concerns about health and quality of life. We take pride not only in "ownership" but also in involvement in their training.

Our need and our children's need to nurture are often filled by our pets. As the family unit has become smaller, our dogs fill the role of child and siblings. In non-traditional families, the dog may fulfill the child's role. What else can fulfill the role of guardian, friend, playmate, child and confidant in addition to providing unconditional love and loyalty?

The first family member to greet the pet owner at the door is usually the dog. No matter how short our leave, the greeting is always exuberant and friendly. People of all ages require and seek this type of unconditional acceptance. The dog does not care if you are rich or poor. There is no race or sex bias in their bonding. They have the capacity to sense our moods and are content to sit by our sides during the most difficult of times.

For many children, the arrival of the puppy for which they have always wished is the beginning of a new and special relationship and responsibility. The opportunity to participate in this care is often the child's first significant responsibility and will provide us with the chance to experience the natural life cycle of all animals (i.e., birth, growth, development, adulthood, old age and death). In our materialistic, disposable society, the dog is different from any other present received. The love and affection that develops for the dog does not have a monetary value. The dog is not to be discarded nor traded; it is not a toy. The passage of time only deepens this bond. For many in modern urban society, the grieving following the loss of a "loved one" is first experienced on the death of the family dog.

The dog also plays the role of protector. Homes with dogs are unlikely to have intruders. People walking dogs are less likely to be accosted or mugged. The purchase of a dog should not be predicated solely on the basis of personal protection, however. They are much more than just "watchdogs."

For many, raising, showing and training the pet dog becomes a family hobby. There are training clubs and specialty clubs devoted to training dogs for show as well as for obedience. Besides encouraging proper handling, obedience and care, these clubs provide an excellent means for pet owners to socialize, to share information and to "network." In many European countries, Schutzhund clubs or French ring clubs abound. These sports are also becoming popular in North America. Dogs have to pass sociability and stability tests before training. These dogs will be trained for obedience, agility, tracking and article searches as well as for personal protection.

The American Kennel Club (AKC) and Canadian Kennel Club (CKC) also sanction matches in obedience training. Dogs can get degrees from

A therapy dog spends a special moment with a resident of a nursing home. Photo courtesy of Teresa Ewing.

Novice to Companion Dog (C.D.) to Utility, tracking and agility. The role of these matches is to encourage the pet owners to develop their pets' abilities to the fullest and to develop well-mannered, obedient dogs with stable personalities.

For those with less competitive instincts, one could consider the AKC Canine Good Citizen program. This test seeks to identify and recognize officially those dogs that possess the attributes that enable them to be enviable personal companions and members in good standing within the community. The test ac-centuates the positives in dogs and owners and requires that pets be well cared for and have current vaccinations and licenses in addition to behaving properly in a variety of circumstances.

SPECIALIZED DOGS

The dog's role in society has gone beyond the role of playmate and a "contact with nature." Dogs have developed specialized roles not only in sporting events (e.g., hunting) but in police work, search and rescue, drug and explosive detection and assisting the physically challenged

Their strong sense of smell makes dogs very helpful in Search and Rescue. This is SAR volunteer B.W. Lightsey and his SAR dog "Puller."

(hearing, seeing and physical). Dogs and other pets have now become recognized adjuncts to "pet-facilitated therapy" and are being used in visitation programs in geriatric residences, hospitals and prisons.

The Seeing Eye dog is well known for helping innumerable individuals to move around more readily in their environment. Less well known and recognized is the "hearing dog." These dogs are trained to a variety of sounds and circumstances and respond by alerting the person that is challenged with a hearing impairment. They can alert owners to doorbells, fire alarms, phones or crying babies by nudging the owner or by turning on specific signal lights.

For the physically challenged, the canine companion has been trained

Dogs with a warm and friendly disposition are ideal for therapy work. This is Timberline's Rocky, U-CD, a Pit Bull with therapy experience in hospitals, nursing homes, and hospice centers. Photo courtesy of Teresa Ewing.

Socialization and training are key to preparing a family dog for therapy work. Canine candidates must learn to tolerate handling by strangers in the company of other dogs.

to open doors and fetch objects on command. By training them to a harness, they assist the physically challenged in moving about. The dog's ability to retrieve articles can save valuable time and effort. In time, the trained dog's vocabulary can be expanded to numerous phrases or words.

The dog (as well as other pets) are now being recognized as important tools in what is called Pet-Facilitated Therapy. Pets are being used to assist therapists in overcoming barriers in communication between the patient and the therapist. In the clinical atmosphere, a non-judgmental, friendly,

Because of their extremely outgoing and people-friendly personality, Golden Retrievers are excellent dogs to use in therapy work. Photo by Karen Taylor.

loving dog may assist a therapist by allowing the patient to relax and "open up."

The Delta Society, a national non-profit organization is dedicated to enhancing the human-animal bond. Having recognized the need and importance of pet-facilitated therapy, the Delta Society offers training workshops and a network of fellow volunteers that visit hospitals, nursing homes and treatment centers. This role has now been expanded by the Delta Society to an animal-assisted activity (AAA) and animal-assisted therapy (AAT) program. Pets are registered as Pet Partners with the Delta Society after they have been properly evaluated by veterinarians to ensure the pet's health and tolerance for noise and new surroundings. Workshops and home-study programs are available by contacting the Delta Society, P.O. Box 1080, Renton, WA 98057-9906, (206) 226-7357.

The role of pets in geriatric medicine is now being recognized. The elderly's sense of time and worth may be distorted. Besides the obvious benefits and need for unconditional love, the canine family member provides an opportunity and responsibility to feed, groom and exercise. Elderly patients living on their own can become consumed with self concerns. The role of the dog can often return a feeling of self worth. The

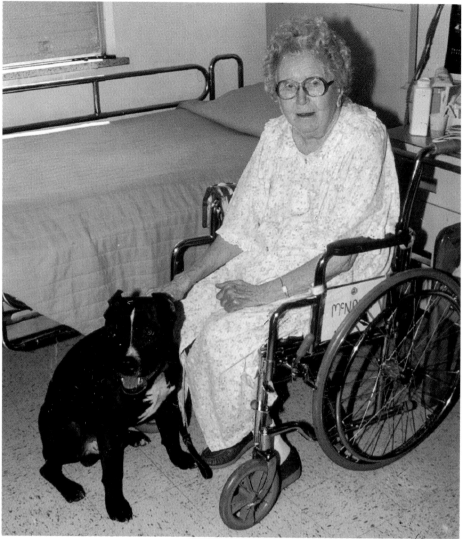

A dog can help return a feeling of self-worth and eliminate the loneliness in an elderly person's life. Photo courtesy of Teresa Ewing.

daily demands of feeding, walking and caring for the pet act as an external biological clock. The canine pet not only restores the schedule of rising, feeding and sleep but can aid in removing the loneliness that an elderly person may feel. The pet also acts as an important link to the outside world by introducing the owner to other members of the neighborhood. The simple truth is that in our fearful and insulated society, people are reluctant to talk to strangers. People with pets are not perceived as threatening or bad. If you own a dog, you must be a gentle, caring person. Hence, people with pets are more likely to be spoken to by strangers as they appear to be more friendly and non-threatening.

Research on the effects of handling a pet (dog) on blood pressure has demonstrated that, for most people, contact with a dog has the effect of lowering blood pressure. In fact, there is the belief that the prognosis for a heart patient that owns a pet is significantly improved over the non-pet owner. It is believed to be due to the positive effects on lowering blood pressure and anxiety as well as the positive physical effects of walking and brushing the dog.

PET SELECTION

Having recognized the importance pets play in our society, it is also prudent to remember that the single largest cause of death in dogs is man. More dogs are killed at humane societies for being unwanted and at veterinary hospitals for behavior problems than for all medical problems combined. The failure of the pet owner is the biggest cause of dog deaths in North America.

Dogs are too readily available in our society, both in terms of cost and numbers. Good intentions are overshadowed by impulse and lack of thought. Responsible pet ownership starts prior to acquiring a pet. In my mind there are six major failures of pet ownership that cause dogs to be needlessly killed:

1. Failure in proper pet selection.
2. Failure to properly train (house and obedience).
3. Lack of animal control (i.e., straying).
4. Failure to consider the "costs" (monetary and timewise) of pet ownership.
5. Failure to have pets neutered in a timely fashion and without "one litter first."
6. Failure to "poop and scoop."

It is my firm belief that the failure of proper pet selection is the most frequent error. We have such a drive to get a dog that little thought is given in selecting a pet. I have observed people spend hours deciding on a a personal article of clothing while people in a pet shop may select a dog in minutes because it looks "cute" or "lonely."

Careful consideration to the following must precede the impulse to "get a dog." You must be able to answer (truthfully) the following questions with a yes before getting a dog.

1. Do you have the time to properly care for a pet?
2. Do you have the commitment to spend the time to care for a pet?
3. Is your life-style stable? (e.g., moving to apartment, new baby, etc.)
4. Do you know what breed, sex, and age of dog is best for you?
5. Do you know how to train a dog or what is involved in training?
6. Do you know where to get information on dog selection?
7. Can you afford the costs of pet ownership?
8. Are you committed to obeying "poop and scoop," leash laws and city ordinances?
9. Are you committed to giving a dog a home for the rest of its natural life?
10. Do you really want a dog and will we make adjustments for it in your life?

If you cannot truthfully and wholeheartedly answer "yes!" to the above questions, *do not get a dog* Perhaps a new stereo or a pair of shoes would be a better choice. For those that have considered the whole process and are sure, man's best friend will pay you back a hundred times over in love and loyalty.

SUMMARY

Pets have become a significant part of our lives and are considered as family members. Despite their importance, the leading cause of death in dogs is us. Dogs are euthanized at humane societies and veterinary clinics as they are either unwanted or have developed behavioral problems due to improper training. Responsible pet selection and ownership are the key to stemming this unnecessary loss of animal life.

ADDITIONAL READING:

Ackerman, L : *Healthy Dog!* Doral Publishing, Wilsonville, OR, 1993, 126pp.

Eckstein, W : *How to get your dog to do what you want.* Fawcett Columbine, NY 1994, 283pp.

Fogle, B : ASPCA *Complete Dog Training Manual.* Dorling Kindersley, London, 1994, 129pp.

A Golden Retriever trained by Helping Paws of Minnesota pushes the button to open the electronic door for her owner Charlene Maki.

Dr. Ernest Rogers and his dog Kodiak. Photo by D. Massie, Virginia Maryland Regional College of Veterinary Medicine.

Dr. Ernest Rogers obtained his Bachelor of Arts in psychology with emphasis on physiological psychology. He also obtained a Bachelor of Science in biology. Both baccalaureate degrees were obtained at University of Guelph, Guelph, Ontario, Canada. In 1991, he graduated with a Doctor of Veterinary Medicine from Tuskegee University, Tuskegee, Alabama. Currently, Dr. Rogers is obtaining his Doctor of Philosophy, with an emphasis in veterinary pharmacology, from Virginia Polytechnical Institute and State University, Blacksburg, Virginia.

Selecting the Perfect Dog for the Family

By Ernest Rogers, BA, BSc, DVM
Virginia-Maryland Regional College
    of Veterinary Medicine
Virginia Polytechnical Institute
Duckpond Road
Blacksburg, VA 24062-0442

INTRODUCTION

The selection of the correct dog is not always easy. It requires patience and forethought to avoid mistakes. Those individuals who arm themselves with the information necessary to make a good decision will be better able to get an appropriate dog-family fit. This will avoid the heartbreak of having to give up a dog due to an unworkable situation.

The dog-family fit (or human-animal bond) relates the type of dog, its activity level, size and disposition (character and personality) to the expectation the family has of how the dog will interact and relate to individual family members and strangers. Family in this context may include all individuals (human and other pets) who interact with the new dog on a regular basis.

This chapter is written for several audiences, the first-time dog owner as well as those individuals with extensive dog handling and training backgrounds. The novice dog owner will use this information to guide their selection of a dog. Even the experienced individual (owner, breeder, trainer, kennel person or veterinary health professional) should find the information helpful. It is hoped that by the end of this chapter the reader will have a basic understanding of the pertinent factors that should be considered to ensure a good dog-family fit.

SOURCES OF INFORMATION

Veterinarians

Many people think of their veterinarian as a source of medical, surgical and emergency services. Your veterinarian and their professional staff are also a source of dog pre-purchase information. Veterinarians, as health professionals, consult and advise many breeders, trainers, and humane societies. This often puts the veterinarian in a position to know where the best sources of dogs and dog-related services are located in your area.

Small-animal practitioners have much training and experience in dealing with dogs. This makes them a particularly valuable resource when discussing the relevant issues pertaining to dog ownership.

An owner may want to gain some basic information about the type of dog he wishes to purchase and then discuss the advantages and disadvantages with his veterinarian. Some practitioners may invite you to a formal appointment in their clinic, while others may discuss the issues with you over the telephone. Whatever the situation be prepared with your potential selections so that you will be able to get the most out of the time the veterinarian will be able to share with you. This will be the start of what hopefully will be a rewarding and beneficial relationship for you, your dog and the veterinarian.

Finding the appropriate veterinarian is often by the recommendations of friends and colleagues. Factors that may be important to the owner before selecting a veterinarian may include: size of the practice, hours of operation, location and rapport with the clinician and staff.

Breeders

The American Kennel Club, United Kennel Club, The Kennel Club (England) and the Canadian Kennel Club are sources of information about breeders of purebred dogs. There are also a number of popular magazines available at bookstores and magazine racks that have advertisements for the sale of purebred dogs.

Reputable breeders are often good resource people, who have taken the time to learn the necessary information about their breed. The characteristics, temperament and quality of any individual animal reflects the knowledge, care and dedication of the breeder as well as to the attention given to the stud, dam and puppies.

Breeders can also be excellent sources of information for both breed characteristics and pet sources. Visiting a dog show before you purchase a pet will allow you to talk to breeders and get a real impression of an adult pet. Breeders may also answer questions concerning trainability, grooming and costs associated with their particular breed(s).

Trainers

The selection of a trainer or training program is critical to the dog-family-fit equation. For those individuals experienced with dogs, many may be able to negotiate the hazards and pitfalls of puppyhood and of introducing a new dog to a household. The rest of us should probably enroll in some form of training / socialization program or, at the very least, read books on training a puppy.

To find a successful, competent and reputable trainer or program, your veterinarian, breeder or humane society may be your best source of information. Be aware that any training program for either puppies or adult dogs is as much to train the novice owner as it is to train the dog! This resource, if used correctly, may make the difference between a good dog-family fit and a catastrophe.

These are not the only sources of information on pets and pet services, but in my experience these are some of the more reliable indi-

Some dogs make excellent pets despite their reputation. It is important that each animal be evaluated as to its suitability to be with children. Photographer: G. Baber, Virginia Maryland Regional College of Veterinary Medicine.

viduals from whom to obtain guidance. These people and the relationship they share with you and your pet will serve you well in ensuring that the dog you select meets your expectations for a good dog-family fit.

SELECTION FACTORS: THE OWNER

We are all individuals with individual needs, life styles, expectations, abilities and resources. Since the uniqueness of the individual shapes the type of pet that would be most compatible with that person, these individual factors should be considered in choosing a suitable canine companion.

Expectations/Function of Dog

Dogs, above all, are companions. Some breeds are more independent than others though all dogs look upon the family as their pack. The dog's position in that pack depends on its training, early socialization and the personalities of the individuals involved with the dog.

To have a dog that meets the behavioral and training criterion of Rin Tin Tin, Lassie or Benji is probably unrealistic for the average pet owner. Most television canines are very well schooled by professional trainers. Just because a dog looks like Benji doesn't mean that he'll act like Benji. The unrealistic expectation of a television dog can lead to disappointment. All pets are trainable when given sufficient time, love and patience, but very few will ever meet the level of training of your favorite movie or television hero!

It seems obvious that a sedentary individual who wishes a companion to spend quiet evenings on their lap probably wouldn't be very happy with a Saint Bernard. Similarly an athletic individual who may run several miles a week may not get great satisfaction from jogging with a Pekingese. Some animals and breeds require, even demand, more exercise and activity than others. This must be considered within the scope of the owner's life style and expectations.

One common expectation of owners in purchasing a dog is for companionship for their children and themselves. This goal can be easily met by the right dog. Where protection of property is an issue, simply the appearance of a large dog at a house can add to the house's security status. Others look for a dog for athletics such as hunting, retrieving, hiking or walking. Competitions such as Frisbee, herding or obedience trials are of importance to some owners. There are also those individuals who have decided that they would like to breed animals for fun or profit. In general, this last category is only for the experienced, dedicated dog owner. It certainly takes a very special person to be a quality breeder.

The likelihood that any individual dog will meet his owner's expectations is directly related to: the owner's understanding of the breed characteristics; the time, effort, knowledge and ability of the owner with respect to training, and; the owner's ability to recognize what needs he or she is trying to meet by purchasing a dog.

Time

Owning a dog takes time. Time and priorities are an important part of everyone's life. We, as prospective dog owners, must assess how much time we have on both a daily and weekly basis to share with our canine companion. Dogs are pack animals and as such require pack interactions and relationships. As the new owner of a puppy, you (and your family) become part of the pack. Responsibilities with respect to being a member of the pack include play times, discipline times, as well as simple physical contact times.

Grooming can be a very time-consuming chore depending on the dog's hair coat and its daily activities. A longhaired dog such as a Old English Sheepdog or Pekingese requires much more grooming than a shorthaired Chihuahua. If that same sheepdog is an outside dog still more time may necessary to remove burrs, sticks and mats. In general, longhaired dogs require more attention than shorthaired dogs. Many owners use a professional groomer; these services add to the cost of upkeep of the dog. Many a beautiful dog's appearance has been ruined by the owner's lack of ability or willingness to groom his or her dog.

Dogs with fur shed! Some breeds shed more hair than others. The shedding process can occur seasonally or year 'round. Proper grooming may reduce shedding, though it is unlikely to eliminate this occurrence. One should be aware that a shedding, dog leaving loose hair around a house can drive a fastidious housekeeper to distraction.

The time required to complete the training and socialization of a puppy can be a drain for the first few months to a year of the puppy's life. Puppies are very demanding. Failure to give the proper care in this critical period will likely precipitate behavioral problems in the adult that may disrupt the bond you hope to form with your puppy. Adult dogs, though less demanding, still have needs that must be filled. In fact, some adopted adult dogs come with problems that could require as much time as a puppy.

Dogs usually have to go out at least three times per day to relieve themselves. With respect to housetraining, setting a fairly constant schedule will improve success. This requires diligent planning by the owner. In general, the puppy requires more attention to its housebreaking needs than the adult dog to ensure success.

Housing

Where do we keep the dog? Inside or outside, apartment, house or farm, free run of the house or limited access (kitchen or basement), to crate train or not to crate train: these are decisions that should be made before the new dog arrives.

Some common sense must be used since shorthaired dogs do poorly outside in the dead of winter, while Huskies may thrive outside with only a dog house. All dogs should have

Children and dogs always seem to find some way to have fun together. Few children, however, are able to take full responsibility for the care of a pet. Adult supervision is always a wise precaution. Photographer: G. Baber, Virginia Maryland Regional College of Veterinary Medicine.

access to plenty of fresh, clean water at all times. In the winter, this may require a special apparatus to prevent the water from freezing. In the summer, the outside dog will also require shade as a place to cool off. Puppies should be confined to limited areas that are easy to completely clean until they are reliably housebroken.

Dogs being pack animals prefer to be with the family. The need of the dog to socialize must be taken into account when deciding on housing. Strictly outside animals can do well when the owners pay sufficient attention to the dog's need to socialize on a daily basis. Some animals without the necessary socialization may develop behavioral problems that are more difficult to resolve than to prevent!

Dogs left on their own outside without supervision should either be trained to remain on their own property or an appropriate conventional or electronic fencing system can be used. This may be more important in the urban and suburban setting, though owners can be held (financially) liable for the destruction of livestock in rural areas. Strictly indoor dogs must be allowed out on a regular basis to defecate, urinate and exercise.

The size of the area in which the animal will be housed should play a pivotal role on the size of the dog. Large dogs requiring a lot of room to exercise may be inappropriate for a strictly urban setting (especially in view of restrictive leash laws). These animals may do better in a suburban or rural setting.

Activities and Interests

An individual purchasing a dog for obedience trials and competition would want to have a dog with high trainability and high intelligence. Those owners who wish to have a canine companion who will spend time outside engaged in athletic activities would want a dog that is high in energy and athletic ability.

Each person intending to purchase a dog must look at how the pet will be able to fit into their life style and activities. It becomes slightly more difficult to select a pet for a family which has multiple activities and interests and wishes the dog to participate in everything. In general in these situations, it is usually best to bow to the wishes of whomever will be the primary caregiver. Considering the dog's role in one's daily activities helps to ensure a good dog-family fit.

Social Atmosphere

This owner factor examines the environment (s) to which the dog will be exposed. A family with young children and adults (dogs view children very differently than they view adults) is a very different situation than a family consisting of a single adult or a family of two adults and other pets. In all these cases the key to success is appropriate early socialization.

Some pets remain within the confines of the family home. Other owners have the good fortune to be able to keep their pet with them all day in public situations, while running errands or working. In one case, the pet's exposure to new situations, people and smells is limited, while in the other case the dog is con-

This adolescent has found a pet that matches his activity level yet can also share quiet times. This interaction is positive because consideration was given to the type of activity and exercise required by both the dog and the owner. Photographer: G. Baber, Virginia Maryland Regional College of Veterinary Medicine.

stantly bombarded by new things. In the second case, it is important to select an animal who is not afraid of new situations, who is likely to have a sociable, friendly personality.

There are many owner factors that must be considered before the final selection of a dog. Though some of the more important factors have been reviewed here, some individuals may have more considerations and concerns before bringing home that perfect canine companion.

SELECTION FACTORS: THE DOG

Dogs' personalities is as variable as the number of dogs that exist. Having reviewed the characteristics of the owner's life style, we now have some idea of the role the dog should play. A good dog-family fit requires that one find the dog with the characteristics that meet the life style and expectations of the owner. To accomplish this task, a sound knowledge of the personality characteristics of each breed is necessary. Let's now review some of the various aspects of a dog's personality that are important considerations in the selection of a dog.

Gender

In selecting a dog, people often have preconceived notions related to which sex they prefer. In many cases, behavioral traits vary between males and females.

One comment with respect to gender should be made here. To own a pet is a responsibility and a privilege. Today, we see many unwanted "throwaway" pets that must be euthanized at our local shelters and humane societies. Part of this problem is due to wandering sexually intact canines. In my opinion, only those animals intended for breeding should remain sexually intact; all others are better off either spayed or neutered.

There are advantages to neutering the male dog. There is a reduction in roaming, escaping, mounting and even some types of aggression. Castration also reduces the possibility of prostate disease and eliminates the risk of testicular cancers. Dogs are castrated just around the onset of puberty or as recommended by your veterinarian.

Spaying a female has been suggested to ruin the quality of the canine as a pet. Some owners even believe that failure to allow a female to have a litter reduces the desirability of the female as a companion. There is no evidence to support these views; in truth, there are health advantages to having your dog spayed before its first heat, such as reduction in the development of breast cancer and virtually eliminating the possibility of uterine disease. Other behavioral advantages include eliminating the male attractant pheromones given off by an intact female in heat. Spaying a female avoids unwanted pregnancy and its associated problems. In short, neutering one's pet is generally viewed as a responsible and wise decision, which saves many headaches in the future for you and your pet.

In general, females are usually less aggressive and smaller than males of the same breed. This can be important to the owner who wishes a small dog of a given breed.

Activity Levels

In general, a dog with a high activity level craves more attention, demands more play time, and needs more exercise than his lower-activity-level counterpart. High-activity dogs that are not given sufficient exercise on a regular basis may tend to run and generally make a nuisance of themselves both indoors and outdoors. These animals probably would be best appreciated by more active people.

Low-activity dogs enjoy a more low-key existence with less of a requirement for exercise. They appear to appreciate the quiet "sit around the house times" as well as quiet walks. Less active dogs require a minimum of activity but may be spurred to action by an intriguing game or other excitement. These animals are for those individuals with a quieter life style.

Intelligence and Problem-Solving Abilities

Many people enjoy the challenge of an intelligent pet. I use the word "challenge" because it can truly be a challenge to live with these animals. These are the pets that keep their owners alert by learning how to open doors. They often become intolerable stealers. These animals are excited about learning. So long as it is a challenge, these animals will try to learn. Trainability can be high when the goal behavior is presented in an appealing way, as in the form of a game. Learning is often quick with a minimum number of training sessions required to reach and reinforce the goal behavior. Exercise and play can be used to reduce the potential for boredom in these animals.

These intelligent animals can be demanding of their owner's time and energy. They may easily get bored. When this occurs with long-term confinement or isolation, behavioral problems may result. These animals must constantly be challenged to get the best quality pet. In some cases, curiosity may override the animal's desire to be obedient, and the animal may become difficult to control.

Less curious breeds may require more energy to train. Training in these cases may take more time, more sessions, and more patience for them to "get it right." These animals make excellent pets as well. They are often eager to please their owner and satisfied with a minimum of attention.

In any case, dogs can be trained to respond to the basic commands. It is necessary for those individuals with minimum experience to seek help to properly train their pet. It is usually best to start short training sessions as early as possible so as to avoid the development of undesirable behaviors. Knowledge of the basic commands ensures that your dog will remain safe and healthy for many years. High intelligence and high curiosity are necessary for working canines but dogs with moderate intelligence and curiosity can also be good pets.

Aggression

Breeds vary in their aggressive tendencies. Aggression isn't only the tendency of a dog to bite either a human or another animal but also the animal's willingness to defend its territory or challenge strangers. Aggression relates the dog's personality to its response in a given situation as either dominant, submissive or somewhere in-between. Aggression as a characteristic is closely related to an animal's socialization history as a puppy.

A dog that is walked off-lead must be well trained (under the owner's control) and in an environment that is safe for both dog and others sharing the area. Training a dog for off-lead walks is not difficult but requires patience, consistency and dedication on the part of the owner. Photographer: E. Rogers , Virginia Maryland Regional College of Veterinary Medicine.

Aggression may be measured on several levels. First there is an animal's tendency to attempt to control its environment and the people and animals within that environment. Behavioral aggression manifests itself in many ways as food guarding, territorial protection, predation and fear aggression. In breeds that tend to be more aggressive (particularly males), severe behavioral problems surrounding aggression may be more likely to occur if less than adequate attention, guidance and discipline are given to the pet's training as a puppy.

In some cases an owner may want an animal for protection of property. This does not necessarily mean the animal must be aggressive. It requires very high standards, abilities and training to properly develop a guard dog. Novices who attempt to train an animal to be aggressive may tend to reinforce inappropriate aggressive tendencies in the animal, and this can result in an animal that at any time may get out of control. Professional training is absolutely necessary if one's goal is to have a working guard dog. Some breeds have a natural tendency to protect their territory or property. In these cases, the dog must be checked to ensure this tendency doesn't get out of hand and become a problem for both the family and visitors.

Each breed may be classified as high aggression or low aggression. It is important to realize that aggression is a very individual trait. Dominant male puppies tend to be more aggressive than submissive female puppies. Fortunately, training, socialization and environment also play a large role in shaping the aggressive nature of most animals. It is for this reason I encourage early puppy training and adequate appropriate socialization.

Some animals suffer from pathological aggression, which may have a physiological or environmental basis. Diagnosis of pathological aggression is accomplished by a veterinarian based on a clinical exami-

Highly sociable breeds such as the Bernese Mountain Dog often work well as pets in families with children. Photo by Isabelle Francais.

nation and the animal's behavioral history.

In most cases, aggressive animals are inappropriate for families with individuals who are in a weakened condition, or elderly or children. Poorly trained aggressive animals may be a severe liability both legally and financially to their owners. It is therefore necessary to ensure that all pets be adequately controlled by training to avoid any harmful or painful consequences.

A concept often considered with aggressiveness is that of sociability. Highly sociable breeds, the Labrador Retriever, Bernese Mountain Dog or Poodle, often work well as pets in families with children and other pets, or where the dog will come into frequent contact with strangers. But again nothing can substitute for good socialization and individual attention as a puppy and good training.

Even the very friendly Poodle needs good socialization and disciplined training. Photo by Robert Pearcy.

Age

Puppy, young adult or mature adult? This is often a difficult question to answer. In general, the puppy is much more malleable to the family life style than an adult dog.

Advantages of purchasing a puppy include: ease of adaptability to the family situation, a clear background/history, and fewer bad habits to break. Another advantage is that the puppy usually may be trained without the liability of inappropriate previous training. The major advantage that many people see is that a puppy is small, cuddly, cute and playful.

The disadvantages include: having to housebreak a new puppy, attending to the inevitable accidents, putting up with the "teething stage" and, in general, spending many waking hours giving care, nurturing, feeding, cleaning, training and walking your new puppy.

The older dog on the other hand may already be housebroken and may only require an understanding, patient, and attentive owner to fit into the new family's schedule. Older animals may also come with knowledge of the basic commands. There are few disadvantages to a properly trained older pet, especially if the family is familiar with the dog before adoption.

Disadvantages of an older pet are often related to why the animal is up for adoption in the first place. Many dogs are given up for adoption for behavioral problems. In some cases, these problems may be eliminated with patience and good training. In general, knowing the dog, the environment from which it came, and the life style of the previous owners are often the best indicators of the success of the adoption. Those animals with an unknown history are, as one might suspect, a gamble both as to their behavioral history and possible problems as well as to their adaptability to a new family situation.

A good dog is one that fits the life style and expectations of the family. Some will be puppies while many others will be adults. The personality of the dog, its adaptability as well as the patience of the family are the keys to success!

Source

In general, two sources of animals exist, the breeder (or other commercial operations) and the shelter or humane society. More recently, several private organizations have initiated programs to rehabilitate former racing dogs to be pets in a family situation; this may prove to be another source of pets for some families.

Reputable breeders set specific goals and criteria for their matings. The cost of a puppy is related to the stud fee (the money paid to obtain the best male), the time to care for the bitch and litter, veterinary fees for any medical and surgical interventions required, as well as the time and energy expended by the breeder. Breeders are rarely adequately compensated for their time simply by the fees paid by those who purchase puppies, despite what might seem to some as high prices. All breeders should be able to supply a complete medical history and give information on both the male and female parents.

This relationship is successful because the dog and owner have bonded. This is the interaction we think of when we talk about the human-animal bond. Photographer: G. Baber, Virginia Maryland Regional College of Veterinary Medicine.

It may be extremely helpful to see the parents (if possible), in order to gain an insight into the temperament, behavior and size expectations of the pup.

Breeders are the usual source of purebred animals. There are often two types of animals that can be registered. The show-quality animal is an animal that, as a puppy, shows potential to meet the breed criterion for conformation and other requirements. These animals often bring a premium price, or may be kept by the breeder for future shows and breeding. The pet-quality animal is an animal who, as a puppy, shows some less than perfect breed traits with respect to conformation, coat or eye color or markings. These animals are no less of a quality pet, though their cost may be less than a show dog. Selecting a purebred dog affords the additional opportunity to further understand the breed and its behavioral, genetic and medical tendencies.

Another source of dogs is the shelter or humane society. Unfortunately, medical and behavioral histories are not always available for most animals. Some adult or young adult animals are put up for adoption for behavioral problems; this must be considered when adopting a pet. A good thorough medical and temperament evaluation by a veterinarian may alleviate some concerns, but the only true test is the animal's ability to adapt to a new situation. One added bonus of this type of adoption is that the adoptee is being given a second chance at a new life. That, in itself, gives some of us a warm feeling. Most humane societies have fees for licensing, spaying or neutering and vaccinations before an adoption can be finalized. There may also be forms to be filled out and other red tape, so be prepared and patient. This is to protect the animal and the adopting family from an inappropriate placement.

Breeder or shelter both have a readily available source of animals for adoption. The right dog for you may be found anywhere. Once the type of dog has been chosen, don't eliminate a source. Careful selection and understanding of the new dog is important to get maximum satisfaction and enjoyment.

Vocalization, Reactivity and Excitability

Breeds vary greatly in their reactivity, vocalizations and excitability. These traits serve as the basis of many a pleased or dissatisfied owner. Owners should be completely aware, as best they can, to these aspects of their newly adopted pet.

Breeds with high reactivity tend to be good alarm dogs (those that bark to alert the owner to an unusual event). Though this may be appreciated by an owner in a single family dwelling in a high crime area, it is unlikely to be appreciated by all one's neighbors in an apartment building. These animals tend to bark at the slightest provocation. Other animals with low reactivity may actually be oblivious to significant changes in the environment.

Vocalizations vary among breeds, from those who rarely bark (the Basenji) to those animals with a

This dog running through tall grass will require extra attention. Dogs can pick up both fleas and ticks. To avoid problems, the owner of this dog will have to take the time to properly groom the dog to protect the pet and the family with which he lives. Photographer: E. Rogers, Virginia Maryland Regional College of Veterinary Medicine.

loud prolonged bays (Beagles). Predicting the likelihood of a dog as being more or less vocal given a certain environment is not an exact science. Fortunately, with proper training, many animals can adapt to a multitude of situations.

Excitability varies almost as much with the environment as it does with the breed. Some breeds are known to be stoic, such as the Basset Hound, while others are of high excitability especially in novel situations or around new people or animals. Again, rarely is a rule about dogs 100% accurate, but often the temperament of the parents gives some indication as to the temperament of the puppy. Environment and training play a very large role in the outcome of any puppy with respect to excitability. In general, puppies are more excitable and playful than adults of the same breed.

ADDITIONAL CONSIDERATIONS

Puppy Personality Tests

There is a fair amount of information in both the popular and scientific literature relating puppy personality tests to the eventual adult personality and behavior. This idea seems reasonable at first glance, though I don't believe the reliability of the prediction is very high. Genetics, intrauterine environment and neonatal experience are some of the factors involved in the development of the adult personality.

In my experience, the factors that play the most importance in the development of the adult personality and final behavior are early socialization, training and the environment of the growing puppy, adolescent and adult. Some individuals go as far as to suggest that there is no correlation between the puppy personality test and the adult behavior. With all of the significant intervening variables from puppyhood to adulthood, I would propose that the best use of the puppy personality test is to demonstrate what potential there is for a problem and then to address these issues with the appropriate training and environment.

Breed-Specific Characteristics

This is a difficult subject fraught with much controversy and personal opinion. Many experienced individuals have had varying experiences with multiple purebred and crossbred dogs.

At one national meeting I attended, a group of veterinarians from one geographical area in the United States described a certain breed of dog as being very aggressive with a tendency to bite more often, with less provocation than other breeds in their practices. A surprising contrast was that veterinarians from another distinct geographical region several hundred miles away, also in the U.S., found the same breed of dog to be gentle, sociable and non-aggressive. This points out that the range and diversity of a breed may vary greatly with the area and even within any one area with the breeder.

There are many books that cover the subject of "typical" adult characteristics for various popular breeds. The reader is referred to these books for a detailed description of the various breeds with the caveat that variations may occur from these standard descriptions. Consultation with a knowledgeable individual in your area is still an advisable step before purchasing a dog.

The Atlas of Dog Breeds of the World has long been hailed as the "Bible" of purebred dogs. Over 400 recognized breeds detailed and illustrated in color. Published by TFH.

Cost : Upkeep and Maintenance

Pets become members of the family and, as such, should have their needs considered and added to the family's budget. Costs associated with owning a dog include, but are not limited to: food, heartworm medications, spaying or neutering, licensing (a neutered animal usually has much lower licensing fees), vaccinations, puppy training, yearly medical examinations, grooming and, when necessary, boarding. Pets, like people, occasionally get sick or injured and may require additional medical attention. The older animal, as with the older person, may require additional treatment or medications to maintain a good quality of life. These may be some of the most commonly overlooked factors in the selection of a dog. Disaster can be avoided by proper planning and consultation with a veterinarian.

SUMMARY

Obtaining a dog for pleasure and companionship need not be a hit or miss phenomenon. The search for the perfect family pet must start with a thorough understanding of reasons and motivations in obtaining a canine companion. Consideration of the owner's life style and needs often makes the type of dog and its characteristics clear to the adopting family. By seeking the advice of local knowledgeable individuals and experts and using the guidelines presented in this chapter, it is hoped that every adoption is a perfect dog-family fit.

ADDITIONAL READING

American Kennel Club: American Kennel Club, *Dog Care and Training*, Howell Book House New York, NY, 1991.

Clark, R; Stainer, J: *Medical and Genetic Aspects of Purebred Dogs II.* Forum Publications, St. Simon's Island, GA, 1995.

Hart, BL; Hart, LA; *The Perfect Puppy.* W.H. Freeman & Co; NY, 1988.

Hart, B: *Canine and Feline Behavioral Therapy*, Chapter 21, Behavioral Aspects of Selecting and Raising Dogs and Cats, Lea and Febiger Publishers, Philadelphia, 1985, 275pp.

GLOSSARY OF TERMS

Dog-family-fit: The social/pack relationship between a dog and the other individuals making up the family.

Human-animal Bond: The specific interaction and relationship between an animal and a significant individual in the family.

Pathological aggression: A type of aggression which is based on some pathological (disease) process that may occur in the body. One example may include some neurological problems that incite an animal to attack.

Pheromones: A smell that conveys information among animals. The information may indicate many things. The start of a male's territory or a female in heat.

Protection dogs: There are basically three levels of training that lead to a protective instinct in most dogs. The most basic level is that of the "alarm dog." The alarm dog serves to enforce it's territory by barking and "sounding the alarm." The next level is the "guard dog." The guard dog is one who will not only bark but confront a stranger on his territory. Both the alarm and guard dog act using their natural instincts to protect their property and territory but may be docile away from home. The "attack dog" is the typical police/sentry dog who will stand his ground or become offensive (attack) on command in any situation. This level of training is only reached effectively with specialized training.

Socialization: The behavioral changes that occur secondary to interaction with one's own species and other species with which one must live or contact. This may be termed "learning to get along with others."

Throw-away pets: The unfortunate matings of non-neutered animals that result in puppies for which there are no homes. Many of these animals are euthanized in shelters daily.

Dr. Sharon Crowell-Davis received her Doctor of Veterinary Medicine degree from Auburn University and her Ph.D. from Cornell University. She has been treating behavior problems of dogs, cats and horses for 17 years and is one of the founding diplomates of the American College of Veterinary Behaviorists. She is a professor at the University of Georgia, College of Veterinary Medicine.

How Dogs Learn: The Role of Rewards and Punishment

By Sharon L. Crowell-Davis, DVM,
   PhD, Dip. ACVB
College of Veterinary Medicine
The University of Georgia
Athens, Georgia 30602

INTRODUCTION

Learning can be defined as changes in behavior which occur as a result of experience. Dogs are constantly having experiences and so they are constantly learning. Learning occurs throughout life, and the myth that "You can't teach an old dog new tricks" is only a myth. There are several different processes by which dogs learn, and, if you understand the underlying process, you can better understand how your dog's environment gradually works to change its behavior. You can also deliberately cause changes in your dog's behavior.

CLASSICAL CONDITIONING

Classical conditioning is a phenomenon that was discovered by a Russian scientist named Pavlov. Hence, it is sometimes called Pavlovian conditioning. Dr. Pavlov discovered that if he rang a bell whenever he offered food to dogs, the dogs would eventually salivate when he rang the bell, even if there was no food present. This phenomenon occurs commonly and affects a variety of behaviors, particularly those associated with emotional responses such as fear or anticipation of food, and physiological responses such as salivation and heart rate.

Classical conditioning is particularly important because it can cause problems of neutral stimuli becoming conditioned stimuli for behaviors you don't want. For example, if a dog is punished too strongly, so that it becomes frightened, stimuli associated with the frightening experience can become conditioned stimuli for being frightened. Subsequently, the dog might be frightened of just the person who punished it, or of people physically like that person, or of all people. It might also be frightened of items associated with the excessive punishment, such as newspapers. Natural phenomena can also cause classical conditioning. A dog that has previously not been frightened by rain or

A. The smell of food normally causes a dog to salivate. The food is an unconditioned stimulus and the salivation in response to food is an unconditioned response.

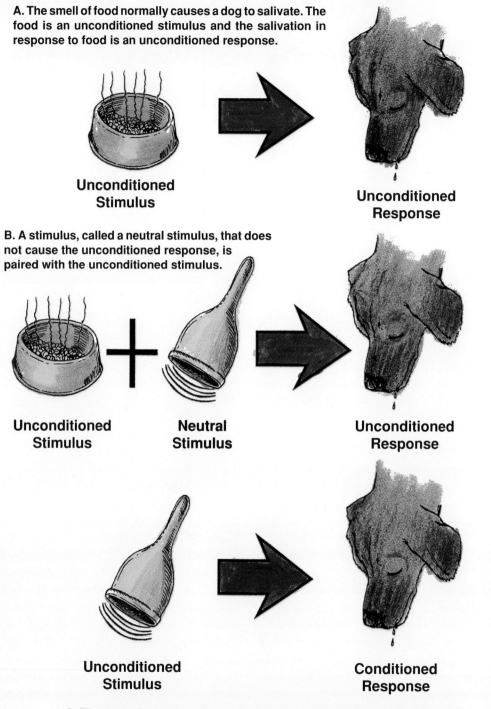

Unconditioned Stimulus

Unconditioned Response

B. A stimulus, called a neutral stimulus, that does not cause the unconditioned response, is paired with the unconditioned stimulus.

Unconditioned Stimulus

Neutral Stimulus

Unconditioned Response

Unconditioned Stimulus

Conditioned Response

C. The neutral stimulus eventually becomes a conditioned stimulus and now causes the same response. When the response is caused by the conditioned stimulus it is called a conditioned response.

If a dog has a frightening experience, things or persons (stimuli) associated with that experience may become conditioned stimuli, and cause fright.

wind may become intensely frightened at the smallest drop of rain or gust of wind once it has been through a hurricane, or even a bad storm.

DENSENSITIZATION AND COUNTERCONDITIONING

Dogs that have developed behavioral problems caused by classical conditioning can be treated by a process known as desensitization and counter conditioning. In desensitization, the stimulus that now causes the undesired behavior is gradually brought closer and closer to the dog. But this is done very slowly, slowly enough that the dog does not show the undesired behavior such as fear. For small problems, this might be accomplished in one short session of 15 or 20 minutes. For severe problems, weeks of working with the dog every day may be required.

The process of desensitization can be sped up by causing the stimulus that now causes the problem behavior to become associated with something that causes a behavior that is incompatible with the undesired behavior. Examples would be getting the dog to eat bits of delicious food or playing with it. It is important that the new, incompatible stimulus not be given in conjunction with the undesired behavior. Instead, the new stimulus must be presented when the dog is showing desirable behavior in the presence of the old conditioned stimulus.

If your dog has a behavioral problem which you believe would benefit from desensitization and counterconditioning, you should contact your veterinarian for specific instructions. Done incorrectly, this technique can make a problem worse instead of better.

OPERANT CONDITIONING

A dog's behavior also changes depending upon what the consequences of a given behavior are. This is called operant conditioning.

POSITIVE REINFORCEMENT

If a certain behavior increases depending upon the presence of a certain stimulus after the behavior, we say that the behavior has been positively reinforced. Positive reinforcement is a very useful tool in teaching dogs of any age. Typically, the reinforcer is something very pleasant, called a reward, such as delicious tidbits of food, praise, petting or play. Using positive reinforcement in training can have beneficial side effects, such as improving the bond between you and your dog and causing classical conditioning of yourself as something associated with pleasant experiences. The very sight of you can then cause the associated conditioned responses, such as relaxation, food anticipation, or playfulness.

Positive reinforcement can be used to shape your dog. For example, if your dog doesn't know how to sit on command, you can try holding a tidbit of food over your dog's head while you say *Sit*. Your dog will probably tip its hindquarters down a bit as it holds its head

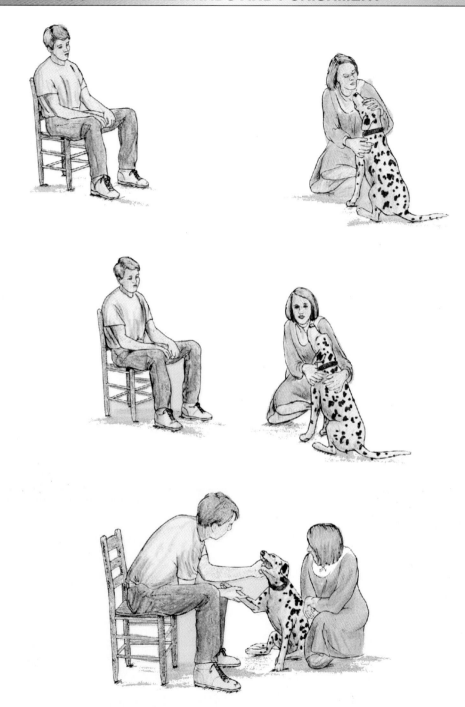

In an example of desensitization and counter-conditioning, the dog gradually comes closer to the stimulus that now causes it fright. At the same time, it has pleasant experiences so long as it does not become frightened.

To teach a dog to 'down' on command by "shaping," give it a reward for lying partway down. With each successive training session, require it to lie down more and more before it is rewarded.

up. When it does that, give the reward. Next time, only give it the reward after it has tipped its hindquarters down a little bit farther. After you've required your dog to be in more and more of a sitting position each time before you give it the reward, you will reach the point where you only give the reward if your dog sits all the way. You can then use shaping to teach your dog to lie down. With the dog sitting, tell it *Down*, then hold the tidbit of food just below its nose so it has to drop its head to get the reward. Again, hold the tidbit lower and lower each time, until your dog must lie all the way down before it gets its reward.

Positive reinforcement can also be used for a different technique, called prompting and fading, to achieve the same results. To teach a dog to sit by this method, you physically manipulate it into a sit. You can do this by saying *Sit* and gently but firmly holding its head stable at the collar, then applying pressure to the hindquarters until it sits. That is the prompt. Then reward your dog. Gradually use less and less pressure and physical manipulation as you repeatedly tell the dog to sit. Always reward it immediately once it is in the appropriate position.

You are probably used to the idea of using rewards to reinforce a dog's behavior in a structured training situation. Using rewards to reinforce desired behavior in everyday life can be useful too. Improperly used rewards can also cause problems in everyday life. You have probably encountered dogs that don't seem to know how to stand still. They jump and whirl and bark and generally act very unruly. They are usually not pleasant to be around. Such dogs act this way because they have been rewarded. They have learned that the way to get attention is to jump and whirl and bark. When they are quiet they do not get attention, so they don't do that very much. You can start a puppy off right and teach it to be a well-mannered dog by making a point of rewarding it when it is simply sitting or lying around being a good dog. This does not spoil the puppy. It teaches the puppy that it can get attention by behaving this way. When the puppy is grown up, you will be glad to have a dog that sits quietly to get your attention rather than one that barks and spins to get your attention. Even if you change your attention from praise, petting, and play to scolding, the unruly dog, which is a very social animal, will have learned that barking and spinning is the way to act to get some kind of attention.

When and How to Reinforce

There are numerous ways to positively reinforce a dog. Most of the common ones include verbal praise, petting, food, and play. Praise alone can be a powerful reward, particularly if a dog has a strong social bond with the trainer. Highly palatable food, however, is almost always a strong reward, which can be very useful if used correctly. When you use food in training, there are two important things to remember. First, make it very palatable. Pieces

To teach a dog to 'sit' by "prompting and fading," push it into a sit, then reward it. Pushing it into the required position is the prompt. Gradually decrease the force of the prompt with each successive training session, while continuing to reward a complete sit. This is "fading."

of kibble aren't very motivating. Chopped up hotdog, liver or cheese, however, will induce most dogs to work very hard for even a small piece. The potential problem with food is that you will not always have a piece of liver available as a reward, and you don't want the dog's behavior to be totally dependent upon the presence of liver. This dependence can be avoided by the use of a phenomenon called "variable ratio reinforcement."

When you are first training a dog to do something new, give it a treat every time it performs the desired action. Once it has learned what to do, as demonstrated by giving the correct response several times, gradually begin to omit the food treat on some occasions. At first, omit the treat only every third or fourth time, then every second or third time that the dog behaves correctly. Next, start giving the treat only every second or third time, then every second, third or fourth time. Gradually give the treat less and less often overall. However, don't ever totally eliminate food rewards and occasionally surprise your dog by giving the treat very frequently, even several times in a row. If you do this, there is no predictability about when the treat is coming. Even as you gradually decrease the frequency of food rewards, always continue using praise and petting.

Punishment

If a certain behavior decreases depending upon the presence of a certain stimulus after the behavior, we say that the behavior has been punished. Punishment usually involves administering some sort of aversive or unpleasant stimulus to the dog, but administering an aversive stimulus to a dog does not necessarily mean that you are punishing it. If you get up in the morning, find the kitchen trash strewn around the floor, grab your dog by the collar, pull it over to the trash and proceed to hit it and yell at it, you are not punishing it. You are merely hitting it and yelling at it. This is because the timing is incorrect for punishment to occur. If you get up the next morning and find the trash strewn about and start heading for your dog with an angry look on your face and your dog cringes, it is not cringing because it knows it should not have gotten into the trash at 2:00 a.m and is now regretting its misbehavior. It is cringing because

Giving a dog attention when it is jumping around, spinning and barking provides positive reinforcement for these behaviors. Dogs that get attention when they behave this way are likely to be unruly. While a dog can be trained, as this one is, to jump only on command, you must be careful to never allow jumping if the command is not given.

you and something about the situation, perhaps the look on your face, have become clasically conditioned stimuli for a fear response.

To be effective, punishment must be appropriately timed, consistent, and of the appropriate intensity. Appropriately timed means *imme-*diately. When you administer an aversive stimulus to a dog you are only affecting the behavior that is going on right at that moment. That means that if you call a dog to you and then scold it, you are punishing it for coming when you call. The dog does not understand your explanation that it is a bad dog because it barked at the neighbors or urinated on your carpet. If approaching you when you say "Come" is followed by a scolding, your dog will be less likely to approach you the next time you say *Come*.

"Consistent" means the punishment must be administered every time the dog engages in the misbehavior. If jumping up on people sometimes results in a sharp, unpleasant *No!*, but sometimes results in petting and sometimes results in brief petting followed by a half-hearted "*no* bad dog" and a push, the dog will continue jumping. To teach the dog not to jump up, the dog must be punished every time it jumps up by everyone it jumps on.

"Appropriate" means that the

punishment must be appropriate for the individual dog. Different dogs respond differently to different types of punishment. You need to use a punishment that is just unpleasant enough to disrupt the behavior but not so unpleasant as to cause fear. If a dog regularly receives punishment that is too intense, it is likely to start developing a generalized problem with fear, which could manifest as hiding, r u n n i n g away, cringing, snarling, biting, or various other behaviors. For a timid dog a simple, sharp *No*! is sufficient. For a very timid dog, even a quiet voiced no may be enough. The punisher, of course is not

Giving a dog attention when it is sitting or lying quietly does not spoil the dog. It teaches the dog that the way to get attention is to behave in a quiet, controlled fashion.

the word. The dog does not innately understand what no means. The punishment is the sharp tone of voice and the fact that the word "no" may have become a conditioned stimulus because it has previously been paired with a spanking or other punishment. Some owners use a light swat on the hindquarters as a quick and easy way to punish a pet. You must be careful if striking a dog, though, as it is easy to cause pain-elicited or fear-elicited aggres-

sion. Also, if you are going to use physical punishment, ask yourself if you're doing so because you realistically expect to achieve an expected change in behavior or because it makes you feel better to hit the dog when you're angry with it. If the latter is your answer, you'd better avoid physical punishment. If you do choose to use spanking, it does not matter whether you use your hand or a newspaper except as a matter of convenience. You may have heard that using a n e w s p a p e r causes the dog to think that the newspaper and not you are causing it the pain. This is not true.

V a r i o u s noises are often good punishers. Things that make screeching, hissing or clanging noises can startle a dog and disrupt the behavior, are slightly unpleasant and do not generally cause injury. An exception would be if you used an extremely loud noise that caused hearing damage.

If you have a dog for which a simple reprimand is not sufficient, and do not have a noise-maker handy, you can supplement a verbal reprimand by taking hold of the loose skin on either side of the dog's neck and mildly shaking the dog while staring it in the eyes and scolding it. This technique has many analogies to "punishments" administered by one dog or wolf to another, and the dog responds to it instinctively as a punisher.

Caution should be taken when considering the use of this approach with aggressive, adult dogs who might respond aggressively to this type of correction.

One punishment technique that should never be used is "hanging" a dog, in which the leash is raised so that the forefeet and even all

For the dog that does not respond to simple scolding, holding the scruff of the neck and staring it in the eye while continuing to scold is a stronger form of punishment.

four feet are raised off the ground. This is abuse, not punishment, and can cause severe injury. The use of electric shock collars for punishment is very problematic. They are very potent punishers and, misused, can cause a great deal of harm. Also, poorly made or maintained shock collars can discharge spontaneously. A thoughtful, knowledgeable trainer can make very effective use of shock collars, especially when training dogs which must work at a distance from their handler. In general, the use of shock collars should be left to experienced trainers.

Negative Reinforcement

Negative reinforcement, like punishment, usually involves the use of unpleasant stimuli. However, there is an important and fundamental difference. Negative reinforcement reinforces or causes an increase in a behavior because the unpleasant stimulus goes away if the dog engages in the behavior.

Negative reinforcement can be used to increase submissive behavior in a puppy. Gently but firmly hold the puppy down, showing your dominance. As soon as the puppy submits and relaxes, release it. If you do this rather than continuing to hold the puppy down, you will reinforce submission.

People sometimes contribute to the development of behavior problems by negative reinforcement. For example, if your puppy growls as you walk towards it while it is eating and you decide to leave it alone, you will have negatively reinforced growling.

Time Out

Just as removal of an unpleasant stimulus can cause a behavior that is followed by removal of that unpleasant stimulus to increase, removal of a pleasant stimulus can cause a dog's engagement in a behavior that results in the loss of that pleasant experience to decrease. One use of this technique, in which a dog is placed in isolation or is ignored until it behaves calmly, is sometimes called "time out." This can be useful with certain unruly dogs. If a dog is behaving in an unruly fashion, it can be placed in isolation, perhaps the bathroom, for a brief period. The dog should only be let out when it is not barking, but it should be let out as soon as it is calm, even if that calmness is only momentary. Carried out incorrectly, even this simple technique will not be helpful. For example, if the dog is simply placed in the bathroom and left there for a long period of time just to give you a break from its behavior, it will not learn anything and it will not be getting even normal levels of exercise. As with all other techniques described in this chapter, talk with your veterinarian about whether this technique would be helpful for your particular dog and exactly how you should use it.

SUMMARY

Learning is a change in behavior that occurs as a result of experience. Dogs of any age can learn through both classical and operant conditioning. Classical conditioning primarily affects emotional responses and related physiological responses. Through classical conditioning, unpleasant experiences may lead to behavior problems of excessive fear. Operant conditioning is that which occurs because a dog's behavior is affected by the consequences of that behavior. A behavior may become more common because it is positively or negatively reinforced. In positive reinforcement, the dog is rewarded for engaging in a behavior, while in negative reinforcement, an unpleasant experience stops if a dog engages in a behavior. Conversely, if a dog's behavior results in an unpleasant experience or in the removal of a pleasant experience, the behavior will decrease. When using punishment, it is important that the punishment be given immediately and consistently and that it be of the appropriate intensity for a given dog.

ADDITIONAL READING

Crowell-Davis, SL: Negative reinforcement is not punishment: Help clients know the difference. Veterinary Forum, 1990; March, 38.

Domjan, M; Burkhard, B: The principles of learning and behavior, 2nd Ed., Brooks/Cole Publishing Company, Pacific Grove, CA, 1982.

Spreat, S; Spreat, SR: Learning Principles. Veterinary Clinics of North America, Small Animal Practice, 1982; 12:593-606.

Reward your dog with his favorite toy for obeying a command or executing a trick. This Australian Terrier will do just about anything for his Nylafloss! Photograph by Karen Taylor.

Dr. Wayne Hunthausen is a pet behavior therapist who works with people, their pets and veterinarians throughout North America to help solve pet behavior problems. Since graduating from University of Missouri School of Veterinary Medicine in 1979, he has practiced in the Kansas City area. He is director of Animal Behavior Consultations, which provides behavior consultations as well as training services. He writes for a variety of veterinary and pet publications and is coauthor of the textbook, The Practitioner's Guide to Pet Behavior Problems. Dr. Hunthausen frequently lectures on pet behavior and currently serves on the behavior advisory board for the scientific journals: Veterinary Forum, Feline Practice, Canine Practice and Veterinary Technician. He is a member of the American Veterinary Society of Animal Behavior and has served on its executive board as secretary-treasurer and currently as its president.

Besides hosting his Kansas City radio talk show, "Animal House," he is a regular, featured guest on the "The Morning News" for the local NBC television affiliate. He lives in the Kansas City area with his wife, Jan, their Standard Poodle, Simon, and their Airedale, Ralphie.

Preventing Common Puppy Problems

Wayne Hunthausen, DVM
Animal Behavior Consultations
4820 Rainbow Blvd.
Westwood, KS 66205

INTRODUCTION

Young puppies seem to have split personalities, sometimes acting the role of perfect angels, and at other times taking on the persona of mindless little devils, hell-bent on disrupting our lives and destroying our homes. There were times when I was raising my Standard Poodle, Simon, that I actually reached for his fuzzy little black head to feel for horns! In reality, puppies are quite innocent little beings whose normal behaviors tend to get them into trouble when not given adequate guidance and supervision.

Most of the problem behaviors in which puppies engage are very normal behaviors, but performed at the wrong time or in the wrong place or directed to the wrong objects. A little forethought, adequate supervision, appropriate confinement, and early training can go a long way toward keeping these guys out of trouble, not to mention saving the relationship and the home.

THE BASICS

One of the first concerns for preventing undesirable behaviors is to provide for the young pup's needs. Adequate physical exercise is a very important consideration, especially as the puppy reaches five to six months of age. At this time, puppies are entering their teenage months and have an incredible amount of energy available. If we do not take the time to provide enough exercise for the puppy, the release of all that energy into undesirable behaviors can have disastrous results. Allowing the pet to romp by itself in the backyard is usually not enough. Vigorous exercise should be encouraged every day. Working breeds, such as Labrador Retrievers, Siberian Huskies and Malamutes should be exercised by speed walking or jogging with them at least two to three times daily. Teaching the pet to play fetch can be helpful. A pet that knows how to play fetch will have an activity that can provide exercise for it when you are feeling lazy or when bad weather prevents outdoor excursions.

Besides physical activity, mental activity is necessary. If appropriate mental stimulation isn't provided for the pup, it will invent its own games which can be virtual triathlons of destructive activity such as: "How many plants can I eat in 30 minutes" or "Let's play mix and match with the sofa pillows." Type "A" personality puppies may spend their extra time pursuing new careers, such as redecorating, remodeling with their teeth or gardening. Early obedience training can help fill this need.

Proper toys are absolutely essential in preventing problems. All puppies chew. It's a fact of life. It is up to the owner to direct that chewing

biggest hurdles of raising a puppy. Always give the pup happy verbal praise whenever it is chewing on one of its toys and, on occasion, give it a small piece of its puppy kibble as a reward. This will help the puppy learn that there is a bigger payoff when it chews its toys rather than the sofa, television or carpet.

Because problems may occur when there is not enough food available or when the puppy doesn't know when its next meal will be

Providing proper toys is absolutely essential to satisfy the chewing needs of your growing puppy. Photo by Isabelle Francais.

to acceptable objects and away from family possessions. First, you need to offer different types of safe toys to the pet until you find the ones it likes. The next important step is to actively reinforce chewing on the toys. If you can make chewing on the pup's chew toys more rewarding than chewing on anything else around the house, you are well on the way to getting over one of the

forthcoming, it's a good idea to establish a regular feeding schedule for the puppy. The quest for food may have the puppy exploring places where it shouldn't be and chewing on things that should not be in its mouth. It is rare for a healthy puppy under six months of age to overeat when it is only fed dry puppy food. Therefore, it usually works best to allow it to eat as much as it wants at mealtime during its first six months of life. Only restrict the amount of food you offer if your puppy begins to put on too much weight. Feed at the same times, two or three times each day, but only leave the food down for 15 to 20 minutes. This feeding schedule will provide an adequate amount of food at predictable times and help curb hunger-related investigatory behavior, as well as aid in housetraining. Another benefit of a regular feeding schedule, as opposed to feeding free choice, is that it helps the pup learn that you are an important figure in its life. The pet is more likely to respect and listen to someone who controls its food.

A sufficient amount of social interaction must be provided for all puppies. This is particularly important during the first three months of the young pup's life when it is developing confidence in interacting with members of its species and others . Dogs make good pets because of their social nature, but because they are social animals they have certain needs for social interaction that must be met. Just how much social interaction is required varies with the individual. Some are quite content with minimal human contact, while others seem to be underfoot wanting some type of contact all the time. Whatever the pet's needs happen to be, you risk making a social mess out of it by relegating it to the backyard or basement most of the time. Puppies in these types of situations usually become starved for attention and act unruly and inappropriate whenever they have the

A Nylabone® is an excellent chew toy that is both safe and healthy for your puppy.

opportunity to be around someone. This generally results in a scolding and more confinement—a vicious cycle that the pup can't win. The more time the young puppy spends with the family, the better it will be because you will have ample opportunities to intervene during its social development in order to shape desired behavior.

Last, but not least, have some rules and stick by them. You should make a mental or written list of everything you want the pup to do and everything you want it to avoid doing. Be sure that all family members agree on the rules and abide by them. Whenever the pet is caught in the act of misbehaving (jumping up when greeting, eliminating in an inappropriate area, chewing on furniture), it should be given a sharp, verbal reprimand. But don't just rely on punishment to enforce the rules. Every time you catch the puppy performing a desirable behavior(greeting without jumping up, eliminating outdoors, chewing its toys), be sure to take the time to give it a lavish reward. To become a good leader, you need to gain the puppy's trust. In order to do this, the pet will need to know what to expect from you every time it behaves in certain ways. Puppies or children who grow up in families never knowing what to expect can develop all types of emotional problems including unruly behavior, severe anxieties and aggression.

SUPERVISION AND CONFINEMENT

Raising a young puppy can be quite a challenge, fraught with peril and requiring the patience of Job. On a scale of difficulty, it can fall somewhere in between getting teenagers to clean up their rooms and squeezing a camel through the eye of a needle. But it can be done. Preventing failure depends on taking action to set the puppy up for success. In order for the puppy to succeed, you must provide adequate supervision and confinement. Because of problems such as destructive chewing and housesoiling, most young dogs cannot be trusted to have free roam in the house until at least 12 to 18 months of age. By that time, housetraining should be completed and normal investigative, chewing and digging behaviors have declined. Until then, the pup should be kept within eyesight or confined to a safe area. A leash can be an invaluable tool for keeping a puppy within eyesight. When I am raising a puppy, I use its leash indoors more than I use it outside. Puppies quickly learn to sneak away to perform their mischief. A leash or tiedown will help keep the puppy with you when you are distracted watching television, cooking or reading. Baby gates can also be very helpful for keeping the puppy in an area where you can keep an eye on it.

When you can't keep the pup with you, it must be confined to a safe area. A confinement crate will serve this purpose nicely. It should be big enough for the pet to comfortably stand up and turn around when it reaches its adult size. When the puppy is in its crate, it is protected from hazards around the home and the home is protected from the puppy. A good way to introduce the pet to the crate is by playing a game that teaches it to go into the crate on command. Just prior to each feeding time, grab a handful of the puppy's dry kibble and take the pet to the crate. With a bit of a flourish, toss a piece of food into the crate. As the pup runs in after the food, say "Go to your crate." Once it has eaten its prize, the pup will run out to play again. Repeat the exercise 15 or 20 more times. Gradually move farther from the crate before you toss the food. Eventually, you should be able to say "Go to your crate" as you sweep your hand toward the crate and the pet will enter on command. Keep the crate in an area of the home where you will be spending time with the puppy. Whenever you pick up toys that have been scattered about, place them in the crate. Occasionally hide a biscuit treat in the crate for the pup to find. By doing theses things, the puppy will be going in and out of the crate many times during the day and associating pleasant events with the crate.

You must be careful not to overdo crate confinement. The pup can be kept in the crate all night when it sleeps and up to three to four hours during the day. But if you are away from home at work or school for a full eight-hour day every day or for a period that is longer that the pet has control over its bowels or bladder, you will need to provide it with more room. In either case, you will need to use a small, puppy-proofed room or exercise pen during the day and the crate at night when the pet sleeps. A crate is just too small an area in which to keep the pet all night and all day, too.

The puppy will also need supervision in the yard. Until the puppy is one year of age or older, I think it's important for a family member to accompany it whenever it is outdoors. The first year of life is prime time for bad habits to develop outdoors such as digging, destructive chewing and barking. Owner-absent, backyard behavior problems can be extremely difficult problems to correct. They are much easier to prevent. If you spend a lot of time with the pet in the yard, you should have frequent opportunities to encourage desired behaviors and discourage undesirable ones. If you must leave a young puppy outdoors by itself during the day when you are away, give it plenty of aerobic exercise before you leave and provide ways for the pup to entertain itself when you are gone. Chew toys and large balls for the pup to push around should help. Another way of making the backyard more inter-

An owner crate-trains her young puppy. Photo by Dr. Wayne Hunthausen.

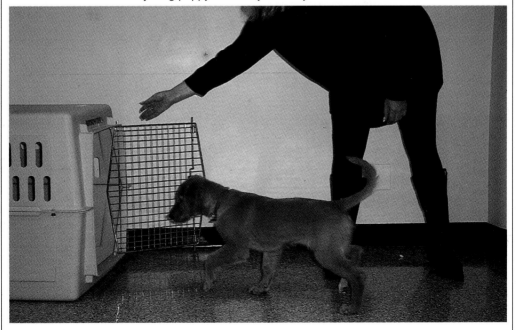

esting is to build boxes, tunnels and ramps for the pet to explore. Of course, be sure to puppy-proof the yard by moving or fencing off objects that could be chewed, securing the fence against escape and removing anything that might be dangerous. Chicken wire can be secured over the ground in garden areas and along the fence line where the pup might dig out and escape. Pups will dig after ground squirrels and other small animals, so ridding the yard of these creatures will eliminate at least one reason for digging.

FOOD BOWL GUARDING

A quite serious adult problem that can easily be prevented during puppyhood is aggression around the food bowl. Adult dogs that growl when approached while eating usually have grown up with little experience with people at dinner time. To prevent aggression, the goal is to teach the young puppy that there is no reason to be anxious about someone approaching its food, that we will not eat it and it will not disappear. Start by making dinnertime a social time. Let the puppy eat out of a bowl in your lap while you stir the food around with your hand, pet it and talk to it. This will make the puppy comfortable having a human present when it eats. You can take this a step further and actually teach it to look forward to having a person present when it eats by occasionally slipping a small piece of lean meat or ball of canned food into its dry kibble as it's chewing away. He'll think you're some sort of food shaman who magically makes the food

get better whenever you hang around. In order to generalize the gustatory, good feelings, it's a good idea to have all family members participate, as well as willing visitors.

PUPPY PROOFING

Once the older puppy is housetrained, has started to calm down and has been taught to chew on toys, you will want to consider allowing it to have more freedom around the home. At this point, you need to take extra precautions to insure that the house has been puppy-proofed. Dangerous, expensive and irreplaceable items should be put out of reach or made to taste bad. Commercial hot or bitter sprays will teach the pet to keep its mouth away from objects around the house. Cayenne, mentholatum, underarm deodorant and oil of citronella are other products that occasionally will work to deter the pet. A quick fix for most pets who chews on plants is to mist the leaves with water and sprinkle cayenne pepper on them. Child-proof locks can be helpful aids to keep the pet out of cabinets. Booby-traps and motion alarms can also be very effective.

EARLY TRAINING

By all means, begin training your puppy right from the first day you bring it home. Early training can be one of the most important things you can do to gain control of the puppy, prevent a wide variety of problems and promote desirable behavior. Owners who wait until the pup is six months of age or older

Puppies are more likely to develop proper chewing habits when the owner spends time teaching them what to chew. Photo by Dr. Wayne Hunthausen.

to begin training have lost valuable time. At an early age, puppies learn at warp speed. Using positive reinforcement methods, training can start as early as eight weeks of age. If all you do is teach the young puppy to sit on command, you will have developed a powerful tool for other types of training and behavior modification.

To gain control of the pup and teach it that you are the boss, simply request it to sit before it gets anything it wants (food, play, a pet on the head). This teaches it that you control everything in its life that it wants or needs and that it must defer to you before getting anything. Sitting becomes the pet's way of saying please. Frequent use of the stay command can be another powerful way of gaining leadership control of the pet. Once the pup learns to stay on command, frequently ask it to stay and wait for permission to move before accompanying you out of a room, through a door or up the stairs.

You can also use the sit command to shape the way the puppy greets people. By requesting a sit every time the pup approaches you, you are not only teaching a proper greeting behavior, but you are preventing the puppy from jumping up. Whenever it meets someone new, have the visitor ask the pup to sit for a small food reward. This teaches a proper greeting and helps prevent handshyness, since an outstretched hand is frequently associated with food.

Early, food-reward obedience training can also be very helpful for

Interacting with the puppy at mealtimes will help prevent adult aggression problems around the food bowl. Photo by Dr. Wayne Hunthausen

the shy puppy. As the pet develops confidence during training, it also learns to associate food rewards with the words used to give the obedience commands. When you take it out to meet people and ask it to sit at the greeting, the word "sit" will cause the puppy to think about getting a treat and make it less anxious about meeting someone it doesn't know.

SUMMARY

Raising a puppy can be quite a challenge, but it will be much easier if you do some research before adopting your pet. Visit your library and talk to dog owners who have recently raised puppies, so that you have a clear idea of what to expect from that fuzzy little ball of energy. With a little preparation, you'll be better equipped and ready to shape the pup's behavior and your relationship with it to be the best it can be.

ADDITIONAL READING:

Ackerman, L: *Healthy Dog!* Doral Publishing, Wilsonville, OR, 1993, 126pp.

Campbell, W. *Better Behavior in Dogs & Cats.* Goleta, California: American Veterinary Publications, 1986.

Dunbar, I. *Sirius Puppy Training Video.* James and Kenneth Publishers. Berkeley, CA, (510) 658-8588

Bohnenkamp G. *Manners for the Modern Dog.* Perfect Paws, San Francisco, CA, 1992.

Hart B. L., Hart L. A. *The Perfect Puppy*, NY: W. H. Freeman and Co., 1988.

Hunthausen, W; Landsberg, G: *Providing Behavior Services in Veterinary Practices.* American Animal Hospital Association Publication, Denver, Colorado, 1993.

Landsberg, G; Hunthausen, W; Ackerman, L: *Canine and Feline Behavior Guidebook.* Elsevier Publications, Oxford England, 1995.

Monks of New Skete, *The Art of Raising a Puppy.* Boston: Little, Brown & Co., 1991.

Meyer, Nikki. *A Pet Owner's Guide to the Dog Crate.* Nikki Meyer Educational Effort Inc., Davis Hill Rd, Weston, CT.

Rutherford C., Neil D. *How to Raise a Puppy You Can Live With.* Loveland, CO: Alpine Publications, 1981.

Vollmer P. *SuperPuppy.* Escondido: SuperPuppy Publications, Escondido, CA, 1988.

Dr. Ian Dunbar is a veterinarian, animal behaviorist and dog trainer, with three books, 15 booklets and eight videos to his credit. Dr. Dunbar received his veterinary degree and a Specials Honours degree in physiology and biochemistry from the Royal Veterinary College (London) and a doctorate in animal behavior from the Department of Psychology at the University of California, Berkeley, where he spent ten years researching the development of hierarchical social behavior and aggression in dogs. Presently, Dr. Dunbar writes the American Kennel Gazette's "Behavior" column, which was voted best dog column by the Dog Writers Association of America. Also, Ian writes for Dog Fancy, Cat Fancy, Dogs in Canada and for Dogs Today in England, where each summer he films his television series about dogs and people. Dr. Dunbar is currently the Director of the Center for Applied Animal Behavior in Berkeley, where he lives with a Malamute, two mutts and a kitty called Mitty.

Lure/Reward Training

By Ian Dunbar, PhD, BVetMed, MRCVS
Director, Center for Applied Animal Behavior
2140 Shattuck Avenue, #2406
Berkeley, California 94704

INTRODUCTION

Successful obedience training really comes down to teaching a pet dog just three simple obedience commands: to sit, to settle-down and walk on leash. Sit gives the owner immediate and momentary control over the dog and it is the simplest positive solution to a plethora of potential problems. For instance, instructing the dog to sit prevents it from jumping-up, bolting, running away, chasing, mounting, or being mounted. It is a matter of counter-conditioning: if the dog is sitting, there are so many annoying things the dog can not be doing. It is much more time-efficient to teach a reliable sit (a single positive response), than to attempt to reprimand and punish the dog for a multitude of problems. Additionally, sit is a much better emergency command than a recall. Sit is the purest and simplest response: either the dog sits or it doesn't. If the dog sits, it is under the owner's control; if it doesn't, it isn't. Depending on the situation, the owner may instruct the dog to resume playing, walk up to the dog and put it on leash, or call the dog. If the dog sat willingly, it will be much more likely to come when called. If the dog does not sit when told, it is an emergency and so, do whatever it takes to catch the dog and then, do not let it off leash again until you have at least trained it to sit reliably.

Instructing a dog to settle down and shush is a simple and effective long-term control command. Again it is a matter of counterconditioning: if the dog is quietly lying down on its mat or bed, there are so many things it is not doing. For example, a peacefully reclining dog can not bother family members, children, visitors, or other animals. Also the dog can not reconnoitre other rooms of the house, to troll the kitchen counters or contemplate petty larceny of smelly socks, priceless underwear, used Kleenex and floppy disks. Also, the dog can not usurp the couch, bark at the window, chase its tail and self-energize. If the dog is lying in its bed or crate, that is what it is doing and nothing else. Teaching the dog to enjoy little quiet moments enables the owner to momentarily relax and enjoy a brief respite from the incessant, rambunctious clamour of living with a puppy or adolescent dog.

Teaching a dog to walk on leash is

Walking a well-behaved dog can bring pleasure to any owner. For the dog, frequent walks lead to healthful, social gain. Photo by Karen Taylor.

essential for the owner to enjoy walking the dog. Frequent dog walks are vital for the dog's well-being. Frequent walks are the single most important ingredient of any socialization program, whereby the dog continues to meet a multitude of people, other dogs and animals each day. Walking the dog offers essential physical and mental exercise and also, the good old dog walk is the very best, most time-efficient, reliable training exercise.

TEACHING THE MEANING OF INSTRUCTIONS

Many moons ago, rather than enjoying the summer months per-

forming repeated rectal examinations on dairy cattle, I set off for the Mediterranean and Eastern Europe with a fellow veterinary student and four fine English ladies in my newly acquired 3-ton ex-RAF Bedford Ambulance. Unfortunately, after a delightful few weeks in Greece, we were refused entry to Bulgaria. A Bulgarian border guard barked an instruction, strangely enough in a language I did not understand and so, I did not respond. The guard barked louder and so I barked back. The guard then barked louder still and thrust the muzzle of an ominous and automatic firearm towards my ventrum and so we left Bulgaria and went back to Greece.

The above little story illustrates the first reality of dog training: Just because you told the dog to do something does not necessarily mean the dog understood your instructions. Consequently, there is no point in shouting. Instead, in the words of the world's best dog trainer, Charlie Wyant, "Go back and train your dog." Without a doubt, not understanding the owner's instructions is the single most common reason for a dog to fail to follow directions. Thus, the prime directive in training is to open interspecific communication channels.

Basically there are only two ways to communicate with a dog: Either we teach the dog our language, or we learn the dog's language. Whereas, it would indeed be possible and amusing to don a doggy suit and communicate our wishes by manipulating ears, by wagging a tail, or by urinating against a tree or lamppost... such antics would be quite impractical and certainly, viewed as a little strange. Consequently, we teach the dog our language. However, it is no good explaining things to the dog, since it does not understand what we say. It is no good demonstrating what we want because dogs are different from people and do not learn by imitation. Instead dogs learn from the consequences of their actions. Initially, dogs learn to associate specific actions and responses (e.g., sitting or lying down) with pleasant and rewarding consequences. And so the dog is more inclined to sit and lie down. Later in training, dogs learn rewards may only be forthcoming if the owner has first requested the specific response or activity. To put it simply, dogs learn good things are likely to happen if they perform a specific desired response following a specific request.

Just as you have chosen your dog's name, pick the words you wish to use for instructions. You do not have to use the words come, heel, sit, down, stand and stay, anymore than you have to call your dog Rover. For example, you may train the dog to settle down by saying down, settle down, settle, relax, chill out, crash, get a grip, or go to your bed. Similarly, you may train the dog to sit by saying, park it, or genuflect, or by giving the instruction in a foreign language, sientate, or o suwari . Train the dog in Bulgarian if you like. The actual words are neither here nor there, just as long as you teach the dog the meaning of the words you choose as instructions.

Body language is more expressive in the dog world than vocal expression. Dogs wag and wiggle every extremity to tell us their thoughts.

Food treats and kibble are probably the best lures for novice owners, but balls, Frisbees, chewtoys, squeaky toys and tug 'o war toys may similarly be used. To test if the lure works, move it up and down in front of the dog's nose and ask the dog "Are you ready to learn?" If the dog nods in agreement, it's time to start training.

Sit

Hold the lure in front of the dog's nose, say "Rover, Sit" and move the

The hound breeds, such as the Dachshund, are arguably the most vociferous of all dogs: they are blessed with resonant, deep voice and a broad range of expression. Dachshunds may rank among the most difficult dogs to train, but do be patient since they are innately very intelligent. Photograph by Robert Smith.

Any favorite toy may be used as a lure... Photo by Diana Robinson.

...and maybe later given as a reward. Photo by Diana Robinson.

lure upwards and backwards towards the dog's eyes, keeping it an inch above the dog's muzzle. As the dog looks up to follow the lure it will sit down. When the dog sits, say "Good dog" and scratch it behind the ear, throw a ball for the dog to retrieve, tell it to go play, or offer a treat as a reward. Usually it is as simple as that. If the dog jumps up, you are holding the treat too high. If the dog backs up, work with the dog in a corner.

Once this simple training sequence, Request-Response-Reward, is repeated a number of times, the dog quickly learns the act of sitting is associated with rewards and in no time at all the dog becomes Sit-happy and will be eager to sit voluntarily and frequently. Later in train-

ing, the dog learns the owner saying "Sit" is the key—the magic word—which controls whether or not it is likely to receive a reward when it sits. Once the dog begins to sit reliably on cue: The dog is beginning to learn the meaning of the instruction; and the owner is beginning to gain verbal control over the dog's behavior.

Settle Down

To teach a dog to lie down, waggle a lure in front of its nose, say "Rover, Down" and lower the lure to the ground between the dog's forepaws. Praise the dog when it lies down "Good dog!" and reward your recumbent critter with a relaxing chest rub, a food treat or two, supper in its bowl, or an invitation to share the

Using a food lure to teach PBGV Dimity to sit in the television program *It's a Dog's Life.*

Using a chew toy bone to teach Phoenix to sit...

...and lie down. Photos by Dr. Ian Dunbar.

couch.

It is easier to get the dog to lie down if it is already sitting, since its hindquarters are already down. Once the dog's nose (and forequarters) have followed the lure to the floor, slowly move the lure away from the dog's forepaws and as the dog reaches forwards leaving its hind end in place, it will flatten out and lie down.

If the dog is standing, hold the lure between finger and thumb and lower the hand (palm downwards) to rest on the floor. As the dog worries at the lure, it will likely place the side of its muzzle on the floor (Good dog!) and then assume a playbow with elbows and sternum on the ground (Go-o-o-o-d dog!). By gently moving the lure toward the dog's brisket and between its fore-

paws, the dogs rear end will collapse backwards and the dog will lie down (GO-O-OD DOG!!!)

On the first couple of trials reward the dog the instant it lies down but with successive trials, progressively delay the reward for a little longer each time: for two seconds, then three seconds, five, eight, 12, 20, 40, 60 and so on. Before you know it, your dog will happily settle down on request for several minutes.

Come and Follow

Call the dog, "Rover, Come" and squat down and pat the ground and waggle, or juggle a lure in your hands. Praise the dog as it bounds towards you and instruct the dog to sit prior to impact. Scratch the dog behind the ear, reward the dog by

Alternative 'stairs' method to teach Oso to lie down. Photo by Dr. Ian Dunbar.

offering a food treat and/or tossing a ball for the dog to retrieve. Once the dog comes and sits happily and reliably, delay giving the reward until after the dog has followed you for a short distance. From the outset, encourage the dog to walk close to one side by holding a lure on that side. Entice the dog with the lure and always keep walking away from the dog: If the dog slows down or stops, speed up; if the dog turns one way, turn the other; if the dog forges on ahead, slow down, or about turn and speed away in the opposite direction. Practice around the house and off-leash in other safe areas such as fenced yards and tennis courts. The dog will quickly learn to follow and to look to you as the leader. Whenever stopping, transfer the lure to the other hand and signal the dog to sit by your side.

Stuffing bone chew toys with freeze-dried liver and dog biscuits...

Other Positions

Since it is so easy, efficient, effective and enjoyable to train a dog using lure-reward techniques, the owner may as well teach the dog a multitude of other responses, such as, playbow, stand and rollover. It is a good idea to teach the dog to playbow at the same time as teaching it to lie down. Teaching a dog to playbow is an extremely useful command, especially for large dogs. To see a dog assume a friendly playbow, quickly puts other dogs (and people) at ease.

Similarly, teaching the dog to stand-stay and rollover-stay for examination will make your veterinarian a happy puppy. To entice the dog to stand, with the dog either sitting or lying down, move the lure half a dog-length away from the dog and waggle it at muzzle height. As soon as the dog stands to investigate, lower the lure a couple of inches to get the dog to look down a little. (Otherwise the dog will stand but sit immediately).

It is easier to teach rollover if the dog is already lying down. Waggle the lure in front of the dog's nose and then slowly move the lure to one side and backwards alongside the dog's muzzle all the way to its withers. As the dog looks backwards over its shoulder, tickle the dog's goolies (the unmentionable nether regions between its hind legs) with

...to encourage dogs to settle down. Photos by Dr. Ian Dunbar

the other hand and the dog will lift a hind leg to expose its inguinal (groin) region and roll over. Once the dog is lying on its back, hold the lure still to keep the dog in position and slowly and rhythmically give the dog a tummy rub or scratch its chest. Now your dog will be a happy puppy too.

EASIER METHODS

Some owners have difficulty using lures, especially with active and rambunctious adolescent dogs. The lure makes the dog more excited and the owner becomes agitated and begins to jerk the lure away from the dog, which is the best possible way to train the dog to snap and lunge. Keep calm: Practice smooth lure movements and hand signals with friend's dogs (which are calmer) and then, use a less exciting lure when working with your dog again. If this does not work, it's time to change to Plan B. Luckily there is an even easier and more relaxed way to teach dogs to sit and lie down, even though it may take a little longer. But then, now you have the time to read a good book on dog training whilst you are training the dog.

Prior to feeding the dog dinner, take a handful of kibble and put it in a bowl on the kitchen table and sit down and ignore the dog. Ignore everything the dog does, unless it sits, which it will do eventually. The dog may paw, circle, bark and playbow—ignore all of these antics and wait for the dog to sit. In fact,

"Oso come..."

"and Sit"

"Good Boy!" Photos by Dr.
Ian Dunbar.

Using a favorite toy to teach Phoenix to heel and sit. Photos by Diana Robinson.

Using easy and enjoyable lure/reward methods, dogs love to learn. Phoenix likes "to be a bear." Photo by Diana Robinson.

time how long it takes if you like. Praise the dog the instant it sits and offer a piece of kibble. Offer an additional piece of kibble if the dog remains sitting, otherwise ignore the dog again and repeat the procedure, except this time you will probably discover the dog takes less time to sit. And next time it will sit even more quickly. After the dog begins to sit promptly, ask the dog to sit, praise it when it does so but delay giving the food treat for progressively longer periods. Now you may handfeed the dog the first course of its dinner as long as it remains sitting.

The above procedure may be used to teach the dog to settle down and also, to teach the dog not to lick, mouth or touch. If the dog becomes excited worrying at the lure, hold a piece of kibble in your hand say "Off" and wait for the dog to lose interest, which it will eventually. Praise the dog and offer the kibble ("Take it") the instant it pulls away its muzzle. After a few repetitions, the dog will grasp two mind-boggling principles:

1. It cannot get kibble by worrying at the owner's hand; but
2. It can easily con the owner into offering kibble simply by withdrawing its muzzle and breaking contact.

Now progressively delay offering the kibble after the dog has broken contact. Thus the dog will learn, it must break contact and not touch for a period of time in order to receive kibble. Once the dog has learned that "Off" means it may watch, sniff and follow the lure but not touch it. Immediately and miraculously the dog calms down and becomes easier to train using lures and rewards to teach other exercises.

OFF LEASH AND ON-LEASH TECHNIQUES

The above training methods fall into two categories: 1. Reward Training—waiting for the dog to respond appropriately and then rewarding it for doing so; and 2. Lure/Reward Training—enticing or luring the dog to respond appropriately and then rewarding the dog for doing so. With both techniques, mistakes are simply ignored for two reasons: 1. By definition, the dog can hardly make a mistake and get it wrong, until we have taken the time to teach it what is right; and 2. Whereas reprimanding and/or punishing the dog during the teaching phases of training would only serve to teach the dog to dislike training, with lure/reward training the dog soon learns to thoroughly enjoy training. Additionally, reward training techniques do not involve touching, guiding, or physically prompting the dog, let alone forcing it to comply.

Even though it was a generally accepted method back in the stone ages of dog training, guiding the dog into position is extremely ill-advised for a number of reasons. If the dog is touched in the course of training it is likely to respond preferentially to the touch rather than verbal commands, i.e., the dog learns to sit when touched on the rump, or tugged on the collar, but it does not learn to sit when requested to sit.

Callahan likes to sit up and beg...

..to play opossum...

...and, of course, Springers love to spring. Photos by Dr. Ian Dunbar.

...to wave goodbye...

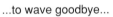

The dog has yet to learn the meaning of the verbal instruction. But surely, this was the whole purpose for training the dog—to teach it our language.

During initial training, the use of physical prompts and especially the leash, quickly become a 'crutch' in training and the owner soon develops an inflated view of their control over the dog. This becomes a significant problem the first time the dog is off leash and at some distance from the owner: The owner instructs the dog to sit, the dog does not respond and the owner can not reach the dog to physically prompt, or force it to respond. In fact the Jekyll and Hyde (on-leash/off leash) difference in reliability is the single biggest problem of traditional on-leash training.

Additionally, some trainers tend to forget that whereas they may be expert dog trainers, novice owners seldom have these skills and no matter how adeptly physical techniques are demonstrated by trainers, they tend to be abused in the home by owners, especially by men and by children. The end result— the dog gets pushed and pulled, and squished and squashed. Physical prompting often becomes force-training in the hands of a novice, whereupon the disparity between on-leash and off-leash control increases still further. With force training, since the dog has been forced to comply, by definition it does not want to comply. In contrast, the primary aim of lure/reward training is to teach the dog to want to comply.

Dogs quickly learn to love following instructions, especially if they are the key to home comforts. Photo by Dr. Ian Dunbar.

Phoenix and Oso sit for their supper. Photo by Dr. Ian Dunbar.

Most owners quickly learn that force-training is notoriously ineffective. The first thing the dog learns is those many times and situations when the 'trainer' can not force it to comply. For example:

1. **Owner-absent problems** - the owner is at work while the dog is left at home alone to misbehave;

2. **Dog-absent problems** - the dog is chasing squirrels and consuming cat doodoo off-leash in the park and well out of reach of the owner's grabbing and jerking little paws;

3. **Owner physically-present but functionally-absent problems** - the owner is at home but taking a shower, changing the baby, chatting on the phone, or watching the TV while the dog trashes the kitchen; and

4. **Owner physically-present but mentally-absent problems** - the less said about this the better.

Therefore, it is preferable to keep your hands and leash off the dog during training. Rather than using your hand to prompt or force the dog to comply, use your hands to reward the dog for complying. Training will proceed much more quickly if the owner trains the dog off-leash in safe (confined) areas. Without a doubt, lure/reward techniques are the most efficient and most effective way for training any animal and dogs are no exception. Non-contact lure-rewards techniques are the *sine qua non* of dog training. As a bonus, the user-friendly and dog-friendly tech-

The good old dog walk is the very best training exercise, both for socialization and for increasing the dog's prompt response and reliability.

niques are as easy and enjoyable for novice owners as they are for dogs.

Walk on leash

Having said all this, there is however one exercise which must be taught on leash, namely—on-leash walking. Even so, leash work may be taught without leash corrections. But first it is worthwhile testing to see whether the dog even wants to walk by your side. A tight leash is evidence the dog would rather be somewhere else—in fact, anywhere else—but by your side. In fact the dog would rather sniff another dog's rectum than walk with you. Remember that! And forget jerking that dog's leash, that'll really make you fun to walk with. The problem is a simple one and the solution may be found by looking in a mirror. It's time to wise up and lighten up. Go back and practice those off-leash following exercises, but this time skip along and whistle a happy tune. Give the dog a reason to want to walk next to you.

Now back to the leash. Rather than continuing to walk while the dog pulls and thereby rewarding the dog for pulling, don't go anywhere. Just stand still and wait for the dog to slacken the leash and sit. Be patient. It will happen eventually. Praise the dog when the leash is slack and as soon as it sits, give the dog a treat and take one step— just one step. And hold on, because the dog will immediately surge for-

ward as soon as you move. Wait for the dog to sit again. It doesn't take as long this time, does it? Now take another step. Once the dog begins to sit promptly when you stop, try taking two steps, then go for three and then four, five, six and so on. Before you know it, the dog will walk calmly on leash and will sit when you stop.

If the dog ever forges or tightens the leash, stop immediately and wait for the dog to sit once more. If the dog forges and pulls when leaving home but walks back fairly sedately, leave home in the fashion indicated above, go to the end of your garden path and then turn around and come back home. Repeat this just a few times and you will find it soon becomes easier and easier to leave the house in a mannerly fashion.

The dog's prompt response and reliability is put into practice by instructing the dog to settle down every 20 yards or so, while you enjoy a good book.

Most training needs to be done around the home and on dog walks so that the dog is well practiced in those settings. However, it is still an excellent idea to go to class, not just to learn how to train your dog but also as an opportunity for the dog to socialize and for the both of you to have a good time. The best time to train your dog is as early as possible (i.e., as soon as the dog has had its puppy shots. So make sure you look around for a good off-leash puppy class. Puppy classes are essential. Miss out on your pup's early education and you and your puppy will regret it for a long time.

The best time to attend puppy class is actually before you get the puppy. It is generally a good idea to find out how things work before you plug them in and with a puppy, the clock is already running. In fact, by the time the pup is just four and a half months old, it will be much (MUCH) more difficult and time-consuming to even try to modify its temperament, let alone to reverse all the bad habits it has learned, courtesy of living with a novice owner who did not know what to do. You need to know what to do the first day your puppy comes home and you need to know it before the puppy comes home. Visit several classes and learn as much as you can and maybe even test-drive one or two dogs. If the trainer does not like you there, then obviously that would not be a good class to attend with your pup later on. You will quickly get a feel for the best class for your prize pup from the other class participants.

It may be a good idea to bring along a chew toy to occupy your dog while you read.

Make sure that you stop at places that have enough room for your dog to rest as well.

Practice at home before you go to class and then once the puppy is old enough, take it to class but also be sure to continue training at home and on dog walks.

TEACHING THE RELEVANCE OF COMPLYING

To some extent the dog will have grasped partial relevance of complying with the owner's wishes from early lure/reward training. The dog quickly learns, if it follows the lure it is likely to be rewarded. Maybe it will receive the lure as a reward, or more likely it will receive all sorts of other rewards. Indeed most new trainees are more than happy to respond appropriately during early training and at home in relatively non-distracting settings. However... when the dog collides with adoles-

cence and/or in unfamiliar surroundings, the dog's eager compliance begins to wane. More than a few owners can be heard to lament their dog's park-side disobedience "But he's perfect at home" And certainly he should be perfect at home, because that is where most training has taken place. But dogs learn differently from people: Whereas people tend to over-generalize, dogs tend to be extremely fine discriminators. For example, if you have mainly trained the dog in the kitchen before dinner time, even though you may have a damn good kitchen-dog, your best friend may still fail to respond when off-leash in the park. If you want a dog to be reliable off-leash in a variety of settings, then it must be regularly trained off-leash in a variety of settings.

Welcome to the second reality of dog training: Just because the dog knows what you want it to do, does not necessarily mean the dog will do it. Ask any Malamute and they will tell you—undoubtedly the quickest learner of any breed but also, unfortunately, the quickest forgetter—they just do not see the point of mindlessly repeating mundane boring exercises at the whim of a mere human. Neither do many other dogs. It is not sufficient merely to teach the dog what we want it to do; in addition the dog must be taught why it should comply, i.e., to teach the dog to want to do what we want it to do. Indeed teaching the relevance of complying is the major ingredient of any successful dog training programme.

Life Rewards

A simple way to teach the dog the relevance of complying is to first make a list of 20 things the dog really enjoys doing and then each time, simply instruct the dog to sit, settle down, or walk on-leash beforehand. For example, to have the dog sit, or settle down before petting it, to sit before opening doors to enable the dog to enter or exit the house or car, to sit before allowing it on the couch or bed, and last but not least, to sit for supper. The owner can get exceptional training mileage with minimum of effort by repeatedly instructing the dog to sit during lengthy, enjoyable, doggy pastimes. For example by periodically instructing the dog to sit for a couple of seconds, while it is playing. Or, when snuggled on the couch watching the TV, briefly train the dog during each commercial break and then invite the dog onto the couch again. In no time at all, all

Be sure to give your dog some attention during your rests along the walk.

dogs (including Malamutes, Basenjis, Shibas and Afghans) grasp the quintessential maxim: "Good things happen when you sit." Similarly, the dog will learn good things happen when it settles down, walks calmly on leash, or participates in any dog-owner activity/game/training exercise.

Certainly for most domestic dogs, and especially suburban dogs, a simple enjoyable doggy walk represents both the very best training exercise and the very best reward. A stroll with the dog provides an ideal time to train the dog in a variety of settings and situations. By walking the dog on leash, (or off-leash in safe areas), and instructing the dog to sit and/or settle down every 20 yards or so, owner and dog may participate in some 250 short training interludes, each in a different setting, and all within a single three mile walk. Moreover, each time the dog responds promptly and willingly the dog is allowed to resume the walk. Thus, the walk may be used as an effective reward over and

over again for prompt and willing compliance. After a while, sitting and lying down become as enjoyable as walking, sniffing and peeing—all doggy activities the dog enjoys with its best friend and coach. The owner calls for a sit before tossing a Frisbee and the dog enthuses "G-r-reat play!" The owner suggests "Go play!" and the dog says "Yes!" And then "Settle-down" and the dog responds "Good call—my favorite!" Certainly, with a well-trained dog it is virtually impossible for dog, owner, or onlookers to distinguish between what is fun and what is training. Indeed, when both become both, the owner has discovered the Holy Grail of dog training.

ADDITIONAL READING

Dunbar, I: *How to Teach a New Dog Old Tricks,* James & Kenneth Publishers, Berkeley, CA.

Dunbar, I: *Doctor Dunbar's Good Little Dog Book,* Spillers Foods, London England, 1992, 46pp. Available from James & Kenneth Publishers, Berkeley, CA.

Weston, D: *Dog Training: The Gentle Modern* Method, Hyland House, Melbourne, Australia, 1990, 96pp. Available from James & Kenneth Publishers, Berkeley, CA.

Dunbar, I: *SIRIUS Puppy Training* (Video), Bluford/Toth Productions, New York, NY, 1987, 90 min. Available from James & Kenneth Publishers, Berkeley, CA.

Dunbar, I: *Training the Companion Dog,* James & Kenneth Publishers, Berkeley, CA 1991. Available from James & Kenneth Publishers, Berkeley, CA.

Practice makes perfect.

Dr. Debra Horwitz graduated from Michigan State University, College of Veterinary Medicine, in 1975. Since 1982, Dr. Horwitz has had a referral practice for behavioral problems in companion animals. From 1990 onward, she has devoted her practice energies exclusively to the practice of behavioral medicine in companion animals. Her practice is located in St. Louis, Missouri where she is now affiliated with Associated Veterinary Specialists. She is a frequent lecturer, both nationally and internationally. Her articles on companion animal behavior appear in both veterinary and popular publications. She appears locally in St. Louis on both television and radio as well as in local print publications and lectures.

Excitable and Disobedient Behaviors

By Dr. Debra Horwitz
Veterinary Behavior Consultations
253 S. Graeser
St. Louis, MO 63141

INTRODUCTION

The unruly dog presents a dilemma to owners. When do you decide that a young dog is unruly and not just high spirited and immature? It is a popular misconception that there is ever a time to condone the unruly dog. True, puppies can jump, chew and bark but there is no reason that these behaviors have to be accepted as the expected and normal puppy behavior. With time, patience and effort the owner can teach a young puppy proper behavior and be well on the way to an appropriately mannered dog.

How does one define the unruly dog? As mentioned, many excitable and rowdy behaviors that we see in puppies will diminish with time and proper training. The unruly dog is one that continues to be difficult for the owner to manage past puppyhood (6-9 months). This is the dog that will not respond to commands to sit, will not walk on a leash, jumps on people, continually barks for attention, frequently steals things and generally wreaks havoc on the household. The problem is compounded in large dogs because of their size.

INDENTIFYING UNRULY PUPPIES

Often these excitable and disobedient dogs can be identified in the early puppyhood. These puppies will continually mouth owners' hands, and resist attempts to control them for even the most minor procedures. At this time you can often head off a potential behavioral problem by understanding what is happening, its basis and possible outcome. Many people do not realize why puppies chew on them and give the incorrect feedback to control the behavior. Puppies chew on each other constantly in play. Besides being an outlet for energy, play in the animal world often has a learning component. We see this in predatory play of kittens as well as the chewing, wrestling play of puppies. One of the lessons that a puppy is trying to learn is how much pressure from their jaws causes pain. The yelping response of the littermate gives feedback to the puppy as to what amount of pressure causes pain. Pet owners on the other hand often do not give this feedback and the puppy may not learn an important socialization message. So when puppies mouth hands of people, it is important to respond in an appropriate manner to the chewing. That response may be to firmly, but gently, hold the mouth closed while saying "no biting!", or even emitting a yelp to frighten the puppy and let him know that the bite caused pain.

Using methods that puppies already respond to can be an effective way to stop biting behavior in an exuberant puppy. This might be emitting a loud "yelp" or "yipe" that will startle the puppy and let it know that it has caused pain. Another method is to walk away and discontinue play time, ignoring he puppy until it calms down. Punishment should be used carefully because it can also cause problems. If the punishment is insufficient to stop the behavior, it may make matters worse. Excessive punishment can cause the puppy to fear the owner, or cause defensive aggression. Physical techniques like grasping the muzzle and saying "no biting" or "quiet" may work with some puppies. Others may struggle excessively and break free and nothing is accomplished. Some puppies can learn an "off" command that means "don't touch" and then be rewarded for removing their mouth from the owner. For very exuberant puppies, a Promise head collar will help get control and avoid struggling with these problems.

Another misconception that owners have is that a puppy cannot be trained until 6 months of age. Nothing could be further from the truth. As mentioned earlier puppies are learning all the time, every thing that they do teaches them some-thing. By waiting until they are 6 months old to teach certain tasks, we allow other behaviors to take form. Then we have to undo behaviors we don't like in order to get the ones we want. It is important to realize that puppies have very short attention spans. It is also important to motivate the puppies to perform using positive reinforcement. By early training, excitable puppies can often have their behavior channeled in the correct direction. The training of puppies is discussed in another chapter in this book.

But what about the dog that is 12-18 months and a total terror? Many owners may have tried traditional obedience training classes without success. The dog still jumps on people, barks incessantly and defies commands. Often times these owners are inadvertently making training and reinforcement errors. They have tried yelling at their dogs, pulling on choke collars and usually have resorted to isolation to avoid the problem. Let's address these training and correction techniques to see what works, what is ineffective, and why.

When dogs misbehave, isolation is a common technique that owners use. However, isolation usually only makes the problem worse. Dogs are very social and want to be with people. The more that they are isolated, the more excited and therefore unruly they will be when they are finally let out of confinement. This then leads to a "Catch-22" situation, the worse a dog behaves, the less the people want it around. When they do see the dog, the more it will

Let's talk about formal training! A dog as large as an Afghan Hound can be a real nuisance if he jumps on you.

act like a dog to gain their attention. In the dog world, running, jumping, licking and barking are means to signal pleasure at seeing the other dog. Unfortunately, people do not greet these behaviors the same way! Instead they may yell at the dog, physically reprimand it or isolate it again. For some dogs, negative attention is better than no attention, reprimands do not stop their improper behavior, and so the cycle just continues.

Another common training error involves owners actually reinforcing the very behaviors that they do not want. A good example is a dog barking to come inside. When a dog is outside barking to come in and the owners ignore the dog for 10 minutes but finally let the dog in, what have they accomplished? The owner probably let the dog in to stop annoying the neighbors or themselves due to the incessant barking. But what does the dog learn? The dog has just learned that 10 minutes of incessant barking gains access to the indoors. Therefore the dog will be willing to bark longer the next time, especially if it also then gains access to the inside. In other words the owners have just reinforced the very thing that they did not want: barking. This is not the only scenario where incorrect training occurs. Another common problem is giving a command, the dog not performing what was requested, so the owner repeats the command. This sends the message to the dog that 2-3 repetitions of the command are needed to get the desired behavior. When you ask a dog to do some-

thing, be sure that you can get the dog to perform the behavior. Remember, if you have not adequately taught the dog how to perform the command, you are doomed to fail. If you tell the dog to sit and he does not, within reason, make him sit. If you can't do that then you need to structure the situation so that you will get the response that you ask for, or do not ask for a behavior unless you know that the dog can perform it on command. It is important to keep in mind that if you never ask your dog to sit on command, there is no reason to assume that he/she will sit when asked unexpectedly or in a very demanding situation. Your dog already knows how to sit, just not how to do so when asked. What can be seen from these examples is that how we train dogs is important.

An essential component of training is appropriate reinforcement of rewards and appropriate punishment. Inappropriate rewards and punishment can lead to the exact behaviors that owners were trying to avoid. The concepts of learning are covered in other parts of this book and will not be dealt with here.

Dogs live in the here and now and, therefore, the timing of rewards and punishment is critical. Unless you reward or punish during or immediately following the act, the dog does not connect your actions with its acts. The dog realizes that your are angry or happy, but not about what. In other words, punishment after the fact does no good and can even lead to the kinds of disobedient behaviors that owners find objectionable and confuse the dog.

How then can owners get control of these excitable dogs so that they can start teaching correct behavior? A recently developed training collar can be very beneficial in accomplishing that goal.

The "Promise™" headcollar is actually a halter-type collar developed by Dr. R.K. Anderson, a veterinarian and Professor and Director Emeritus of the Animal Behavior Clinic at the University of Minnesota and Ruth E. Foster, Past President of the National Association of Dog Obedience Instructors. The headcollar is marketed by Ameri-Pet. The headcollar uses a dog's natural instinct to follow a leader using pressure sites that cause the dog to respond in a behaviorally appropriate way. One strap goes behind the ears over the back of the neck, which simulates the pressure control that a mother dog uses on her puppies. The second strap encircles the dog's nose and simulates how the leader dog would put his mouth over the muzzle of a subordinate dog and stimulate submissive behavior. Dogs have a natural instinct to pull against pressure, so when you pull backward with a traditional choke collar the dog instinctively pulls ahead. But with the Promise™ headcollar, when you pull on the lead, the pressure is exerted on the back of the head and the dog will pull backwards to avoid the pressure, rather than forward, and stays by the owner's side. Lastly, since the headcollar does not encircle the lower neck, the dog is not choking while the owner is trying to train. The headcollar also comes with an indoor lead for added control in the home.

Like any type of collar or restraint, it does take some getting used to when a dog first puts on this collar. Dogs will buck, try to rub it off and try to get out of it. However, they quickly adjust-especially if the owner does not give in. Also owners encounter people who ask why their dog is wearing a muzzle. This halter is not a muzzle; the dog can open its mouth, eat, bark and bite! The headcollar is a humane way to train dogs, as it does not rely on choking the dog for control.

These collars are particularly useful in the excitable, disobedient dog, but any puppy could be trained with one from 8-10 weeks on. Like any other collar, the Promise™ headcollar can be left on the dog all the time when owners are home. If the dog is a problem, the indoor lead can be left attached for further control. This way, as soon as the dog begins to engage in behavior that is unacceptable, the owner can grab the lead, stop the behavior and have complete control. By the same token, if you give the dog a command and he does not obey, with a collar and leash on the dog you can get the compliance that you require. It is especially effective for dogs that jump on people and for dogs that pull their owners while walking. It can be used on any size dog, by any size person. Strength is not a factor in the use of the Promise™ system. It also does not rely on controlling the dog by choking it. Instead it uses the dog's natural instincts and behavioral signals to encourage compliance. The Promise™ system also comes with a handbook detailing how to train your dog.

Often, the key to turning an unruly dog into an acceptable pet is having continuous control until you reliably can get the behaviors that you want. This is most easily accomplished by having the dog on leash. Although this seems like a simple solution, it is not often tried. Once the dog begins to engage in the unwanted behavior, prolonged attempts at control are frustrating to the owner and do not really teach the dog the correct lesson. In fact because often people are unable to stop the behaviors that they do not want, they actually end up reinforcing them by allowing them to continue. An integral component of controlling an unruly dog entails restructuring the situations so that the unruly behavior is not able to take place. This can take various forms such as keeping the dog on leash so that they can not run through the house, closing doors to other rooms and limiting the access of the dog to areas where he is unsupervised, only interacting with the dog in a positive manner and setting up situations so that the dog will do as the owner asks.

This brings up another vital issue in controlling excitable and disobedient dogs. Many owners are so frustrated by the behavior of their dog that the only interaction that they have with the dog is negative. Unfortunately, they have lost the joy of pet ownership. But worse than that, they do not reward the behaviors that they do want. It is just as important to tell the dog when it is doing the correct behavior as to discipline the bad. It is also important to train the dog in the correct behavior even when you are not sure you will need it. An example of this is training the dog to sit and stay in the front hall. Why you may ask? How will the dog know to sit and not run out the door when people come to visit, a highly excitable event, if the dog never practiced doing so when things were calm? *Teach the dog what you want it to know before you need it.*

What about other unruly behaviors like barking, food stealing, door charging, jumping up, getting on furniture and pulling on leash? Lets take a look at each one of these and then discuss some solutions that can be used to help with these problems.

BARKING BEHAVIORS

What can an owner do about a barking dog? To determine a treatment approach, a few questions need to be asked. Is the dog barking outside while the owners are gone? If yes, why is the dog outside all day? Perhaps the dog is not housetrained or is destructive and cannot be left in the house while people are gone. Then the barking problem is really a housetraining problem or destruction problem that needs to be attended to first. When the problem is barking while the owner is home, one approach is to teach the dog a command for quiet. To start training, allow the dog to bark a few times, say after the doorbell rings, then hold a food treat right by the dog's nose. The dog will

Puppies at Play with a Nylafloss™.

stop barking to sniff the treat. Immediately couple this pause with the phrase "quiet," then give the dog the treat and verbal praise. The next time, the dog should be required to be quiet longer in order to receive the treat. The quiet interval should gradually be increased so that the dog learns the meaning of the word.

Another method to stop barking is to use punishment. When the dog begins to bark, startle the dog with a loud noise, like pan lids clanging together. Usually this will stop the barking temporarily. When the dog stops, say "no barking" or "quiet" and praise the dog for silence. You will need to repeat this each and every time the dog barks for it to be effective. If the pet is trained with a Promise™ Halter, a pull on the leash is all that is needed to retrain most dogs.

For barking that continues in the owner's absence, anti-bark collars or debarking are sometimes advocated. These are controversial is-

Use of a Promise halter (photo provided by Dr. Debra Horwitz).

sues which should be discussed between owners and their veterinarians.

DOOR CHARGING AND JUMPING UP

Another behavior that causes problems for owners is door charging. Door charging is the behavior of the dog speeding to the door whenever anyone knocks or rings the bell. How can an owner deal with this problem area? Start by teaching the dog to sit and stay for a food reward in the entry area. Gradually phase out food treats when the behavior is learned and can be reliably repeated. Then, practice with visitors, keeping the dog on leash and making it sit and stay. When a dog is sitting and staying in place, then the dog is unable to jump on people. Require your dog to always sit before it gets petted and you can go a long way toward eliminating jumping behavior. If the dog has never even practiced the task without distractions, how can you expect the dog to perform the task when visitors come over?

FOOD STEALING AND GETTING ON FURNITURE

These two problems have something in common; they most often occur when the owner is not looking. Therefore, in order to stop the behavior, you need to be able to punish it without being there. This usually requires the use of "booby traps." The use of remote punishment devices allows the punishment to come from the object while the act is occurring and is more helpful in correcting problem behavior. Examples of these

An excellent means for restraining your dog is a halter which discourages pulling. Quality halters are available in pet shops. Photo courtesy of Four Paws.

devices are shaker cans, Snappy Trainers™, Scat Mats™, and motion sensors. Shaker cans are empty soda cans that have a few pennies in them. By rigging them to fall easily, they will startle a dog when disturbed. Snappy Trainer™ is a mousetrap that has a large red flap on the end. This flap not only prevents the dog from being injured when the trap is sprung, it also sends a visual message to the dog. Scat Mats™ are mats to place on furniture that administer a mild shock when touched. Motion sensors are available at many electronic and hard-

Dogs left alone outdoors can become problem barkers. Owners must attend to curbing this behavior before it becomes a serious problem.

ware stores. Some sense vibration, while others sense movement. When disturbed, either type emit a noise that scares away the dog. Certainly, a very effective method to deal with food stealing is to make sure food is not left available for the dog to take.

CHASING BEHAVIOR

Chasing and running after prey is a normal dog behavior. This behavior is more strongly motivated in some breeds of dogs than others. In order to control this behavior it is necessary to train the dog to do something different than it was doing before. It is not enough to yell "no" and punish the dog. This alone will not stop a behavior that has a strong instinctual motivation. In-

The only safe place to leave food where a Dalmation is concerned is on or in the fridge.

stead, counterconditioning and desensitization are necessary to control this behavior once it has gotten out of hand.

First, let's talk about prevention of chasing behaviors. As soon as you witness the young dog engaging in an inappropriate chase, immediately start training. Get a leash on the dog, teach it to sit and stay and then you can present the dog with the stimulus that it would normally chase and reward the dog for good behavior. Remember, when off the leash, the dog may revert to its old habits. Therefore, try to avoid those situations until you feel confident that the dog will behave.

Once the dog has been engaging in chasing behaviors for some time, it will be more difficult to stop the behavior. The very fact that the object the dog chases runs, is reinforcement enough. Again, a program of desensitization and counterconditioning is needed. This consists of teaching the dog to sit and stay, gradually introducing objects the dog chased and rewarding the dog for good behavior. It will be necessary to first start with objects the dog does not chase and progress to more tempting items. If the behavior is extreme, a consultation with a behaviorist may be necessary.

PULLING ON LEASH

It is always a shame when owners are unable to engage in the simple joy of walking their dog due to extreme leash pulling. One answer is the use of the Promise headcollar that was mentioned earlier. With the headcollar, dogs can easily be

Dog pulling owner by the leash. Headcollars and harnesses work better than traditional collars if your dog is a puller.

taught to walk at their owners side without pulling. Best of all, since the headcollar is not a "choke" collar, it is better for the dog. Early puppy training is another way to teach a dog not to pull on leash. Anti-pull harnesses also work very well but do not give the owner the extra control afforded by the halter devices.

SUMMARY

Many of the problem behaviors that annoy owners are really normal dog behaviors. By channeling them into acceptable outlets or training the dog how to behave owners can enjoy and keep their pets.

ADDITIONAL READING

Campbell, William E., *Behavior Problems in Dogs*, American Veterinary Publications, Inc., Santa Barbara, CA, 1985.

Dunbar, Ian, Dog Behavior: *Why Dogs Do What They Do*. TFH Publications, Inc.,Neptune, NJ, 1979.

Monks of New Skete, *How to Be Your Dog's Best Friend*, Little, Brown and Company, Boston-Toronto, 1978.

Pryor, Karen, *Don't Shoot the Dog!*, Bantam Books, New York, 1984.

Tortora, Daniel F. PhD, *Help! This Animal is Driving Me Crazy*, Wideview, New York, 1978.

Dr. Lowell Ackerman is a nutritional consultant in addition to being board-certified in the field of veterinary dermatology. To date, he is the author of 13 books and over 150 articles dealing with pet health care and has lectured extensively on these subjects on an international schedule. Dr. Ackerman is a member of the American Academy of Veterinary Nutrition and the American Veterinary Society of Animal Behavior.

Nutrition and Behavior

By Lowell Ackerman, DVM PhD
Mesa Veterinary Hospital, Ltd.
858 N. Country Club Drive
Mesa, AZ 85201

INTRODUCTION

There are many ways in which diet and behavior can be linked, and it is only recently that these have begun to be properly explored. It now appears that some problems may have a nutritional basis, while others are responsive to nutritional manipulation. It is not outlandish to assume that some dogs might have behavioral problems related to their diet. After all, many dogs eat high-calorie, high-protein commercial diets, liberally laced with additives, flavorings, preservatives and other processing enhancements. All of these features have become suspect by different investigators pursuing different aspects of behavior problems. This discipline is still in its infancy and not immune to controversy. However, let's take a look at some of the ways that nutrition and behavior may be linked.

EFFECT OF DIETARY INGREDIENTS ON BEHAVIOR

Most veterinary behavior specialists have considered the role of protein in behavior problems. Both the quantity of protein and its quality and extent of processing have recently become suspect. High-meat diets can result in lowered levels of the neurotransmitter serotonin in the brain, which can make some animals more aggressive. Conversely, high-carbohydrate diets result in higher levels of serotonin in the brain. Can feeding high-carbohydrate diets be an effective treatment for some forms of aggression? This concept is being explored, but clear-cut answers are not yet available. For animals that do respond to this regimen, supplementing the diet with vitamin B_6 (pyridoxine) might also be beneficial because this aids in the production of serotonin.

Casomorphine is derived from the digestion of casein and exorphines from the digestion of gluten. Together with hormones, hormone-like substances, and pheromones naturally present in many dog foods, all have been shown, scientifically, to alter normal dog behavior. Casomorphine and the exorphines, which would be provided by milk proteins and cereals respectively, can trigger behaviors in dogs not unlike giving them morphine or other opioids. The overall effect of casomorphine and exorphines from commercial dog foods has not been adequately investigated.

Another concern, often posed by dog trainers, is that training problems are more common in dogs fed dry food than those fed a canned

Can diet influence behavior? Photo courtesy of Dr. Gary Landsberg.

ration. Trainers often blame moisture content but there is probably a better explanation. Most dry dog foods are heavily preserved with antioxidants so they can last on store shelves for months without going rancid. Since canned diets are heat sterilized before packaging, additional use of preservatives is not needed. Some of the preservatives getting increased scrutiny are ethoxyquin, butylated hydroxyanisole (BHA) and butylated hydroxytoluene (BHT). Only recently has any scientific research been directed in this area.

Testing the Theory

It's not enough to make claims and hypotheses about health care issues.

There must be a way of proving or refuting such theories for individual animals. This is possible to a limited extent, as long as certain provisions are accepted. The hypothesis of high-protein or preservative-rich diets contributing to behavior problems can be easily tested by feeding a high-quality but low-protein diet for as little as seven-ten days. This time frame is not long enough to uncover adverse food reactions (up to 12 weeks would be necessary) but is sufficient for judging the impact of protein and preservatives on pet behavior. The diets must be homemade protein sources that are suitable, including boiled chicken, lamb, fish or rabbit combined with boiled white rice or mashed potatoes. This also limits problems that might occur from high cereal-based diets (e.g., exorphines), milk proteins (e.g., casomorphine), and preservatives. The meal should be mixed as one part meat to four parts carbohydrate and fed in the same amount as the pet's regular diet. Only fresh water should be provided during the trial. No supplements, treats or snacks should be given. This diet is not nutritionally balanced, but that should make little difference for the seven-ten days in which the trial is being conducted.

If there is a response to the diet trial, it is advisable to follow up on the process by challenging the pet with specific potential offenders. The first test would be to increase the protein component of the diet (50:50) to see if there is a behavioral change. If so, this helps confirm the suspicion that it is the protein component that is contributory. Adding commercial foods or treats with specific preservatives is the best way of determining the role of food additives in the problem.

What to Do About It

For animals that respond to a homemade low-protein, preservative-free diet, there are many options available. Regular use of a homemade diet should be discouraged unless a completely balanced ration can be formulated. Low-protein diets are commercially available and are the most convenient option. Remember that low protein should not mean low quality. Look for diets with high-quality protein in moderate amounts and an easily digested carbohydrate

source. Cereal-based diets tend to have a lot of exorphines, which may contribute to behavioral problems. Start with canned diets, which tend to have few if any preservatives. Dry foods have the most preservatives, and semi-moist foods have too high a sugar content. If the condition worsens when the pet is put on a commercial ration, there are likely more problems than just protein content to consider. Home-delivered, preservative-free, home-prepared and frozen pet foods are all options with which the veterinarian should be familiar.

For dogs with reactions to preservatives, canned foods are an option; and there are also preservative-free diets commercially available. Both of these are usually acceptable, but current regulations make it almost impossible to be assured that there are actually no preservatives in preservative-free diets. Manufacturers need only list on the label those preservatives that they add during ration preparation. However, there is no guarantee that the manufacturer did not purchase the raw ingredients already preserved. If a pet responds well to the homemade diet, and challenge feeding fails to uncover a culprit, consider additives as a likely candidate. When commercial diets cannot be used, homemade diets remain a final option. At this point, it is worth having a diet recipe prepared by a nutritionist to ensure that nutritional requirements will be met. Alternatively, computer software is available (e.g., Small Animal Nutritionist: N-squared Computing, Silverton, Oregon) so that custom diets can be formulated by practitioners.

FOOD ALLERGY/INTOLERANCE

It is not unusual for pets to react adversely when fed certain foods. Occasionally, diet-related problems can affect systems other than the skin and digestive tract, and behavioral problems have been reported. Some animals can even develop diet-related seizure disorders.

When it comes to allergy and intolerance to foods, individual ingredients are always to blame. Pets are likely allergic to specific ingredients in a diet, such as beef, chicken, soy, milk, corn, wheat, etc. However, many owners tend to blame brand names, preservatives, or a suspicious ingredient listed on the package. Many others fail to get the correct diagnosis because they refuse to believe that the problem they are seeing is diet-related. They may be hesitant because they have been feeding the same diet for years without problems or they feel that the problems are not worsened at feeding time. It's time to lose all your prejudices about what you think about adverse food reactions and learn some basic truths.

Some individuals suspect that hyperactivitiy can have a dietary component. Photo courtesy of Dr. Gary Landsberg.

How Do I Know if My Pet Has a Food Allergy/Intolerance?

It is almost impossible to confirm the diagnosis by switching from one brand of commercial food to another. Since most of the ingredients in pet foods are similar, merely changing brands or types of food is helpful only if you are lucky enough to change to a food which does not include the problem-causing ingredient.

A home-made elimination (hypoallergenic) diet is the best way to confirm suspicions. It must consist of ingredients to which the pet has never been exposed. This will diagnose an adverse food reaction in most cases, but not differentiate between allergy and intolerance. A single protein source (a protein source to which the pet has not been exposed) can be combined with a carbohydrate source such as rice or potatoes and the entire diet fed for 6-12 weeks. The meat can be boiled, broiled, baked or microwaved (but not fried), and the rice should be boiled prior to serving. They are mixed at one part meat to 2 parts rice or potatoes. The mixed ingredients should be fed in the same total volume as the pet's normal diet. During the trial, hypoallergenic foods and fresh, preferably distilled water must be fed exclusive of all else. Absolutely nothing else must be fed, including treats, snacks, vitamins, chew toys and even flavored heartworm preventive tablets. Access must also be denied to food and feces of other dogs and cats in the household.

If there is substantial improvement while on the diet, further investigation is warranted. If there is no improvement, diet is not a significant part of the problem, and the diet can be discontinued. The intention is not to feed these diets indefinitely. They are not nutritionally balanced for long-term feeding. They are meant only to be fed for the six-12 weeks necessary to determine if food is implicated in the problem. If the condition improves while on the diet, challenge feeding will be needed to determine which ingredient(s) is (are) causing the problem.

By now, most pet owners have heard about blood tests that claim to be able to diagnose food allergies. Surely this is a lot easier that having to prepare and feed homemade diet for many weeks. That would be true if the blood tests actually lived up to their claims. Unfortunately, these tests can be very misleading since the results are often quite inaccurate, being reliable perhaps only 10% of the time. This is not surprising because not all diet-related problems are allergic (these tests don't identify intolerance), and those that are allergic are not necessarily caused by the antibodies measured in the blood

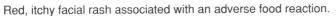
Red, itchy facial rash associated with an adverse food reaction.

tests. Therefore, blood tests should never replace a hypoallergenic food trial as a screening test. More often than not, the results supplied will not prove helpful and can be misleading.

What Do I Do if My Pet Does React to His Diet?

If there is improvement by the end of the elimination diet trial, further investigation is warranted. Challenge feeding with individual ingredients should allow you to determine the dietary cause of the problem. This is accomplished by adding one new ingredient each week to the hypoallergenic diet. You then create a list of ingredients which your pet can tolerate and those which it can't. The recommendation then is to feed a balanced commercial ration that does not include the problematic ingredients. Rarely is it necessary for pets to remain on specialty (e.g., lamb-based) diets, nor is it advisable. Commercial hypoallergenic diets are suitable for owners that don't want to determine the specific cause of their pet's problem. These diets are effective about 80% of the time, for pets with documented adverse food reactions.

Crusty footpads in a young dog with generic dog food disease.

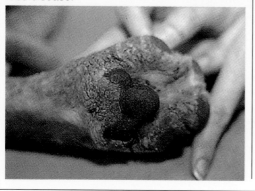

LINKING BEHAVIOR TO MEDICAL/ NUTRITIONAL DISORDERS

It is tempting to speculate on ways that nutritional intervention could be used to treat behavioral problems. After all, nutritional therapy could offer a relatively safe form of therapy, free from many of the adverse effects seen with drugs. Preliminary studies in humans as well as animals suggest that some conditions may indeed be amenable to nutritional intervention. Let's take a look at some examples that have been documented in pets.

When dogs have liver problems, they have a difficult time metabolizing protein into useful amino acids. One of the by-products of incomplete metabolism is ammonia, which can cause behavioral abnormalities (hepatic encephalopathy). Some dogs may just act confused, some have personality changes, some are transiently blind or experience seizures, and others may press their heads against walls or other objects. The key to treatment is to correct the underlying liver problem and to feed small quantities of high-quality protein that are easily digested and metabolized. Meat is generally avoided in favor of boiled rice, vegetables and cottage cheese or egg in small amounts for protein. It is also recommended that three-four meals a day be fed rather than one or two, so that the small intestine has more opportunity for complete absorption. For those dogs that suffer hepatic encephalopathy because of copper retention in their livers, zinc supplementation has been found to be an effective remedy.

Coprophagia is a baffling condition in which dogs consume their own stools. Although nutritional imbalances have long been suspected, no organic reason has been found for this condition. However, in a recent study, it was found that most of these dogs did have a medical/nutritional problem that could explain the condition, such as borderline to low trypsin-like immunoreactivity (TLI), or abnormalities in folate, cobalamin, or other nutrients. About half of these dogs did indeed benefit from enzyme supplementation. This probably explains the anecdotal reports of success of adding meat tenderizers (which usually contain the enzymes papain and/or bromelain) to the dog's diet. Further clinical studies are needed to determine which enzyme supplements are most effective for this disorder and what accounts for the other cases that are not enzyme-responsive. If the cause of the coprophagia cannot be determined, environmental modifications are the best chance for therapeutic success. Denying access to the stool is the first step. The yard should be cleaned regularly and not in the direct sight of the dog with the problem. On walks, the dog should be kept on a leash or halter and "corrected" when it attempts to sniff or ingest other stool. The pet must be in constant supervision while outdoors.

SUMMARY

Nutrition is an important aspect of medicine, including behavioral medicine. Although the impact of nutrition on behavioral disorders is only now being explored, its importance should not be minimized. This chapter reviews some of the more common ways that nutrition and behavior cross paths and some theories that warrant future study.

ADDITIONAL READING

Ackerman, L.: Adverse Reactions to Foods. *Journal of Veterinary Allergy and Clinical Immunology*, 1993.

Ackerman, L.: Effects of an Enzyme Supplement (Prozyme™) on Selected Nutrient Levels in Dogs. *Journal of Veterinary Allergy and Clinical Immunology*, 1993.

Ackerman, L.: Enzyme Therapy in Veterinary Practice. Advances in Nutrition 1993.

Ballarini, G.: Animal psychodietetics. Journal of Small Animal Practice, 1990.

Fernstrom, J.D.: Dietary Amino Acids and Brain Function. *Journal of the American Dietetic Association*, 1994.

Halliwell, R.E.W.: Comparative Aspects of Food Intolerance. *Veterinary Medicine*, 1992.

Mugford, R.A.: The Influence of Nutrition on Canine Behaviour. *Journal of Small Animal Practice*, 1987.

Schoenthaler, S.J.; Moody, J.M.; Pankow, L.D.: *Applied Nutrition and Behavior. Journal of Applied Nutrition*, 1991.

Wallin, MS; Rissanen, AM: Food and Mood: Relationship between Food, Serotonin and Affective Disorders. Acta Psychiatrica Scandinavica, 1994.

Dr. Donal McKeown graduated from the Ontario Veterinary College and then practiced small animal medicine in Washington, D.C. for 16 years. In 1974, he was appointed Associate Professor of Small Animal Surgery, Department of Clinical Studies at the Ontario Veterinary College. In 1984 he became Associate Professor of Ethology in the Department of Population Medicine. Dr. McKeown retired from the College in 1994.

Dr. McKeown has contributed to several books, written many scientific articles and lectured widely in Canada, the United States and Europe. He has received the Distinguished Teaching Award and the Teaching Excellence Award from the Ontario Veterinary College and was presented with the Veterinarian of the Year Award from the Ontario Veterinary Medical Association in 1989. He is past president of the Ontario Veterinary Medical Association, vice-president of Veterinary Medical Diets Inc., president of International Bio Institute Inc., and president of the Fergus-Elora Rotary Club.

Eating and Drinking Behavior in the Dog

By Donal B. McKeown, DVM
Guelph, Ontario

INTRODUCTION

We often take eating and drinking behavior for granted, but there are several aspects of the process that are worth considering. Before we look at abnormal variations in feeding and drinking, let's first take a look at some interesting facts:

1. Eating and drinking behavior are, for the most part, genetically acquired reflexes that have not changed significantly from those of their wild predecessor, the wolf.
2. Dogs are omnivorous and thus can thrive on commercial rations that contain large proportions of cooked carbohydrates. Carbohydrates must be cooked to be assimilated by the dog.
3. Dogs use their teeth to tear their food into pieces small enough to be swallowed and do very little chewing or grinding.
4. Eating and drinking stimulates the gastro-colic reflex about 10-15 minutes after eating and thus regulates the performance of urination and defecation. Giving food and water at regular intervals simplifies house training in puppies.
5. Giving dogs free access to dry food after the dog is fully house trained simplifies the feeding of dogs because the dog can eat whenever it desires (dry food, unless moistened, will not spoil or deteriorate in the bowl) and the owner does not have to worry about volume or feeding schedule. If the diet is too palatable or the dog inherently eats too much or is suffering from a problem that increases food consumption, then the food must be rationed and meal fed. This is best accomplished by giving the dog access to the food twice daily for about ten minutes and then removing it, or by giving a measured amount of dog food.

The amount of food required by the dog can be calculated from the information found on the label or supplied by the manufacturer. This supplies a very rough estimate of daily requirements and must be modified for each individual by observing the results of feeding. If dogs overeat, it is advisable to divide the daily requirement into two equal feedings.

This Bull Terrier is happily distracted with his Gumabone® and is not looking for trouble.

6. Most dogs do not digest milk after weaning because of the lack of the digestive enzyme, lactose. Dairy products given dogs may reduce assimilation of nutrients from the intestinal tract and cause diarrhea or constipation.

7. The inherited nursing reflex drives the new born to find, suckle and bond to a breast. The nose, a heat-sensitive probe, quickly finds the breast based on body temperature, position of the bitch's body and smell. The dominant puppy usually gains ownership to one of a larger posterior breasts.

8. In rare cases, bitches still ex- hibit a regurgitation reflex of partially digested food in response to licking of the bitch's muzzle by weaning age puppies.

9. Changing a dog's diet rapidly may result in gastrointestinal disturbances. Thus, it is recommended to change the dogs diet slowly over a period of 5-7 days by gradually increasing the amount of the new diet and decreasing the old.

BEHAVIORAL CHANGES INDUCED BY NUTRITION

It has long been speculated that dogs, like children, show an increase in excitability when fed elevated levels of certain carbohydrates. Also, It has been suggested that high levels of protein, fat, preservatives and food coloring have an effect on behavior. These ingredients have not all been studied in detail but there is no evidence to suggest that they have any influence on behavior in dogs.

APPETITE

Appetite is the drive to ingest calories and is controlled by complex interaction of internal and external stimuli. Hunger and satiety (a feeling of being full) controls are primarily associated with areas in the brain but current energy levels in the body, liver metabolism, and certain hormones influence appetite. External stimuli such as the physical characteristics and nutrient content (levels of fat, sugar, etc.) of the diet, social pressures, previous experiences, etc.

The appetite of some dogs can be stimulated by the presence of another dog. This competitive effect of increasing appetite is generally transitory.

Appetite can be increased by improving the palatability of the food. Palatability of food for dogs is based on smell, mouth feel and taste, in this order. Palatability of dog food can usually be increased by adding such ingredients as moisture, cooked meat, cooked onions, garlic, sweets (ketchup), salt, bitter and by heating the food to body temperature. Once the dog is eating the food, the additive can gradually be eliminated. If the dog is healthy, one could also increase appetite by with-holding food for several days and not give any treats.

In rare cases, drugs such as progesterone, cortisone, and certain antianxiety drugs may be given with the above additives and methods to stimulate the appetite.

DIET FIXATION

Diet fixation occurs when the dog has been conditioned to eat only one type of highly palatable food, such as table scraps. This bad eating habit can be very difficult to change and becomes a problem when the diet being fed is not well balanced or it is required to alter the diet because of a change in heath status or change in life stage.

Owners can also condition dogs to eat only after they have received a special treat or only after they are presented with a special situation. For example, the dog will eat only if the owner hand-feeds it or the dog will not eat unless it first receives a piece of cheese.

LEARNED FOOD BEGGING

Begging for food is a conditioned response and is usually related to a specific time and place or to a specific stimulus such as the noise of the can opener, the refrigerator door or the smell of food. Begging can become an annoying behavior, and also lead to bad eating habits, malnutrition and obesity.

The best advice to stop begging is to stop rewarding it. If the dog does not receive any more food rewards for begging, the behavior will eventually go into extinction. Extinction refers to a behavior that disappears

If you allow your dog to beg at the dinner table, he will soon learn how to steal food from your plate.

something else, such as play ball. Feed the dog well away from the table while the family is eating, prevent access to the situation by keeping it out of the room by closing the door, or train the dog to accept cage confinement. Another option is to train the dog to sit or stay quietly in the corner of the room and only reward the dog if it remains in that location. Then, slowly increase the time before the reward is given so that the dog ultimately stays in its spot quietly for the whole meal.

when it fails to be rewarded. The client should be reminded that when you stop rewarding a previously conditioned response, it will cause the behavior to increase in frequency and intensity for a short period, before it goes into extinction. Furthermore, if someone in the family rewards the dog occasionally for begging, then begging becomes rewarded on an irregular schedule and thus becomes more resistant to extinction. Therefore rewards must be stopped completely, and the behavior will be expected to increase initially before it stops.

It is useful to interrupt the behavior whenever it occurs by distracting the dog and train it to do

LEARNED TASTE AVERSION

Learned taste aversion occurs when an animal eats a novel-tasting food and is stricken by nausea or illness even several hours after eating and learns from this one event that the novel food is dangerous. This learned behavior is useful for survival in the wild, but has little or no practical application in dealing with the behavior of pet dogs.

GARBAGE EATING

Roaming and eating garbage is thought to be related to hunting behavior. This selfrewarding, difficult-to-change behavior can cause intestinal pathology and toxicity.

Dogs that eat previously buried and decaying food stuffs, rotting carcasses, hoof trimmings etc., are performing normal inherited behavior that appears very rewarding and thus difficult or impossible to control. The surprising aspect of this behavior is that the eating of these obnoxious foodstuffs causes few problems.

GRASS EATING

The eating of small amounts of grass by dogs is normal. The causes of eating excessive amounts of grass are unknown but may suggest an attempt by the dog to ingest bulk to appease a gastrointestinal irrita-tion. Grass is a bulky, rough material that cannot be digested by dogs and thus may induce vomiting or act as a laxative.

DESTRUCTIVE CHEWING AND PICA

The licking, biting, chewing or eating of things that are not considered food, is pica. Chewing on physical objects may be due to play behavior, exploratory behavior or teething in young puppies. In rare cases, diseases such as gastroenteritis, rabies, hormonal imbalances, central nervous system disturbances, etc, may cause

Puppies will chew on everything. Branches can be dangerous to your dog: besides the possibility of their being toxic, they can cut a dog's gums open.

pica. Nutritional deficiencies, (except for a severe lack dietary salt and starvation) do not induce pica in the dog.

Preventing the puppy from having access to the chewed object and supplying the appropriate items to chew is the first step in the treatment. It is important to supply chewables and toys that are not similar to household objects. For example, do not give the puppy an old shoe or sock to chew on. Encourage the puppy to interact with the object by playing with it or by making it attractive; for example, smear it with a highly palatable paste like cheese or liverwurst. If the puppy is teething, supply several toys that have a variety of mouth feels. Puppies usually stop excessive chewing by five to six months of age unless the owner is conditioning the dog to chew by stimulating mouth activities (playing tug of war or mouthing games).

Once pica is expressed, the behavior can be increased and prolonged by the owner paying attention to the dog while it is performing the behavior. Mild punishment is often interpreted by the dog as a reward. Do not punish the behavior but interrupt the behavior by distracting it and train the dog to play with a ball or to do something else unrelated to chewing or mouth activities.

Dogs suffering separation anxiety commonly express their stress by redirecting it to eating non-nutritional objects like walls, doors, carpets, furniture, etc., or lick a specific place on an object (carpet) or themselves (lick-granuloma).

The most common causes of pica in adult dogs are environmentally induced anxieties or severe environmental conflicts or inconsistencies that can result in obsessive compulsive disorders.

CHEWING AND EATING STONES

The chewing and eating of stones is a redirected behavior due to conflict in the environment and is augmented by the self-rewarding activity of chewing. The intensity of this behavior can increase to become an obsessive-compulsive disorder. This form of pica may result in the teeth being ground down to the gum level. Some dog even swallow the stones, which may cause significant damage to the intestinal tract unless they are removed surgically.

Because chewing of stones is rewarding, it is important to prevent all access to stones by placing a muzzle on the dog for several months or keeping the dog on a leash or treat the problem in the winter when the stones are frozen to the ground. The dog, when it is outside, could be trained to play with or carry an appropriate object that is more enjoyable than chewing on stones.

If possible, the cause of the conflict should be eliminated, drugs administered and the dog trained.

HYPERPHAGIA

Canines in the wild normally eat large volumes of food quickly every three or four days. "Wolfing" of large volumes of food quickly

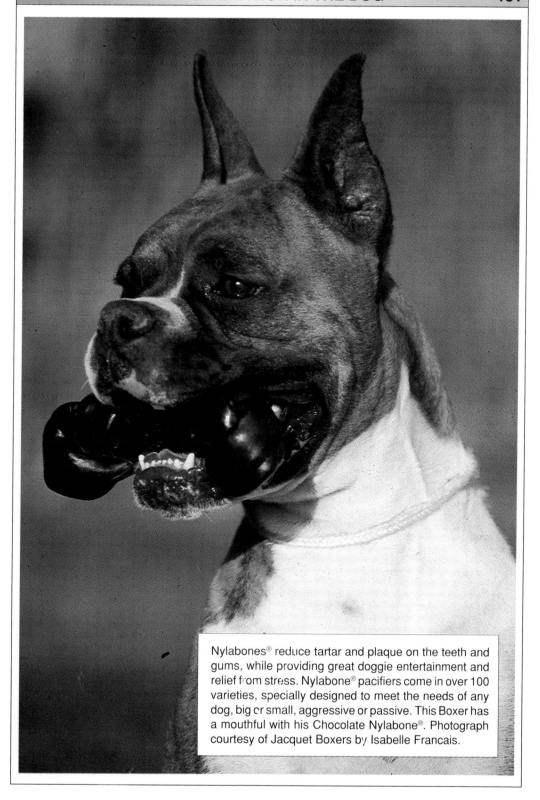

Nylabones® reduce tartar and plaque on the teeth and gums, while providing great doggie entertainment and relief from stress. Nylabone® pacifiers come in over 100 varieties, specially designed to meet the needs of any dog, big or small, aggressive or passive. This Boxer has a mouthful with his Chocolate Nylabone®. Photograph courtesy of Jacquet Boxers by Isabelle Francais.

may be seen in adult dogs when they have had to compete for limited amounts of food, have a metabolic disease or have an obsessive-compulsive disorder (psychogenic polyphagia). Dogs that eat too much too rapidly may vomit immediately after eating, develop intestinal gas from swallowed air or diarrhea.

These dogs should be examined by a veterinarian to eliminate the possibility of concurrent disease. If it is a behavioral problem, the dog should be fed by itself in a quiet location, given a calculated amount of food that should be divided in multiple small meals given throughout the day. Dogs with an obsessive-compulsive disorder should be given drugs, conditioned and the source of the environmental conflict eliminated.

THE EFFECTS OF ANXIETY ON EATING AND DRINKING

Eating is a powerful emotional stimulus for dogs as evidenced by the fact that stereotypys and narcolepsy can be induced by the act of eating. Hunger increases tension and anxiety, while eating general reduces it. Dogs exhibiting a high level of tension and excitement generally do not eat. Dogs may refuse a food reward if training becomes too stressful because the trainer is inconsistent, training too rapidly or the task demanded of the dog is too difficult. Dogs already showing signs of separation anxiety because of being separated from a highly bonded owner cannot be distracted by food treats. The fear and anxiety induced by a longer term of separation, observed when dogs are

Golden Retriever relaxing contentedly with his Gumabone®. Photograph by Karen Taylor.

boarded or hospitalized, may result in depression and anorexia for several days.

Excessive drinking (psychogenic polydipsia) induced by anxiety is rarely seen in dogs and should be differentiated from diseases that are the more common cause.

PREY BEHAVIOR

The prey drive is highly inherited and is augmented by learning from the emotional experience of performing the kill. The hunting reflexes of tracking, chasing, biting, shaking, killing and the burying of excess food has largely been selected against. This serious behavior is still observed in some breeds, such as Bull Terriers, German Shepherds, etc. and in certain families of dogs. Prey aggression is the only aggression programmed to kill. The prey drive is usually directed to one or two specific species (squirrels, ground hogs, cats, rabbits, birds, etc.) and rarely generalizes. No studies have been undertaken to establish how readily dogs will change their target prey. This behavior can be very serious if the prey drive is directed to food-producing animals, other pets or people. The hunting behavior is accentuated in packs and is not necessarily related to hunger. It has been shown however, that most dogs that killed humans, were single dogs acting alone and not in packs, and were not wild dogs but pets owned by people.

Because the prey drive is so highly driven by inheritance and the learned component so intense, training a dog not to attack prey is largely impossible. Owners are requested to prevent access to the prey, keep the dog under control at all times and wear a muzzle. Euthanasia may be required in most cases.

COMPETITIVE AGGRESSION

Food or treats may stimulate competitive dominance aggression that can be directed to either humans or other dogs. Growling or biting may result if the dog perceives that its food source is threatened.

This competitive drive can be used to temporarily stimulate the appetite of one dog by bringing a new dog under leash control close to the food. The effect of the competitively induced appetite drive generally lasts only a few days but may be longer to induce eating in a finicky dog.

COMPULSIVE EATING AND DRINKING DISORDERS

Psychogenic polydipsia (drinking too much), polyphagia (eating too much) and anorexia (not eating) can be caused by various diseases and by environmental conflict. The conflicts cause increased arousal and anxiety that in turn result in either a redirected or obsessive-compulsive behavior.

The obsessive compulsive disorder of attacking the food in the bowl interferes with eating and is sometimes associated with growling. In one rare case a dog that had coprophagia subsequently developed an obsessive-compulsive disorder of attacking its food in the bowl. This dog would also attack and growl at its stool while eating it. Attacking food has been observed experimentally in dogs who were given excessive dosages of the stimulant amphetamine.

After the presence of any primary disease has been eliminated by a thorough examination, the cause of the anxiety should if possible be eliminated and treated for the obsessive-compulsive disorders. Compulsive disorders are covered in more detail elsewhere in this book.

COPROPHAGY

Coprophagy is a very common, repugnant behavior in which the dog eats it own stool or that of another dog or another species. It has been observed naturally in some wild canines and is a routine behavior expressed by bitches who eat their puppies' stool during the nesting period. The eating of stool in the dog is normal and is never associated with another disease and it rarely causes any significant problems. Dogs that eat stool could pick up a variety of viruses like parvovirus or a number of internal parasites such as giardia and coccidia. Dogs that eat stool have dirty mouths and foul-smelling breath.

The cause of coprophagy is largely unknown, however there is strong clinical evidence that the trait is inherited and is expressed more frequently in certain breeds and families of dogs. The behavior usually begins to be expressed around six months (plus or minus two months) and generally disappears around a year of age. If coprophagy begins after one year of age, it is likely to be the result of a redirected behavior or an obsessive-compulsive disorder. Diets that have a low digestibility, contain relatively high levels of starch and low levels of fiber, may increase the tendency to stool eating, whereas, diets high in fiber may reduce it. Palatability of the stool is increased or decreased by the presence of undigested nutrients in the stool and its consistency or mouth feel. If the palatability of the stool is high, then stool eating could be self rewarding. Fecal material of horses and sometimes cat feces seems to be very palatable to many dogs. One of the most important factors affecting palatability of food for dogs is the mouth feel. Thus the consistency of the stool may be an important reason to encourage the dog to eat its stool. When the stool is hard or frozen, the drive to eat the stool is increased and conversely, if the stool is soft or the dog develops diarrhea, stool eating may stop.

Owners may condition stool eating by paying attention to the dog when it is eating its stool, thus augmenting and maintaining the behavior though learning. Discipline rarely works to stop stool eating. In fact, mild discipline may be perceived by the dog as rewarding (attention). If you catch the dog eating it stool, do not reward it by attention but distract the dog and reward it for the performance of another behavior. It is also speculated that by just performing the behavior and thus satisfying the innate drive to eat stool may be rewarding.

The best treatment for coprophagia is to prevent access to the stool. This can be accomplished by placing a muzzle on the dog each and every time the dog goes out. If the stool eating is still present after using the muzzle for one month, replace it for another month or until the behavior is no longer expressed.

If you do not use a muzzle, feed the dog consistently with a highly digestible diet, in sufficient amounts to keep the dog full and divide it in two or three equal feedings over the day. Certain products are available from your veterinarian that contain pancreatic enzyme and when added to the food, may inhibit some dogs from stool eating because it changes the flavor of the stool. It is not recommended to place bad-tasting substances such as hot pepper on the stool, because owners will be inconsistent in its application. It the dog gets access to an occasionally untreated stool, then stool eating is placed on an irregular schedule of reward (the dog gets a reward of eating an untreated stool) and thus the behavior is likely to increase in frequency and intensity. Constantly picking up the stool before the dog gets an opportunity to eat it is useful, however, owners cannot be consistent enough for this to work.

Dogs that eat the stool of other dogs, cats, cattle, rabbits and horses must be prevented from having access to them. In the case of dogs eating horse's stool, the palatability appears so great and the behavior so rewarding that it may not be correctable. Keeping the dog on a lead, using a muzzle, counter conditioning or otherwise preventing access are the only practical methods of preventing and treating this behavior.

OBESITY

Obesity is the most common nutritional disease of dogs. It affects approximately 35 to 45% of pet dogs and may lead to many serious health problems such as: cardiovascular, respiratory and liver disease as well as diabetes mellitus, osteoarthritis, dermatitis and neoplasia.

Obesity is caused by the owner conditioning the dog to eat uncontrolled amounts of highly palatable energy-dense pet diets, human food or treats. Palatability of a food for the dog is based on smell, mouth feel and taste, in this order. Palatability of the diet can usually be enhanced by increasing the temperature and moisture and by adding cooked meats, sugars, fats, and also certain other ingredients such as garlic, salt and cooked onions.

Obesity can be caused by an inherited factor observed in certain breeds such as Dachshunds and retrievers and is generally expressed in middle-aged dogs. Obesity can, in rare cases, be related to a number of diseases such as hyperinsulinemia, hypothyroidism, pancreatic neoplasia, hyperadrenocorticism and other hormone imbalances.

Spaying or castrating does not contribute to a reduction of physical activity levels or weight gain in the dog. This belief probably occurs from incorrectly transferring information concerning the behavioral effects of castrating from other species to the dog. The effects of castra-

Obesity is the most common nutritional problem seen in pets. Photo courtesy of Dr. Lowell Ackerman.

tion varies widely between the species and between individuals. The other reason to falsely suspect that neutering causes obesity is the fact dogs are generally neutered at the end of the growth period (six to nine months of age) without considering the necessity of decreasing calorie intake for maintenance. The dog stops growing, the owner keeps on giving the same amount and type of high-protein, energy-dense food needed for growth to a dog that requires fewer calories for maintenance.

Appetite may be temporarily increased by the presence of chronic, low intensity, environmental stress. Chronically stressful environments may induce obsessive-compulsive eating and drinking disorders such as anorexia, pica, coprophagia, psychogenic polydipsia (drinking too much) and polyphagia (eating too much) (see obsessive-compulsive disorders).

Treatment of obesity in dogs should start with a thorough physical examination, urine analysis and blood chemistry in order to diagnose and treat concurrent disease. One should next obtain the current weight of the dog and establish an ideal target weight for optimal health.

To be successful, we not only have to change the pet's diet but educate the owner and change his or her behavior related to feeding the dog. It is very helpful when establishing a program to keep a log of the amount of food and treats given to the dog, who feeds the dog, where it is fed and by whom.

The correct diet should be chosen for the dog and an accurate amount

Pointer smiling with Nylabone®. Photograph by Karen Taylor.

of food established for a twice-daily feeding schedule. The dog should receive only the recommended commercial or homemade diet.

Giving of treats to dogs is important for the human/pet relationship and for training. The owner should understand that a small low-calorie treat can be as valued to the dog as a large high-calorie one. The owner can give a controlled number of commercial treats that are low in calories, or small pieces of celery, carrot or other uncooked vegetables such as apple slices, green beans or broccoli. It is very important to change the treat from food to other equally valued rewards such as play, praise and exercise. The owner should make every effort to reestablish good eating habits by giving the dog food only in its bowl and food treats only during training periods.

The failure to get compliance from the owner for a weight-loss program is the most frequent reason for a lack of success. The program should be explained carefully and written instruction given to the owner. In order to get compliance, the owner must understand the serious health consequences of obesity and the length of time required to obtain the desired weight loss. The owner should be encouraged to keep a daily record of the quantity of food, the number and types of treats given, amount of exercise and also weekly records of the dog's weight. This diary should be presented to the veterinarian with the dog for a reevaluation and adjustments of the program every three or four weeks. It is important to gradually reduce the calories as the dog loses weight and not calculate the calories according to the end maintenance weight as this may be too severe a reduction at the beginning of the program. That is why it is necessary to monitor the weight loss every few weeks in order to adjust for individual metabolic requirements and to continually readjust the calorie level as the dog loses weight. Starvation is not an acceptable approach to weight loss. If the dog does not eat the new diet for two to three days, it should be checked by a veterinarian.

Exercise causes an increase in energy expenditure and may slightly influence weight loss but the calories used during exercise are small compared to the effect of reducing the intake of calories. The value of exercise in contributing to weight reduction is more significant when the animal is on a calorie-restricted program. The amount and type of exercise is decided by the condition and age of the animal and is only a rough estimate at best. Some recommend 30 to 40 minutes of walking exercise daily or 15 to 20 minutes of vigorous exercise five times a week.

The behavior and the history of the dog should be evaluated to decide if there are any environmental stresses. These stressors should if possible be removed or the dog given low level of antianxiety or antidepressive drugs together with the weight reduction program. Serotonin reuptake blockers will decrease anxiety due to environmental stress, stop or greatly reduce redirected behaviors and may induce some degree of appetite suppression. The feeding schedule should be regular, no snacking and no begging. Reward correct behavior with praise, touch and low-calorie treats.

When the desired weight is reached, an ongoing program of diet, exercise and training should be started to prevent the recurrence of obesity.

SUMMARY

Although we rarely give eating and drinking a second thought, these natural functions can be an important cause of behavioral problems. Whether it's a dog begging for food at the dinner table or chewing on grass in the back yard, eating disorders must be dealt with in a comprehensive manner. This chapter reviews normal eating and drinking behavior as well as problems that involve these functions.

ADDITIONAL READING

Bradshaw J., Thorne C.: Feeding Behavior, in Thorne C. (ed): *The Waltham Book Of Dog and Cat Behavior,* ed. 2. Pergamon Veterinary Handbook Series, 1992, pp 115-129.

Hart B. L., Hart L. A.: *Canine and Feline Behavior Therapy.* Lea & Febiger, Philadelphia, PA., 1985, pp 104-110.

Houpt, K. A. *Domestic Animal Behavior for Veterinarians and Animal Scientists.* Iowa State University Press, Ames, Iowa, 1991, pp 279-286

Houpt K.A. Feeding and Drinking Behavior Problems, in Marder A. R., Voith V. (ed): *The Veterinary Clinics of North America,* Small Animal Practice - Advances in Companion Animal Behavior, Philadelphia, WB Sauders Co. vol. 21, no. 2, March 1991, pp 281 - 298.

Exercising your dog will help ensure that he remain the proper weight. The Nylabone® Frisbee® is a favorite of most dogs. Photo by Karen Taylor.

Dr. Patrick Melese is director of VETERINARY BEHAVIOR CONSULTANTS, a veterinary practice dedicated to preventing and treating behavioral problems in animals, and the Tierrasanta Veterinary Hospital, a general practice in San Diego, California. Dr. Melese's training includes both Bachelors (1979) and Masters degree (1980) from the Department of Zoology at the University of California, Davis where his subjects were Animal Behavior and Neuroscience. From 1980 to 1982 Dr. Melese worked as a research associate doing behavioral research and publishing papers in physiological psychology. Dr. Melese continued to participate in behavioral research and assisting with the Behavior Service in the Veterinary Teaching Hospital while he attended veterinary school. Dr. Melese earned his Doctorate in Veterinary Medicine from U.C. Davis in 1986.

After receiving his veterinary degree, Dr. Melese has been a veterinary medical, surgical and behavioral practitioner. He has kept abreast of advances in the behavior literature, taught classes in veterinary behavior, given presentations to public and professional groups, and consulted with colleagues in the field throughout the world. For the past several years he has developed and taught a 6-week behavior class for young puppies (age 10-18 weeks) that is currently taught in several locations in San Diego County.

Housesoiling Problems in Dogs

By Patrick Melese, DVM, MA and
Carol M. Harris
Veterinary Behavior Consultants
10799 Tierrasanta Blvd.
San Diego, CA 92124

HOUSETRAINING PUPPIES

Your first few hours and days with a new puppy are critical in establishing certain habits including where the puppy will do its business. When attempting to housetrain a new puppy there are several important principles to keep in mind: (1) consistency, (2) being gentle, (3) encouraging desirable behavior and (4) patience.

In general, puppies want to please you and have a natural tendency not to eliminate in what they perceive as their den area. A puppy will look upon any space where it sleeps or spends a great deal of time as its den. If a puppy gets to spend most of the time inside, it is more likely to regard the home as an unacceptable toilet spot. Your goal is to use these tendencies to help the puppy realize you want him to eliminate only outdoors, and save your home to sleep, eat and play in.

To begin with, you need to understand that most young puppies need to urinate every 45-60 minutes, shortly after waking up, after eating, playing, and about 20 minutes after drinking. Bowel movements usually occur 3-6 times daily. This will happen after waking in the morning, about $1/2$ hour after meals and whenever the puppy becomes excited or frightened. The number of times needed for elimination begins to drop as your puppy nears 3 $1/2$ to 4 $1/2$ months of age. By this time most puppies are able to "make it through the night" and are capable of holding their waste for 4-7 hours during the day. If, however, you find you must leave your "not completely housetrained" puppy alone for five or more hours, make every effort to have someone come and let the puppy out to go to the bathroom somewhere in the middle of those hours. This will prevent the possibility of him having an accident in his crate or confined area, thus perhaps creating a larger problem than simple housetraining.

Establishing a consistent, daily routine is critical to efficient housetraining. Take the above points into account and set your schedule accordingly. Be consistent in your meal and exercise times. Remember that puppies up to 12 weeks old need 3-4 meals per day.

For puppies three to six months of age, 2-3 meals per day should be sufficient. Do not overfeed your puppy; take the day's total amount of food and divide it by the amount of meals he should receive that day. When determining how much your puppy should be eating, follow the feeding guides of the manufacturer and check with your veterinarian. They will be happy to suggest appropriate food for your puppy as well as proper amounts. After feeding your puppy spend some quiet time with him for 10-15 minutes, perhaps doing some handling and bite inhibition exercises. These exercises will help your puppy to learn to enjoy gentle handling and that biting should be reserved for playing with other puppies. Watch for any signs of needing to eliminate (such as floor sniffing, circling, squatting, etc.); when these are seen, distract the puppy (clap, call its name, toss a can with pennies in it near pup, say "no!", etc.) then take him outside immediately to the location you want him to use. It's best to choose only one location as his toilet area (again be consistent!). As soon as your puppy has eliminated outside, give him lots of praise and a small food reward. Be sure to wait until the puppy is finished doing his business so as not to distract him. Always take the puppy's preference into consideration when choosing food rewards. These treats should be something your puppy absolutely loves. It is also important to use small treats. You do not want these rewards to substitute for your puppy's regular meals. Make sure you have food rewards available (on your person or at the outside location) for immediate use. Do not lose the moment by having to run to get a treat!

Puppies will become trustworthy in the house much faster if they are not given the opportunity to make mistakes and are consistently allowed to succeed and be praised for that success. This means that initially the puppy should not be allowed to have free run of the house. Your puppy should either be with you (with your attention on the puppy), temporarily outside in a safe environment, or inside in a small enclosed area such as a crate or a gated-off area of a kitchen. It is always necessary for you to keep in mind your pup's elimination needs and see that he is taken outside frequently enough to preclude the possibilities of him making a mistake.

At all times in your dog's life remember that they are social animals and need to be with their pack (you). Avoid leaving your puppy or dog isolated for long periods of time outside, in a separate room or garage, etc. Spend quality time playing with, grooming, training and just being with your puppy. Ignoring this social need can lead to housetraining difficulties now as well as other behavior problems later. Keeping the puppy in the bedroom with you at night can fulfill part of his social needs at minimal time cost to you as well as allow you to deal with his elimination needs before he has an accident in the night (i.e., be aware of your puppy's need to be taken out to relieve himself). If you find that in spite of all your precautions the puppy has had an accident there are a few rules you need to follow.

1) Never punish your puppy by rubbing his nose in his excrement. It is ineffective and cruel.

2) Never use any form of physical punishment such as hitting or otherwise striking the puppy. Don't pick the puppy up by the scruff of his neck and throw him outside.

3) Never, never punish more than a few seconds after the act has occurred.

Remember that dogs only understand immediate reward and punishment. "Immediate" to a puppy means a few seconds or less! Any reward or punishment delayed longer than this will not be associated with the act. By punishing after the fact you are only destroying the close bond you are trying to establish during this critical period in your relationship. If you do find a mistake has occurred, hold your temper and remember that it was your job to watch or confine the puppy and ensure that he has adequate and appropriate opportunity to eliminate outdoors. The best thing to do at this point is to act indifferently. Gently put your puppy away so you do not let him see you cleaning up; you do not want to draw attention to this location. Clean up the mess and (this is vital) using a good odor neutralizer (such as Anti-Icky-Poo®, Outright®, Dog Off®, or other product available through your veterinarian to prevent your puppy from thinking the spot smells

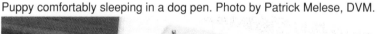

Puppy comfortably sleeping in a dog pen. Photo by Patrick Melese, DVM.

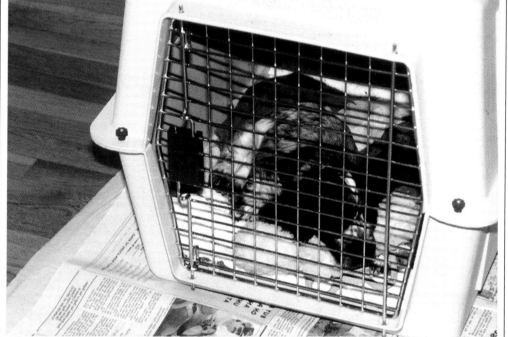

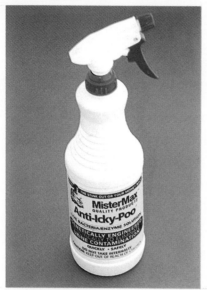

Example of an odor neutralizer. Photo by Patrick Melese, DVM.

like a toilet area. If you are being very vigilant and you see your puppy making intention movements (looking like he has to go), remember to distract him and get him outside, and praise him immediately for eliminating appropriately. You may even wish to add a command such as "Go Potty" as you bring him out so that the pup learns to eliminate on command. This comes in handy when you are in a hurry to have the puppy do his business and go back into the house. Puppies who enjoy walks can also be taught that they must go into the yard and empty their bowels and bladder prior to being taken out on a walk. This will certainly make your neighbors happy and keep you from walking around with a plastic bag filled with your pet's stool.

We have intentionally not mentioned paper training until this point. If at all possible, we recommend avoiding paper training since housetraining is much faster and less confusing for the puppy if it is done in the one step process of "you only go outside." If there are any circumstances, however, which require you to paper-train your puppy (such as long-working hours, top floor apartment, physical disability, etc.), you must follow similar guidelines to those of outdoor training with a few modifications. Everything I have stated earlier in this chapter still applies, except that you are substituting a paper-covered area for the outdoors. You would begin by choosing your puppy's toilet area (best would be an easily cleanable surface like linoleum) and covering the entire surface with newspapers (or commercially available housebreaking pads). A good thick layer makes cleanup easier. Take your puppy to this area when it is time to eliminate and use the same praise and reward techniques described earlier. Gradually decrease the size of the papered area until your puppy is using a spot the size of an unfolded sheet of newspaper. If you then train your puppy to use the outdoors you can take newspaper to the area outside that you wish him to use and retrain him to go there. You will eventually remove the newspaper from indoors and out by folding the paper making it smaller and smaller day by day until it is completely removed. This is a more time-consuming process and your puppy is more likely to make occasional mistakes. You also need to keep in mind that some dogs never fully make the transition from paper to outside and will continue to use paper indoors if it is left in an area accessible to them.

HOUSESOILING IN ADULT PETS

Housesoiling problems in adult dogs occur due to a variety of reasons. Perhaps the dog was not properly housebroken to begin with; the dog has changed homes; a major change has occurred in the dog's home (maybe the owner is home more or less than before, there is a new family member, a new family pet, a change in relationship with a family pet or human, etc.); or the dog's environment has changed. There are also certain breeds which can be extremely difficult to housebreak (certain of the small and toy breeds can fall in this category). If house soiling occurs in a pet that has been well housebroken in the

Pet shops sell puppy housebreaking pads that are effective and economical. Photo courtesy of Four Paws.

Examples of urine eliminating products. Photo by Patrick Melese, DVM.

past, be sure to first have your dog examined by a veterinarian. He may have a physical condition that requires professional attention and treatment (for example, a bladder infection).

Regardless of why the dog is having house soiling problems, the solution remains basically the same. Start by reviewing the principles for housetraining a puppy...(1) consistency, (2) being gentle , (3) encouraging desirable behavior and (4) patience. You must read the section on puppy housetraining above and start as if you had a new puppy. Your healthy, adult dog can control his bladder and bowels longer than a young puppy so the frequency of his outings can be cut back from those recommended for puppies. Dogs with this problem should not,

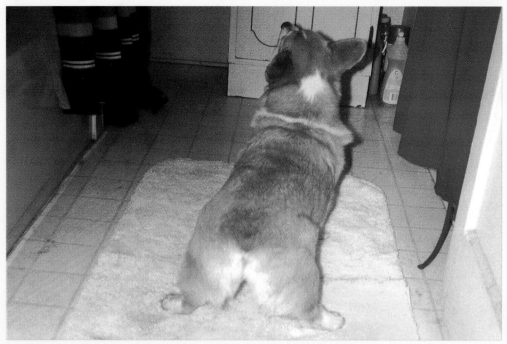

Confining an adult dog to help with housebreaking. Photo by Carol Harris.

however, have free run of the house. You must confine or restrain a poorly housetrained adult the same as you do a puppy. Housesoiling is a self-reinforcing behavior in that once the dog goes inside, he has already reinforced himself by the relief that comes from the very act of emptying his bowels or bladder in the home. Allowing this learning process to continue while attempting to housetrain the dog greatly slows your success. One method of confinement that is extremely successful with both adult dogs and puppies is crate training. The first thing to understand when crate training your dog is that they are animals that use dens by nature. Crate training your dog or puppy has many advantages in addition to being a major aid in housebreaking. It provides your dog with a safe place to be when you are unable to watch him; the cage provides a bed of his own and makes him comfortable with an enclosed area so being boarded or staying at the veterinary hospital is less traumatic. You are providing your dog with his very own den within your own (your house). This provides him with a sense of security and belonging. Among the best type of crate for housetraining purposes is a sturdy airline kennel. These come in sizes suitable for most any breed of dog from the tiniest on up to the giant breeds. When purchasing your crate be sure to buy one just big enough for your dog to stand up, turn around comfortably, and lay down in. Do not purchase an oversized crate with the idea of the more room the better. Dogs naturally do not wish to soil their sleeping area. If you provide

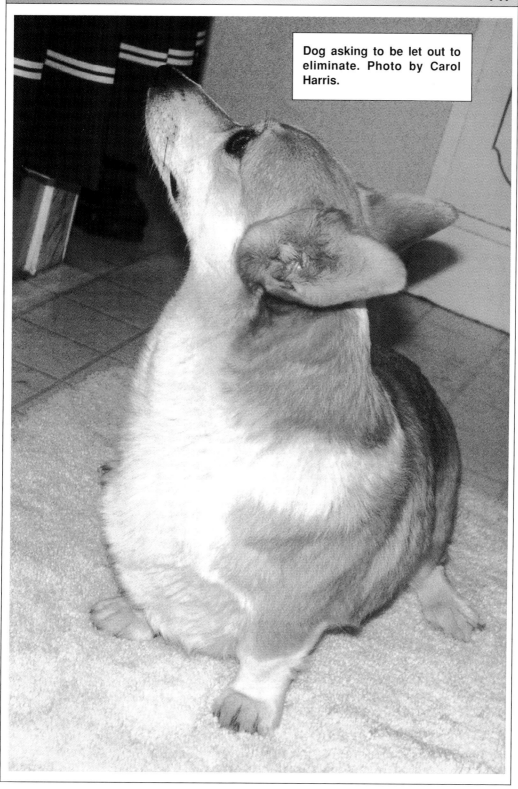

Dog asking to be let out to eliminate. Photo by Carol Harris.

an oversized crate it can allow the dog to soil one area while sleeping in another, thus defeating its usefulness as a housetraining aid. Once you have obtained the appropriate sized crate, set it up in your house where the dog is to sleep. Let your dog adjust to its presence for a day or two with the door left open. Begin to familiarize your dog to the crate by tossing dog biscuits or other food rewards into the crate and letting him retrieve them. As soon as he is comfortable with this, throw his toys in and let him retrieve those. Start feeding him in the crate at first with the food dish at the front of the crate and gradually moving it toward the back. Make sure you are continuing to leave the door open. Very soon your dog should be walking in and out of the crate quite willingly. With most young puppies you can skip the previous steps and go straight to the next step.

Bells on door handle to help signal that dog wants to go out. Photo by Patrick Melese, DVM.

You next put his bedding inside the crate, and gently place the dog inside with an enthusiastic command such as "go to bed". Close the door very matter-of-factly and walk away. Ignore your dog if he cries or carries on. As soon as the dog is quiet, go to the crate and quietly praise him and casually open the crate door. The less fanfare you attribute to letting your dog out of the crate the less importance he will attach to it as well. Repeat this routine leaving him in the crate for longer and longer periods of time, until he settles down and relaxes. A good time to let your dog adjust to the crate is at night when you are sleeping in the same room and he can hear your breathing. This is soothing to him and allows a regular bonding time for you and your dog (sleeping with the pack leaders). While your dog is crated at night you are assured that he is not forgetting the housetraining (and many other) rules elsewhere in the house. This prevents nighttime accidents and allows you to greet each other cheerfully in the morning.

Using the crate during the day when you cannot directly supervise your dog will prevent daytime accidents as well. Avoid using the crate as a punishment or banishment; it is best used as a safe and pleasant refuge. Many dogs choose to sleep in their crates when they are looking for a quiet place to rest, or get away from any annoying pets or children in their environment. Owners often have the crate set up as a bed long after it is no longer needed for housetraining purposes.

Although confining your adult dog will help prevent accidents, you must do your part as well. Ensure that your dog is taken to his outside toilet area regularly. Initially you need to provide many opportunities a day for your dog to relieve himself. A reasonable initial schedule would be to take him out first thing in the morning, mid-morning, noon, mid-afternoon, after dinner, last thing before going to bed, and just prior to the dog being left alone for any prolonged length of time. If he does have an accident, treat it exactly as described earlier in the puppy section of this chapter. Each time you take the dog outside and he eliminates, praise him and give a food reward. Just as you would a puppy, be sure you have the rewards immediately available and be sure your dog likes them.

Keep your dog with you as much as possible during this training period. You will soon begin to recognize your dog's personal ways of asking to go outside. When you see him asking to go out, praise him, take him out immediately and follow the routine of reward once he eliminates. You may even want to teach him to go to the appropriate door, sit and perhaps bark to signal his need to go outside. If he does not bark easily, one can shape a behavior in which the dog hits a set of bells to be let outside. Sometimes a dog door can help by providing continu-

ous access to the outside in households where people are not always attentive to the dog's needs. With diligence and patience you will quickly have your dog reliably housetrained.

SUBMISSIVE AND EXCITEMENT URINATION

A problem often mistaken for a housetraining problem is submissive urination. Submissive urination is urination that occurs when your dog is excited, frightened, or just being greeted enthusiastically. This is not a regular housetraining problem and should never be punished. Punishment will only make the problem worse and occur more frequently. When a normal, subordinate dog becomes frightened, feels threatened, or just gets over-stimulated, he will often show active signs of submissive behavior. In dogs, this includes opening up the hind legs to expose the genitalia, rolling on their back, and often urinating in an effort to express their subordination. This is normal behavior and

Dog being enthusiastically greeted can trigger urination in a scared, submissive or easily-excitable dog. Photo by Patrick Melese, DVM.

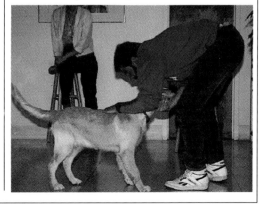

escalation of threat (punishment or yelling, for example) can only exacerbate the problem. Learn the signals that your dog interprets as threats. Standing or leaning over the dog, deep loud excited speech, staring at and reaching over the dog's head or body can all be interpreted as possible threats which leads the dog to respond the best he knows how (trying to communicate his subordinate status as above).

The best way to handle the dog or puppy who submissively urinates is with a great deal of patience and gentleness. Try to greet dogs or puppies who have this problem outside and with as little fanfare as possible. In some cases it is best to even ignore the puppy (walk by, do not make eye contact, move in a smooth, predictable manner). A very relaxed greeting on your part will elicit less submissive or excited behavior and therefore less urination on the dog's part. You can also teach your dog or puppy a command for urination, such as "go potty." Give him the command when you know he's going to urinate (outside) anyway, then praise and reward him. He will soon associate the command with the act of urination. You can then use the same command when greeting your dog outdoors and it will remind him to empty his bladder before coming indoors and greeting you. Later on you can begin to greet by quietly kneeling down and gently hold out your hand (avoiding direct eye contact) and quietly speaking to the dog in your best calm, loving voice. It also lets him know that he can relax; you are pleased with him. If

you remain patient and calm most puppies will grow out of this behavior. It is important to remember that dogs or puppies with this problem get worse if you become angry or overexcited with them. Remain calm and build their confidence.

Obedience training often helps to enhance a dog's confidence. It allows them ever-increasing opportunities for success. The more your dog learns to accomplish (for example sit prior to greeting people) and the more you can honestly but gently praise him, the better chance your puppy has of moving beyond his submissive behavior. You may find that initially food rewards are helpful during greeting (when the puppy has not urinated) since they indicate a clear signal that you are unquestionably happy with the dog's behavior and have no intention of challenging your dog. If the dog does urinate it is best to just instantly walk away without a sound, completely ignoring your pet for 10-15 minutes afterwards. This subtle social reprimand can serve to indicate to the dog your displeasure without any confrontation which would make the problem worse.

As in housetraining, consistency from all family members is vital. Often one individual in the household has been able to eliminate this problem when they interact with the pet. This person can share how they accomplish this "safe" greeting with other family members. Dogs learn much faster when the rules are the same regardless of who they are dealing with.

Dogs that urinate when excited can be helped by following much of the same techniques. In addition, avoid the situations which seem to over stimulate the puppy. Find a way to interact with your pet which does not cause this unacceptable urination by determining exactly which factors lead to this behavior in your dog. Occasionally some dogs seem to have such a weak urinary sphincter that they do not seem to be able to control their leaking urine even with these techniques. Be sure to discuss these with your veterinarian who may decide to prescribe a medication to help (for example, phenylpropan-olamine) if there are no underlying medical problems identified. By following these guidelines, you will be able to take the frustration out of solving your dog's elimination problem, and spend more time enjoying the companionship of your four-legged friend.

Good luck and enjoy your pet !

SUMMARY

Housesoiling problems are one of the most common reasons for owners to seek a behavioral consultation. There is no doubt that a pet that isn't housetrained, or one that urinates involuntarily or when excited puts a lot of stress on the owner-pet bond. This chapter will help you train your dog right the first time, and also offers some tips for dogs who need some extra assistance.

ADDITIONAL READING

Doctor Dunbar's Good Little Dog Book: by Dr. Ian Dunbar; Spillers Foods; James and Kenneth Publishers; Berkeley, CA.

Manners for the Modern Dog: by Gwen Bohnenkamp; Perfect Paws; James and Kenneth Publishers.

Dog being greeted in a non-threatening, friendly posture, except for direct eye contact. Photo by Patrick Melese, DVM.

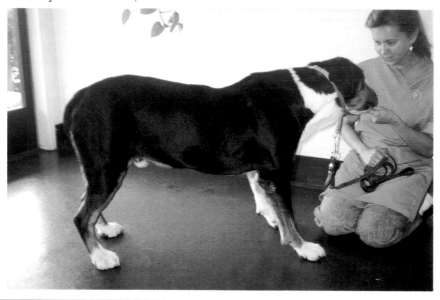

Dr. Walter Burghardt is a veterinary graduate of the University of Florida, College of Veterinary Medicine and currently practices in Coral Springs, Florida. He is a member of the American Veterinary Society of Animal Behavior.

Dr. Burghardt received his DVM from the University of Florida in 1980, and was awarded his PhD in Biopsychology from the University of Maryland, College Park in 1989. From 1980 to 1984, Dr. Burghardt practiced general and emergency veterinary medicine and conducted a veterinary behavioral practice in Maryland and Virginia. He has been the Hospital Director of Abacus Animal Hospital and the Director of the Behavior Clinic for Animals in Coral Springs, Florida since 1984. He is also past president of the American Veterinary Society of Animal Behavior and is the veterinary behavioral consultant to the United States Department of Defense Military Working Dog Program at Lackland Air Force Base, Texas. His special interests in behavior are currently the diagnosis and treatment of canine hyperactivity with or without attention deficit, behavioral problems of the aging patient, and the effects of drugs on learned canine behavior.

Destructive Behavior

By Walter F. Burghardt, Jr., DVM,
   PhD
BEHAVIOR CLINIC FOR ANIMALS
10872 Wiles Road
Coral Springs, Florida 33076

INTRODUCTION

Chewing and digging are normal canine behaviors. Puppies and dogs are normally motivated to chew and dig, just as they are to eat and run. As such, people who have the expectation that their canine pets will never dig or chew on anything are being just as unrealistic as if they expected their pet never to breathe or sleep. These behaviors are not abnormal or unusual.

Unfortunately, sometimes the objects of chewing and digging behaviors are unacceptable to owners. At other times pets chew or dig excessively, usually for the same reasons that people watch TV excessively or engage in any other habitual behavior.

Just why is it that dogs chew and dig? In general, there are a few consistent reasons which we can identify for these behaviors. First, chewing and digging are "adaptive behaviors." This means that these behaviors serve a useful purpose in the life a "real" dog (that is, the kind of dog one might find living off the land in a relatively wild setting). These dogs need to be able to use their teeth and paws to uncover and catch their food source, to tear and break open parts of their meals, and to deal with their environment to obtain resources such as water and shelter.

Secondly, especially in puppies, chewing provides specific exercise for developing and changing teeth, and in the older dog, chewing is a natural way to exercise the jaw muscles, stimulate the gum tissue, and remove tartar accumulation from the teeth.

Finally, each of these behaviors provides the dog with a way to burn off excess energy. In effect, these behaviors are also recreational or "play" behaviors (much like a human child playing in the bath).

When do chewing and destructive behaviors become a problem? Firstly, as mentioned above, these behaviors can become a problem when the targets of the chewing or digging are unacceptable to the owner (such as chewing on a good pair of slippers, or digging a hole in the middle of a flower bed). Secondly, the behaviors may be considered problematic when they become habitual in nature, replacing other normal behaviors. This might occur

In order to prevent inappropriate chewing habits, you should provide acceptable toys and train your dog to chew only those. Photo by Karen Taylor.

when the dog digs in the yard on every occasion on which it is let outside or chews (even on an acceptable item) to the exclusion of other normal behaviors (such as interacting with the owner or with other dogs). Finally, these behaviors may become a problem when they are directed towards unusual targets (such as chewing at parts of the dog's own body or digging in the middle of a hard indoor floor).

Rarely would I characterize destructive behavior as "spiteful" or "malicious." This is for two reasons. First, these motivational concepts are really difficult to demonstrate, and secondly, methods of treatment attempting to lessen these presumed motivational factors almost always are unsuccessful.

PREVENTING DESTRUCTIVE BEHAVIORS

Are there ways of preventing destructive behaviors? Absolutely! We'll first look at chewing behavior below, but keep the principles in mind, because they are also applicable to destructive digging, which we will discuss more briefly at the end of this chapter.

First, obtaining puppies at an appropriate age (8 to about 14 weeks) can really help, and is always good advice. This can often avoid situations where the puppy becomes overly attached or focused on one or two humans as its sole source of social contact. Puppies obtained at a very early age or much past 16 weeks of age appear to have a much higher risk of displaying "separation anxiety." This behavioral syndrome often includes destructive behaviors of digging and chewing while the owners are away.

Another way of preventing inappropriate chewing is to teach puppies from an early age to chew only on their toys. This is done by providing an acceptable set of chewing toys to the pet. These toys would include some selection of soft "mouthing" types of toys (such as soft hollow rubber toys), medium texture chew toys (such as soft nylon toys and rawhide), hard chew toys (such as commercially sterilized bone, hard nylon toys), and "tug" toys. Each of the toys selected should, of course, be safe for the pet, but should also be selected for appropriate size and kind which the

pet prefers. It is also important to make sure that the selected toys are not too similar to objects toward which your pet may already be showing some inappropriate attention. Another important facet of this approach is to "puppy proof" its environment, making unacceptable chewing items as unavailable and unattractive as possible (more on this aspect below).

Once you have selected a collection of toys, it is very important to spend time playing with these toys with your puppy or dog. This serves three important functions. First, it makes the toy more valuable to the pet. Second, it associates your approval for playing with the toy. Third, it helps build a better relationship with you while burning calories and

Chewing is a natural canine past time. Don't provide inappropriate objects for chewing. Photo by Dr. Gary Landsberg.

Provide chew toys designed for dogs and reward your dog when he uses them. Photo by Dr. Gary Landsberg.

meeting the chewing needs. Let's face it, a ball continually associated with good times and "good boy" is likely to have a lot more value than a slimy old squeak toy with which a puppy never comes in contact.

DEALING WITH DESTRUCTIVE CHEWING BEHAVIORS

While building the playtime and toy value, it is equally important to identify, discourage, and redirect inappropriate mouthing and chewing. Set the rule, "only food and toys are allowed in the mouth." Any time an object not meeting this description passes your pet's lips, do the following steps. First, get your pet's attention (for example, clap your hands or use another loud noise). Use a sight or sound intense enough to get the pet to release the inappropriate chewing object, turn and look at you. Second (although saying "NO!" is OK sometime during this process, it is not necessary), IMMEDIATELY coax or take your pet to another location and spend at

LEAST 3-5 minutes playing with it with an acceptable chewing toy, and use lots of praise (and an occasional treat) to encourage the play. Incidentally, initially using a good taste or smell (for example, tuna oil or peanut butter—food items not usually found "left out" in the open) in or on appropriate toys is perfectly acceptable, and may help to further distinguish between acceptable and unacceptable items. Finally, especially if the unacceptable item has been targeted more than once, use an nontoxic but "aversive" taste or odor treatment on it frequently (at least daily). However, remember that just because a product is marketed as a chewing deterrent doesn't mean that your pet will find it objectionable. Most products are "bitter" or "peppery," and your pet may actually like it! Remember that even some people love "el scorcho" Mexican food or eat lemons plain, so test out a product before relying on it.

If you have been following up to here, you will immediately realize that the above procedures require some time and attention towards your pet. This is especially true with redirecting inappropriate chewing to acceptable items. Anytime that your pet chews on an unacceptable item without redirection towards an acceptable toy gives your tacit approval of that chewing behavior. Therefore (especially with young puppies or pets with chewing problems), if you cannot supervise the pet's behavior, it is wise to confine your pet to a "safe" area in which there are few or no unacceptable chewing targets, but where there are plenty of acceptable and preferred toys.

Using a sound strategy can prevent and eliminate many chewing problems before they become serious, if the strategy is applied consistently and persistently. In more severe cases, or in situations where these relatively simple suggestions don't help, professional intervention may be needed. The best place to start? See your regular veterinarian for assistance and a referral, if needed.

DEALING WITH DESTRUCTIVE DIGGING BEHAVIORS

Digging behaviors seem to serve several useful purposes as noted above. If our pet is digging for one of these "adaptive" reasons (escape, shelter, finding food), the intuitive answer to preventing and treating these behaviors is easy;

meet the pet's needs better to reduce its motivation to dig, and redirect the digging to an acceptable behavior which produces needs satisfaction. This alternative behavior is usually some other energetic play behavior, so that it will meet the dog's need to expend energy and pass time.

If your pet is digging because it is bored (recreational digging), the simple answer is to provide a more interesting environment and to reward a competing behavior. Unfortunately, in the real world, simple answers are not always the whole answer. Just as in chewing (discussed above), real control and behavioral change in inappropriate digging involves preventing the animal from digging inappropriately to begin. This may be difficult, especially if the pet is digging primarily when it is alone. Al-

Using a sound strategy can prevent and eliminate many destructive chewing behaviors. Photo by Karen Taylor.

Muzzles can be a temporary solution for dogs that chew in an owner's brief absence. They should not be left on for long periods of time. Photo by Dr. Gary Landsberg.

though there are "high-tech" (remote electronic training aids) and "low-tech" (putting concrete in the usual digging site) solutions to this dilemma, this step usually involves some time, effort, and creativity. As with chewing behaviors above, the concepts are to make the unacceptable digging target as unavailable and unattractive as possible, while making the alternative (non-digging) behavior as attractive and rewarding as possible.

Unfortunately, there are some situations in which the urge to dig or the habit of digging are so strong that it is extremely difficult to refocus the pet on an alternative behavior. In such cases it is not considered "losing face" to allow the pet its digging pleasure, but redirecting it to a more acceptable location. This may be done with a sand box or other clearly delineated digging area which could be

rewarded preferentially over other unacceptable locations.

As noted above for chewing behaviors, if these simple preventive and corrective steps do not prove successful, or if the problem appears to worsen or change despite control efforts, it is wise to consult your veterinarian to obtain more definitive and personalized professional care.

SEPARATION ANXIETY

Now that we've covered the major problems of destructive digging and chewing, I'd like to take a side path on a related problem,"separation

Using a halter to offer guidance to a wayward canine. Photo by Dr. Gary Landsberg.

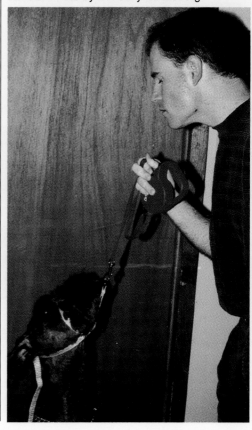

anxiety." We mentioned this problem briefly above, but it deserves special attention as a problem in and of itself.

Separation anxiety is a behavioral syndrome which occurs with some regularity in pets. Animals with this problem show some combination of behavioral signs when they are left alone which include: apparent anxiety or tension (panting, salivating, pacing, trembling), increased vocalization (usually barking, howling or crying), housesoiling, destructive chewing and/or digging, and "escape" behaviors (such as breaking through windows or screens). These behavior problems may range from very mild to extremely severe. Some animals can produce tremendous damage to themselves or their environment.

Because separation anxiety may express itself as destructive chewing or digging, it requires some discussion here. The problem often is seen in pets which are obtained by their owners at very young ages or after the time at which they would normally be socialized with people (the period from about 8 to 16 weeks of age). Sometimes these pets come from litters that were separated early because of some disease or other misfortune, and sometimes they were "the last puppy left" (by itself). Unfortunately, not all puppies show such an abnormal beginning, and still show separation related misbehaviors.

Mild forms of separation anxiety may be treated similarly to destructive behaviors, as outlined above. The key to improving their

This dog isn't looking guilty because of his actions. He has developed a conditioned fear or submissive response to the owner's arrival. Photo by Dr. Gary Landsberg.

behavior seems to be in rewarding calm behaviors, enriching the pet's environment (with preferred toys and treats, familiar sounds) while the owner is away, preventing unacceptable behaviors as much as possible (using barriers or confinement if needed), and making periods of being alone somewhat unpredictable to the pet. Before departing, the dog should receive a vigorous attention and exercise period, and then be allowed a few minutes at least to calm down. When the owner leaves it is critical that the pet is not worked up and anxious so allowing the pet to calm down and giving the pet some food or a new toy to keep it occupied while the owner departs can be

Providing your dog with acceptable chewing devices will aid in preventing destructive behavior. Photo by Karen Taylor.

extremely helpful. When the owner is at home, training sessions should take place so that the dog learns to lie quietly in one room while the owner is in a different room. Obviously, if the dog does not tolerate sessions of being alone when the owner is at home, it will be extremely difficult for the dog to accept being left alone when the owner is away from home.

More serious cases of separation anxiety require medical intervention, and the owner should contact their veterinarian early. Often, these pets may need extensive behavioral treatment and environmental change, and may benefit from treatment with some behavioral medications. Often, your veterinarian will seek the assistance of a behavioral specialist.

SUMMARY

Destructive behavior in dogs is a common reason for them becoming unwanted housepets. This chapter reviews the most common destructive traits exhibited by dogs, the reasons for them, and how they are best corrected and prevented.

ADDITIONAL READING:

Kohlke, HU; Hohlke, K: Animal behavior therapy - Characteristics and specific problems from the psychological point of view. Kleintierpraxis, 1994; 39(3): 175-180.

Polsky, RH: The steps in solving behavior problems. Veterinary Medicine, 1994; 89(6): 5504-507.

Watson, M: *Basic Dog Training.* TFH Publications, Neptune, NJ, 1990, 93pp.

Katherine Houpt, VMD, PhD is a Professor of physiology and the Director of the Behavior Clinic at the College of Veterinary Medicine, Cornell University. She is a charter diplomate of the American College of Veterinary Behaviorists and author of Domestic Animal Behavior (Iowa State University Press). Her research involves the behavior and welfare of companion animals.

Dr. Concannon teaches physiology and reproductive endocrinology at Cornell University. He conducts research on the reproductive biology of dogs and cats, with a special interest in the hormonal control of ovarian cycles and pregnancy. He is the author of over 100 publications in reproductive biology and the editor of two books on dog and cat fertility and infertility.

Canine Sexual Behavior

By Katherine A. Houpt, VMD, PhD
Diplomate, American College of
   Veterinary Behaviorists
and Patrick W. Concannon, PhD
Department of Physiology
College of Veterinary Medicine
Cornell University
Ithaca, NY 14853-6410

INTRODUCTION

Canine sexual behavior and physiology is unique and interesting. Nevertheless, many of the reasons that people do not want (or give up) their dogs are related to sexual behavior, in particular, male sexual behavior. Mounting people's legs, roaming, leg lifting and urination in the house are all elements of sexual behavior. These are all excellent reasons to neuter a male dog. Only those dogs with exemplary behavior should be used for breeding. Canine maternal behavior is an interaction between the altricious (requiring nursing care) puppies and the bitch, but some bitches are not good mothers.

THE MALE

In most mammals the male plays a more active role in courtship and consummation than the female. This is true of dogs as well. Canine male sexual behavior consists of roaming in search of a female, scent marking and mounting. If the female is receptive, or if she can be subdued, copulation occurs. She is mounted and the penis penetrates the vagina. The dog thrusts several times and then ejaculates, often thrusting so forcefully that his hind legs leave the ground. Ejaculation is followed by a lock, in which the male dismounts from the female but is still joined to her because his engorged penis is lodged within her. The lock results from swelling of the glans penis after the male has penetrated the female and from tightening of the muscles of the bitch's vagina. The male dismounts and turns so he is facing away from the female. The lock can last from 10 to 30 minutes. The reason for the evolution of this aspect of copulation is unclear because the animals are particularly vulnerable at that time. Dogs may mate five times a day, which will enhance chances of success in fertilization.

Scent marking

Male puppies engage in sexual play, mounting and thrusting from 3 weeks of age onward, but puberty does not occur until 6 to 12 months. One indication of puberty is that the dog will begin to lift his leg rather than squatting to urinate. This is a form of scent marking. Presumably dogs communicate information as to their sex, and possibly their individuality, and obtain that information by sniffing marks of other dogs. Marking—lifting the leg and urinating—can be a problem, especially indoors. Dogs are well known for their habit of lifting their legs and urinating on vertical objects such as fire hydrants, but they may urinate on indoor vertical objects such as stereo speakers and bedspreads.

Tongueing

An interesting, but subtle, behavior of male dogs is called tongueing. The dog flicks his tongue against the roof of his mouth. He is most apt to do that when he has just sniffed the urine of a bitch. The function of the behavior is to introduce urine or some other substance into a duct that leads to the vomeronasal organ. This organ lies between the nose and the mouth. The duct leading to it opens just behind the incisor teeth and, therefore, is called the incisive duct. The vomeronasal organ apparently is used by animals—and all animals except humans have them—as a special kind of smell or odor recognition. Things that are not airborne can be sucked and pushed by the dog's tongue into the vomeronasal organ and enable the dog to detect and respond appropriately to a bitch

Copulation by dogs. Note that the dog's hind feet are off the ground as he ejaculates.

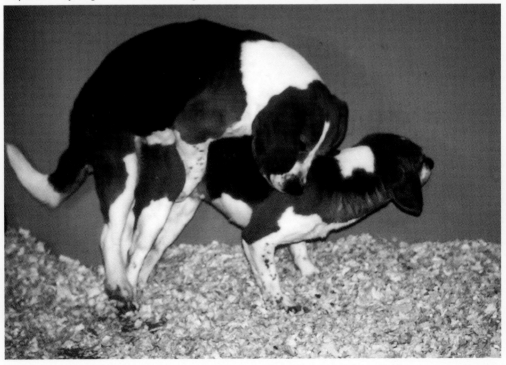

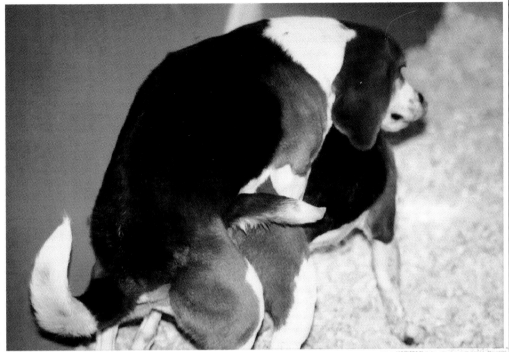

Receptivity in the bitch and normal mounting by the dog. Note that the bitch's tail is deviated to the side to facilitate intromission of the dog's penis.

in heat. This may be the sixth sense of animals.

Mounting

Mounting, a behavior in which one dog stands on his hind legs and straddles another with his fore legs, is a very common behavior. Because dogs have a limited repertoire of behaviors by which to express a wide range of messages, mounting serves to convey several intentions. Therefore, mounting of other males by a male dog or female-female mounting is not necessarily homosexual behavior.

Mounting occurs in a variety of situations, not all of them sexual. Male dogs, especially young ones, mount in play. In fact, play mounting may function as practice for later sexual behavior. Puppies deprived of the opportunity to play with other dogs may have plenty of libido, but may be very clumsy in their attempts to mount, penetrate and copulate with bitches. Mounting also serves as an expression of dominance. A dog may mount another dog in the household as a means of reinforcing his superior position. The mounted dog may not accept that and a squabble may ensue.

Dogs may mount people for the same three reasons: play, sex or a means of asserting social superiority; i.e., dominance. Because the mounting dog is dominant, the owner should discourage the behavior no matter what the dog's motivation may be. Sexual behavior can usually be distinguished from dominance because in the former case the dog will clasp the owner (usually a leg or arm) with his forelegs and thrust.

ABNORMAL MALE SEXUAL BEHAVIOR

The most common reason why a male fails to breed a female is that she is not in full heat although the owners thinks she is. Heat, during which the vulva is swollen and uterine fluids discharge through the vagina and vulva, is composed of two phases: proestrus and estrus. Just before estrus the bitch is attracted and attractive to the male, but will not accept him. This is called proestrus. The owners may try to breed the bitch during the proestrus, which is too early. The male knows better and will not breed her. The owner may mistake this normal behavior for poor libido. Following several days of proestrus, the bitch usually accepts the male (i.e., estrus or full heat).

Sexual behavior in the dog may be inhibited by anything that frightens him. For that reason it is more important that the dog be in a familiar environment. He can also be distracted if too many people are present. He may have been punished for mounting a bitch that the owners did not want him to breed so that he is now afraid to mount any female. There may be social problems also. If the male is subordinate to the female he will not (or will not be permitted to) mount her. Some, but not all dogs may be reluctant to mount their mother either because the mother is dominant or because there is an innate reluctance to breed a closely related animal, i.e., an incest taboo. Dogs may develop preferences or antipathies for bitches of a particular coat color based on past positive or negative experiences. Some males have adequate libido, but do not have the agility to mount and mate properly. This could be due to musculoskeletal problems or to a lack of play experience. Any dog that does not show normal sexual behavior should be examined by a veterinarian to eliminate diseases or injury as a cause. Lack of the male hormone, testosterone, is rarely a cause, but can be determined on the basis of a blood sample.

Two males may live together for many years with no sign of sexual interaction, when suddenly one male will begin to show great interest in the other, sniffing, licking and mounting the other. The most common cause of this behavior is an anal sac infection. The anal sacs are small structures located on either side of the rectum, just inside the anus. They are about the size of a grape in a large breed dogs. Many owners are familiar with anal sacs because they frequently become impacted and irritate the dog. The dog will scoot his rear end along the ground to seek relief. Infection of the sacs can result in production of an odor which must be similar to the odor of a bitch in heat because the infected dogs will attract males.

Both sexes have anal sacs so impaction or infection can occur in either. The normal contents of the anal sac have a very strong and unpleasant odor. Dogs empty the sacs with a resulting stench when they are very upset.

Another reason why a male dog may begin to attract other male dogs is if he has a tumor that secretes female hormones (estrogens). The tumor must be removed. The tumor occurs much more frequently in testicles that have not descended into the scrotum, but which remain in the abdomen, a condition called retained testicle or cryptorchidism (hidden testicle). Cryptorchidism is usually a genetic problem.

REASONS FOR CASTRATION

There are several reasons, ethical, medical, financial and behavioral, why dogs should be castrated (neutered). The most important reason is the ethical reason—to reduce the number of unwanted dogs. The next most important reason is the health of the dog. Several types of cancer are less likely to occur in neutered dogs. The intact (non-neutered) male is of greater risk for developing cancer of the testicles and perianal glands. Furthermore, like his human counterparts, he may develop prostate enlargement, which interferes with his ability to urinate. If the male dog has any behavior problems such as ag-

Mounting behavior. In this case one spayed female is mounting another in what is probably a dominance display.

gression, destructiveness or barking, castration will ensure that the genetics of these problems are not passed on to future generations.

Each of the activities of normal canine sexual behavior can become a problem for the owner. Roaming or running away is an inconvenience at best and can become costly if the dog is picked up by animal control officers. Furthermore, the dog can cause traffic accidents as people swerve to avoid him or he himself may be struck and injured. For these reasons, and because license fees are usually lower for a neutered animal; a castrated dog is a less expensive one.

Castration reduces or eliminates mounting of people in 67% of dogs. Scent marking in the house is reduced in 50% of dogs, roaming in 90%, and 60% of intermale fighting is reduced. Neutering may also help reduce the domineering aggressive behavior of some dogs. These statistics, plus a lower licensing fee and health benefits, should encourage owners of male dogs to neuter their male dog. There is no evidence that castrated males "miss" their sexual urges. Castrated dogs are not depressed. In fact, removing sexual urges probably results in a dog that is more content.

Cocker Spaniel nursing Himalayan kittens. This is an example of excessive or inappropriate maternal behavior. Photograph by Dr. Elinor Brandt.

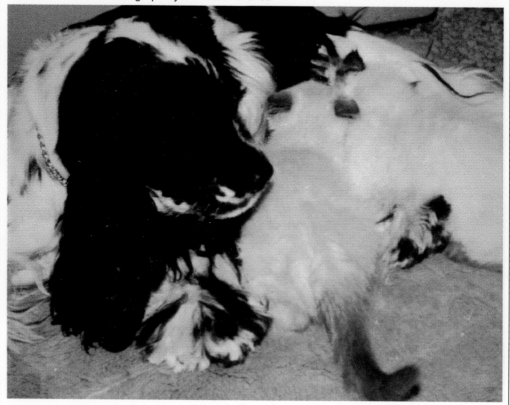

The statistics given above indicate that male sexual urges persist in some dogs. Mounting and marking can usually be controlled by establishing dominance, or if necessary, by medical (hormonal) treatment by the veterinarian. Sometimes, as simple an activity as staring into the dog's eyes until he looks away serves to establish that the human is dominant. This should not be done if the dog is at all aggressive because it is a challenge which might be met with growling or even with biting.

THE BITCH

The bitch usually reaches puberty and has her first heat or estrus at 5 to 18 months of age. Smaller dogs become sexually mature earlier than large breed dogs. Most dogs have two heat or breeding seasons a year except the Basenji who has only one. In other breeds the heat periods are about 7 months apart.

Stages of female cycle

It is important to be aware of the stages of the bitch's reproductive cycle in order to understand her behavior and to be able to breed her at the proper time. There are four stages to the cycle: 1) a 3-20 day proestrus which usually lasts about 9 days, 2) a 5-15 day estrus which also usually lasts about 9 days, 3) diestrus which lasts 50-80 days and 4) anestrus which lasts for several months until the bitch enters proestrus again. An observant owner will note that the bitch's vulva is swollen and most are aware that there is a blood-tinged discharge from the vulva. Some bitches lick themselves more than others so the owner may be unaware of the discharge. This blood is not a shedding of the uterine lining that occurs in humans as menstruation. Instead, red blood cells are able to move from blood vessels through the lining of the uterus to the vagina. During proestrus the bitch may seek out the dog and attract him, but she will not stand for him to mount. As she comes into estrus, her behavior will gradually change from active rejection, in which she might even snap at the dog, through passive acceptance of mounting to active acceptance in which she will stand to be mounted and deflect her tail to facilitate his intromission. She will sniff at the male's head and his genitalia. She will bow, that is stand with her forequarters and head low while her hindquarters are high. This is a canine communication that can mean play or sex. She may stimulate sexual behavior in the male by mounting him. She may run from the male and then suddenly crouch or sit. She may urinate frequently. When the male approaches she will "present" her hindquarters, deflect her tail to the side (an action called flagging), and tip the vulva dorsally.

If the bitch is not bred she may become pseudopregnant. This is caused by the hormone progesterone that is produced by the ovary after ovulation. The mammary glands (breasts) of the bitch may become engorged and she may even demonstrate maternal behavior toward inanimate objects such as toys or slippers.

MATERNAL BEHAVIOR

Whelping

The bitch gives birth (whelps) 63 days after she ovulates (the egg leaves the ovary) which may be 58-68 days after the last breeding. It may be worthwhile to have blood tests taken while the bitch is in heat to determine the exact day of ovulation so the birth date can be calculated. Although most canine births are uneventful, some bitches do not remove the fetal membranes from the puppies in time so the puppy suffocates. More rarely, labor is not normal. A puppy, especially a large one in a small litter, can become wedged in the bitches pelvis. Prolonged labor (more than two hours) or labor that ceases before all the puppies are delivered indicates that veterinary assistance must be sought. Occasionally, it may be necessary for the veterinarian to perform a cesarean section; that is to open the abdomen and the uterus to deliver the puppies. Dystocia, wedging of the puppies, is most common in breeds with large heads and relatively small bodies such as Boston Terriers. If the bitch whelps outside her nest box the puppies may crawl away and become chilled. Fortunately, even tiny puppies have loud distress cries that attract the owner if not the mother. For all those reasons the owner should be present, but non-obtrusive, at the birth of the puppies.

There are ways to predict the birth of the puppies. The bitch's temperature can be taken daily. If the temperature is lower than 100°F, she is likely to give birth that day. Because dogs vary somewhat in normal temperature, a baseline should be established by daily measurements of rectal temperature at the same time of day because there are circadian (night-day) differences in normal body temperature.

The bitch also gives behavioral cues that she is about to whelp. She will try to make a nest by tearing up material in a den-like area. If the owner is lucky the bitch will tear the newspaper provided, but bitches have also been known to excavate couches for the purpose.

Once a puppy has been delivered, the bitch licks it, chews the umbilical cord, thus breaking it, and devours the placenta or afterbirth. Eating the afterbirth serves two purposes: 1) organic matter that would otherwise attract predators is removed; 2) the tissue is recycled so that the bitch, who will now be under considerable nutritional strain while lactating (producing milk) will not lose the energy and protein contained in the placenta. Although many hormones are produced by the placenta eating it does not influence the bitch or the puppies because the hormones would be digested in her stomach and intestines. Licking by the bitch stimulates the puppies to breathe, as well as drying them.

The bitch usually pauses in her

licking to deliver the next puppy, presumably due to the pain of uterine contractions. Once all the puppies are whelped the bitch will lie beside them. The puppy's task is to find a teat (nipple) to obtain nourishment. This is an innate or instinctive behavior in which the puppy reacts to certain cues. He nuzzles through the bitch's hair. If he encounters a hairless area, he roots upward. If he encounters a teat he opens his mouth while moving his head up. The teat should slip into his mouth. Puppies may have difficulty finding the teats especially if the bitch is high chested.

Weaning

During the first few days the bitch spends most of her time with the pups. Nursing reaches a peak at the end of the first week. After that, the amount of time that she spends with them decreases with time. If the puppies leave the nest they will cry and this vocalization alerts the bitch who may attract them back to the nest by licking them so that they follow her back, or, less frequently, she may carry them.

The undisturbed litter will be weaned gradually by the bitch; weaning usually will be complete by 60 days. During early lactation the bitch always approaches the puppies to initiate a nursing bout. By 3 weeks the puppies have opened their eyes and can locomote well. They then approach the bitch and initiate most of the nursing bouts. Bitches rarely punish their puppies until the third week. Even during the weaning process the punish-

ment is mild enough, such that it may momentarily deter the pup's attempts to nurse, but it will not inhibit it from trying again. The punishment may consist of a growl, a snarl or an inhibited bite. The level of aggression of the bitch toward her puppies increases and the number of nursing bouts per hour decreases after the puppies' third week.

Some bitches may regurgitate food for their pups during the weaning process at 4 to 6 weeks. This behavior, commonly seen in wild canids, helps to maintain adequate nutrition in the young during the transition from a milk diet to a raw meat diet, when their powers of mastication and digestion may not have matured enough to enable them to survive on the raw meat. Wolf pups beg for regurgitated food by licking at the mouth of the adult. This behavior is occasionally seen in domestic dogs and may be the basis of face licking and licking intention movements directed toward people by adult dogs.

ABNORMAL MATERNAL BEHAVIOR

Abnormal maternal behavior may be directed toward an inappropriate object or it may be excessive or insufficient. There are few problems with excessive maternal behavior unless aggression toward the owner by the over-protective bitch is considered excessive maternal behavior. Some bitches may try to steal puppies. This excessive maternal behavior may be used to foster orphaned or rejected puppies onto that bitch. Abnormal maternal behavior is mothering of another species or an object. Bitches will sometimes allow kittens or other newborns to suckle. It is relatively easy to introduce a new puppy or even another animal to a litter; dogs do not seem to count their offspring.

Much more common, especially in bitches whelping for the first time, is insufficient maternal behavior. Some bitches may ignore the puppies; others may actually attack them. Still other bitches carry their pups constantly rather than nursing them. The bitch that ignores her puppies may have missed the critical period for acceptance of the young. The critical period occurs as the result of the puppies passing through the vagina and stimulating a reflex to the brain that results in the bitch accepting the next small, wet, wriggling object as her own. If the bitch has to have a cesarean section she may miss that period. If she has had a difficult labor she may be too stressed to accept the puppies. Wetting the puppies later may stimulate her to lick them and she may then accept them. Some bitches seem irritated by puppies and bite if the puppies walk over them. These bitches can be muzzled, but then she will not be able to stimulate the puppies' urination and defecation by licking the urogenital area. The owner will have to do that by rubbing gently under the tail with a moist cotton-tipped applicator stick.

The most frequent problem is the bitch who consumes the afterbirth and consumes the puppy as well (cannibalism) or chews the umbilical cord and part of the puppy. In such cases, or in bitches who have exhibited the problem several times, the puppies should be removed immediately after birth and reintroduced when the litter is complete and the afterbirth removed.

REASONS FOR SPAYING

People are much more likely to neuter (spay) their bitches than their male dogs because of the nuisance of cleaning away the bloody discharge that bitches produce for 2-3 weeks during heat and because male dogs may be attracted to her and have to be repulsed by the owner.

There are several more important reasons to spay a bitch. The most important reason is to reduce canine overpopulation. If the bitch has any behavior problems such as aggression, destructiveness, excessive barking, etc. she should not be bred because her offspring are likely to have the same problems. Canine aggression is so serious and frequent a problem that no dog that has bitten should be bred. The problem of aggression would be solved very quickly if no aggressive dogs reproduced to add more aggressive offspring.

Spaying has definite benefits to the bitch also. If done early enough spaying prevents or greatly reduces the incidence of mammary cancer, a very common cause of death in bitches. She will not be at risk of pyometra, a uterine infection (literally pus in the uterus) that occurs in older bitches and which can kill quickly because the bitch shows few signs until the infection is overwhelming and only emergency spaying may save her. A bitch nursing

Cocker Spaniel nursing a Himalayan cat. This is an example of persistent maternal behavior on the part of the dog and persistent suckling behavior on the part of the cat. Photograph by Dr. Elinor Brandt.

puppies, especially a large litter, may develop a calcium deficiency called lactation tetany, go into convulsions and die unless treated promptly. Owners should be sure that a lactating bitch has an adequate diet and observe her for irritability, muscle tremors and a high fever that are signs of lactation tetany.

There are ethical reasons for spaying bitches and considerable economic ones. License fees are lower. Medical bills are lower and the animal should lead a longer, healthier life.

SUMMARY

Sexual behavior of dogs involves a prolonged intromission, called lock. Bitches in heat attract males and may court males. Castrated males may continue to show sexual behavior such as urine marking or mounting but spayed bitches rarely show either sexual or maternal behavior.

ADDITIONAL READING

Cain, J. and D.F. Lawler. 1991. *Small Animal Reproduction and Pediatrics*. St. Louis, MO, Ralston Purina Company. 68 pp.

Holst, P.A. 1985. *Canine Reproduction, A Breeder's Guide*. Loveland, CO. Alpine Publications, Inc. 223 pp.

Houpt, K.A. 1991. *Domestic Animal Behavior for Veterinarians and Animal Scientists*. Iowa State University Press, Ames, Iowa, 408 pp.

Dr. Robert Eckstein received his Bachelor of Arts (BA) degree in biology from the University of Colorado. He graduated from the School of Veterinary Medicine at Colorado State University in 1990, and served a one-year internship at Oklahoma State University for advanced training in small animal medicine and surgery. He has been a resident in the Behavior Service of the University of California School of Veterinary Medicine, and an adjunct instructor for physiology and behavior since 1991. While at the University of California, he has earned the degree of Master of Science (MS) in the field of Animal Behavior, and is working towards a Ph.D. in Applied Animal Behavior. Dr. Eckstein also works privately as a consultant for pet behavior problems.

Fears and Phobias

By Robert A. Eckstein, DVM, MS
School of Veterinary Medicine
Department of Anatomy, Physiol-
   ogy, and Cell Biology
University of California, Davis
Davis, CA 95616

INTRODUCTION

Behavior problems in the dog related to fears and phobias are commonly seen by those working in the
field of animal behavior therapy.
Some dogs may have very general
fears, acting timid in many different
situations. Other dogs have problem
fears that are very specific, perhaps
limited to a certain person or a certain situation. Phobias are fear reactions that are considered to be out of
proportion to the actual danger of
the situation. Distinguishing between fears and phobias can be quite
difficult when working with animals.
Both will be referred to here under
the general term "fears." This chapter will cover the nature of the fear
reaction, the prevention and treatment of fears in general, and will give
treatment and prevention recommendations for a number of specific
common canine fears. Fear aggression is covered separately in the
chapters on canine aggression.

THE NATURE OF FEAR REACTIONS

The Fear Reaction

When dogs are fearful, they often
give characteristic postural signals
which we can use to identify this
emotional state. One signal is holding the ears back, although this
may not be easily seen in dogs with
floppy ears. Another signal is tuck-
ing the tail tightly under the body
between the legs. These body signals are also part of the more general posture that dogs use to indicate submission. Fearful dogs will
commonly try to escape from the
situation that is provoking the fear,
and this tendency towards escape
or avoidance can help us to identify
the fearful state. Some dogs however, may crouch down in the face
of a fear-producing stimulus. This
is especially likely if there is no
means of escaping from the situation. In extreme cases, the fearful
dog may become outwardly aggressive or become completely immobile, and may involuntarily urinate
or defecate. In such a case, it is
important to realize that the elimination behavior is not a break in
housebreaking training, but is
rather a part of the fear reaction.

The Function of Fear

The fear reaction is a natural
and normal part of a dog's behav-

ioral repertoire, and may have important survival value. It is easy to see how the impulse to escape from a dangerous situation may be adaptive for the dog by promoting survival. Similarly, the impulse to remain immobile in certain dangerous situations may also promote survival. For example, by freezing, a dog may avoid being attacked, or may avoid going deeper into dangerous territory. The fear reaction may be serving the important role of self-protection and self-preservation. However, even behavioral patterns that are "normal" may still be problematic and inappropriate in the domestic setting as a household dog. For example, it may be natural, normal, or even adaptive for a dog to avoid entering tightly confined spaces with limited air flow that smell of gasoline and oil. However, it may be important for the well-being of both the dog and the dog owner for the dog not to be afraid of riding in the car.

The Origin Of Fears

Genetics undoubtedly play some role in the development of fears in the dog. There are differences between breeds with regard to a wide variety of behavioral tendencies, including aggression, trainability, and general reactivity. It is reasonable to expect that the tendency to develop problem fears is also enhanced in some breeds and reduced in others. Genetic influences may also lead to behavioral differences between individuals of the same breed. For example, the offspring of two "fearful" dogs of a certain breed may be more likely to develop problem fears than the offspring of "non-fearful" dogs of the same breed.

Learning is an important factor that contributes to the development of most, if not all problem fears in the dog. The learning that occurs during early puppy-hood is particularly important. It is during this time that the puppy may form relatively firm associations with diverse stimuli such as adults, children, other dogs, car rides, the veterinary office, and loud noises. Learning by association continues to occur in dogs beyond puppy-hood and throughout adulthood. Dogs may learn to be afraid of particular people, things, or situations once they are associated with unpleasant or aversive experiences.

In most cases, it is likely that fear problems have both genetic and learned components as parts of their origin. Practically, it is often difficult, and of limited value, to try to separate out the relative importance of these two forces for a given problem.

Prevention of Fears

Although many problem fears can be treated, it is much better for all involved if the fears can be prevented. Habituation is the process by which an individual learns not to react to harmless, repetitive stimuli, even though the stimulus may have initially caused a startle response. For habituation to occur, the stimulus needs to be repeatedly presented, without any reward or punishment following it.

Puppy classes are a great way to socialize young dogs and expose them to a variety of different stimuli. Photo by Dr. Gary Landsberg.

The individual essentially learns that the stimulus involved is an inconsequential part of the environment, and is best ignored. This is a very widespread and important process in nature, as animals learn to attend to the environmental stimuli that have consequences, and to ignore those that do not.

The habituation process can be used intentionally to prevent the development of many canine fears. However, since young animals habituate more readily than adults, it is best to begin this type of training early. The general technique is to intentionally and repetitively expose the young dog to the stimulus with which we are concerned. This may be a stimulus that is already beginning to trigger a mild fear reaction, or one that we anticipate may lead to a fear reaction in the future.

Many dogs habituate to a wide range of stimuli without any intervention on our part. A young dog may be afraid of the noise of a vacuum cleaner for the first few exposures. If each time the dog is in the presence of the vacuum noise there is no aversive result, then the dog is likely to become progressively less reactive with each following exposure. The dog will learn that this noise is an inconsequential part of the environment.

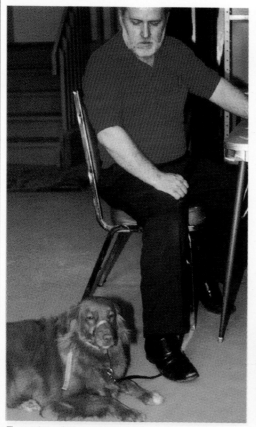

Exposing dog to problem situation with halter and leash. Photo by Dr. Gary Landsberg.

Gentle use of the halter to gain control of the situation. Photo by Dr. Gary Landsberg.

Dogs may also habituate to stimuli, even though we might prefer them to remain apprehensive. During early curbside leash walking, a young dog may be startled by passing cars. As car after car passes, with no consequences resulting, the dog will soon habituate to the passing cars, and lose the initial startle reaction. The dog may thus lose what could have been a very healthy fear of moving cars.

When working to prevent fears in the dog, we often combine repetitive presentation of the problematic stimulus or situation (the driving force of habituation) with a pattern of positive reinforcement, or rewards. For example, if we wanted to prevent a young dog from developing a fear of strangers, we would expose the puppy at an early age to as many people as possible. Additionally, we could make these exposures rewarding, so that the puppy begins to associate the presence of strangers with positive things such as food treats, praise and attention.

This simple approach can be very effective, and is easily applied to many other potential problem areas. In a very general sense, the young puppy should be exposed to

Using positive reinforcement to encourage a "heel" with the halter. Photo by Dr. Gary Landsberg.

a wide and varied set of stimuli and situations, with special emphasis on potential problem areas.

Our efforts to prevent fears may be completely undermined if the dog is punished when the stimulus or situation is encountered. Although we would be unlikely to do this intentionally, punishments may be delivered without our intent. For example, if a young dog has the annoying habit of jumping up on people, the owners may begin to quickly put the dog in an enclosed room when visitors are coming, for the comfort of their guests. Social isolation is a very powerful form of punishment in the dog. If the dog learns that the appearance of strangers means social punishment is about to follow, then a fear of strangers may be unintentionally created.

Problem fears can also be created if the owners inadvertently reward the fear reaction. This is actually a very common occurrence, since the natural reaction of many people is to comfort and reassure the fearful dog. When this occurs, the dog is given an attention reward every time the fear is exhibited. In essence, the dog is being trained to express the fear reaction. When working to prevent the development of fears, we must be very careful to only reward calm, non-fearful behavior. If a fear reaction occurs, it should neither be punished nor rewarded, but should simply be ignored.

GENERAL TREATMENT TECHNIQUES

There are a number of general techniques that can be used when working to eliminate an already existing fear reaction in the dog. Treatment of existing fears is generally more difficult than prevention or early treatment would have been. However, if applied correctly, the techniques described here have a fairly good chance of reducing even long-standing problems fear reactions.

Systematic Desensitization

This technique is the one most commonly used, and most likely to be effective. It is often combined with counterconditioning, which will be described next. With this technique, we expose the dog to the offending stimulus at a level too low to induce a reaction. This is done repeatedly, and the level of the stimulus is very gradually increased. If the fear reaction occurs, we back down a number of steps in the level of the stimulus, and continue the training even more gradually. It may take weeks to work up to the full level of the stimulus. It is very important that the dog not be exposed to the fear-inducing stimulus under non-controlled conditions during this period. With this technique, we want to avoid triggering the fear reaction. The process can be enhanced by offering rewards of food and affection for calm behavior in the presence of the low-level stimulus. The biggest drawback of this technique is that it is time-consuming and labor-intensive.

The most challenging aspect of systematic desensitization is the creation of a gradual gradient for all components of the problem fear. This often requires detailed analysis of the exact conditions that are most and least likely to induce the fear reaction, and may include factors such as distance from the stimulus, the intensity of the stimulus, or specific characteristics. In most cases, more than one factor is involved. Training should begin with all factors at their lowest level, which is the condition least likely to trigger the fear. As training progresses, one factor at a time should be increased. Once the dog can tolerate the full level of one factor, we can back down somewhat, and raise the level of another factor. The ultimate goal is for the dog to tolerate the full level of all factors, which is the top of the gradient, without a fear reaction.

Counterconditioning

This technique aims at replacing the emotional state of fear with a different, inconsistent emotional state. This is best achieved by training the dog to play a very easy game of obedience and reward. The dog is told to sit and stay, and is given a food or affection reward after a short wait. Most dogs learn this game very quickly, and seem to enjoy it. We presume that the likely emotional state accompanying this game, one of expectancy and frequent satisfaction, is not consistent with a state of fear.

The next step is to begin to pair these fun play sessions with low levels of the offending stimulus, progressing as described for systematic desensitization. Conceptually, the low level of fear is overwhelmed by the higher level of positive emotions. These play sessions should then only occur in the presence of the fear-inducing stimulus at the appropriate level. Counterconditioning and systematic desensitization make a very effective combination for the treatment of canine fears.

Flooding

This technique is practically identical to the process used in

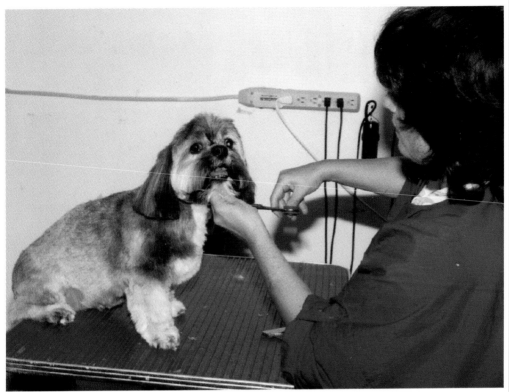

Gentle handling for the dog afraid of grooming. Photo by Dr. Gary Landsberg.

habituation already discussed. In flooding, we present the fear-producing stimulus again, and only stop when the fear reaction stops. This process is repeated as many times as necessary. The advantage of flooding is that behavior changes may occur fairly rapidly.

For flooding techniques to be successful, the dog, the environment and the stimulus must be well controlled. Begin by presenting a mild form of the stimulus in an environment where the pet cannot escape or do any damage. Rewards can be given and the stimulus can be stopped or removed only after the pet calms down. During future training sessions, the dog should then be exposed to slightly higher levels of the stimulus. This technique, where flooding is performed with a reduced or modified stimulus is known as controlled exposure or controlled flooding. Preventing the dog from escaping, while ensuring good control, is a critical component of flooding techniques. The use of a halter and leash or placing the pet in an open wire cage are practical ways of controlling the dog while exposing it to the stimulus.

The drawbacks of using this technique are the possibilities of property damage, physical harm, and emotional stress. Once a dog has developed a deeply rooted fear reaction, repeated exposures to the offending stimulus, may drive the dog into a destructive panic. Even if this occurs, we must stay committed to continuing the exposure, or else we will be rewarding the panic reaction by removing the offending stimulus. Due to these major drawbacks, flooding that involves full-stimulus exposure is very rarely recommended for treatment of existing canine fears.

Drug Therapy

There are a number of drugs that have shown some effectiveness in reducing fear reactions in the dog. They are most useful for extreme fears, used in combination with the above described training programs. The drug may reduce the dog's reactivity, and can give us another gradient to manipulate by gradually reducing the drug dose. However, the majority of problem fears in the dog can be treated with the training techniques alone. A veterinary behavior consultant can help advise on the use of drug therapy for treating fearful behaviors.

SPECIFIC PROBLEM FEARS

Fear of Thunderstorms

Dogs that are afraid of thunderstorms are usually reacting to the sound component, although some may be reacting to the visual component as well. A sound gradient can be created with a thunderstorm recording. The visual component can be simulated with a strobe light, although this should not be required for all cases. Alternatively, a homemade video can be used to mimic both the sights and sounds of a storm.

The recording should be played quite loudly at first, to insure that it is capable of inducing the fear reaction. It can then be played frequently at a low volume, and the dog can be rewarded for calm behavior. The volume can be gradually increased on following training periods. If the fear reaction occurs, it should not be rewarded with comfort and attention. It should simply be ignored, but the next training session should be conducted at a lower volume, and the training should progress more gradually. If the thunderstorms are seasonal, training should begin during the off-season, so the dog is not exposed to the real thing in the middle of the training program.

Once the dog is able to tolerate full volume recordings, the strobe light effect may be added. This can also be done gradually by covering the light with layers material, and gradually removing the layers. The counterconditioning game could be added to both the sound and light training, simply by playing the game during the training sessions. The thunderstorm recording could also be useful if we wished to prevent this fear by exposing a puppy to these sounds repeatedly to encourage habituation.

Fear of Loud Noises

Treatment of this fear is very similar to the treatment for fear of thunderstorms. The main difference is the means of creating a gradient. If we consider the fear of gunshots, one approach would be to use a starter's pistol, and to create a muffler with wrapped towels, or nested cardboard boxes. It is important that the muffler be removable in gradual stages. Once the muffler system is established, systematic training could progress in the fashion described above. The counterconditioning game would be a helpful addition when working with this fear. This fear could be prevented by repetitively exposing the young puppy to harmless loud noises.

Fear of Strangers

This is one of the more common problem fears in the dog. The combination of counterconditioning and either systematic desensitization or controlled flooding is the most effective approach to this problem. An in-depth analysis is usually needed to determine the factors that can be used to set up the gradient. Potential factors include male vs. female, with facial hair vs. clean shaven, plain clothed vs. uniformed, child vs. adult, and young child vs. older child. The distance between the strangers and the dog is almost always used as part of the gradient.

The program begins by pairing the fun counterconditioning game with the presence of a stranger who is the least likely to induce a fear reaction, and at a very safe distance. The distance between the safe stranger and the dog can be gradually reduced, and then the characteristics of the stranger can be changed gradually as well. For example, if the dog was most afraid of bearded men, somewhat afraid of men in general, and only mildly afraid of women, the early training sessions would be only with various women at a safe distance. Once women at a close distance were well tolerated, training could progress to shaven men at a safe distance. Only when the dog could tolerate the presence of shaven men at a close distance would we progress to bearded men, but again dropping back to safe distance at first.

Another option is to desensitize the dog to a familiar family member wearing an artificial beard. For dogs afraid of people in uniform, a family member could put on a uniform to begin desensitizing techniques. Or, if the dog was afraid of young children, training should begin with older children, then younger children playing at a distance (or even a tape recording of children playing).

Treatment of this behavior problem does present certain difficulties. It may be difficult to find enough volunteer strangers to participate, and thus the gradient is likely to be very uneven. It is highly recommended that steps be taken to prevent the onset of this problem by exposing young puppies to many strangers of various descriptions. These do not need to be strangers to the owner, only strangers to the puppy. It will also help if both the owner and the stranger provide food treats and attention to the puppy.

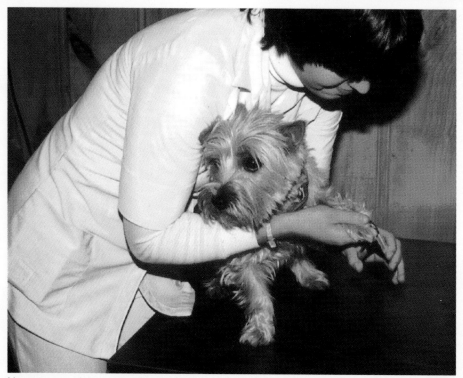

Never use punishment for the fearful dog. Here, gentle handling and rewarding appropriate behavior are used for the dog fearful of having its nails trimmed. Photo by Dr. Gary Landsberg.

Fear of General Situations

Some dogs may become fearful of certain situations, such as going into the backyard, or going into the car. The important part of treating this type of fear is to identify the specific factors that are triggering the fear reaction, and to convert them into a gradient as we would for other problem fears. For example, a dog may be very afraid of car rides, moderately afraid of being in a starting car, mildly afraid when the car door opens, and unafraid of being near a silent car with closed doors.

A good starting point would be to teach the dog the counterconditioning game, and to play it near the car. The game can then be played next to the car. Next, the game could be played near the car with the doors already open, progressing to opening and closing the doors inconsequentially during the game. Getting into the car to receive the treat could then be incorporated, progressing finally to starting the car and taking progressively longer trips. Any time the fear is triggered, it means that we need to back up in the training and go forward more slowly.

The same approach could be used for a variety of problem situations. The key points are to identify the specific factors that can be used to create a gradient, to progress very gradually, and to avoid triggering the fear during the training period. This type of fear is also preventable by exposing the puppy to a wide variety of stimuli and environments and pairing these exposures with rewards.

SUMMARY

Fear-related behavior problems of the dog are commonly encountered. Many of these problems are preventable by the simple technique of repeatedly exposing young dogs to the likely fear-inducing stimulus and rewarding calm behavior. If problem fears do develop, they are often treatable by behavioral training, but this requires a strong owner commitment, since it is often labor-intensive and time-consuming. It is important to remember that punishing the fearful dog is likely to make the situation even more fear inducing, while comforting the fearful dog may actually train the dog to continue expressing the fear reaction. It is recommended to take appropriate steps to prevent problem fears. If fear-related problems do occur, treatment should begin early in their development. In this chapter, we have provided a brief overview of some of the techniques that can be used to successfully treat canine fears and phobias. For serious problems, please consult your veterinarian, who may wish to refer you to an appropriate behavior consultant.

ADDITIONAL READING

Hart, B.L. and Hart, L.A. Canine and Feline Behavioral Therapy. Philadelphia, Lea & Febiger, 1985.

Hart, B.L. and Hart, L.A. The Perfect Puppy. How to choose your dog by its behavior. New York, Freeman Press, 1988.

Monks of the Brotherhood of St. Francis. The Monks of New Skete. How to Be Your Dog's Best Friend. Boston-Toronto, Little, Brown and Co., 1978.

GLOSSARY OF TERMS

Counterconditioning–A behavior modification technique that replaces the emotional state created by a stimulus with an alternate emotional state that is inconsistent with the original.

Flooding–A behavior modification technique that involves exposing the individual to the fear-inducing stimulus continuously, until the fear reaction subsides.

Habituation–The process by which an individual learns not to react to harmless, repetitive stimuli, even though they may initially cause a startle reaction.

Phobia–A fear that is out of proportion to the actual danger.

Systematic desensitization– A commonly used behavior modification technique that involves presenting the fear-inducing stimulus to the individual at a level too low to induce a reaction, and increasing the level very gradually.

Dr. Ilana Reisner graduated in 1984 from the Oregon State University College of Veterinary Medicine and then completed an internship at Michigan State University. After practicing for several years in the Boston area, she came to the Animal Behavior Clinic of the College of Veterinary Medicine at Cornell University where she received her PhD in the field of behavioral physiology. A former Fellow of the Morris Animal Foundation, Dr. Reisner has completed a residency in Animal Behavior and is currently continuing her research in the area of canine aggression, seeing clinical cases and speaking to many groups on the subject of companion animal behavior. Dr. Reisner is a Diplomate of the American College of Veterinary Behaviorists.

Aggression of Dogs toward People

By Ilana Reisner, DVM, PhD
Animal Behavior Clinic
Cornell University
New York State College of Veterinary
  Medicine
Ithaca, NY 14853-6401

INTRODUCTION

Few problem behaviors in dogs cause as much distress and conflict as aggression directed toward people. When dogs become dangerous and cannot be trusted, the solution for many owners is surrender or euthanasia. In either case, the special bond created between dog and owner has been disrupted and, often, people have been injured. Aggression is the most common problem for which pet owners seek the help of specialists in animal behavior; whether the dog is threatening visitors to the home, other household pets or even the owners themselves, biting behavior is seldom tolerated.

Aggression can be defined as behavior intended to threaten or to injure another animal or person. Biting is aggressive, regardless of the context in which it occurs. In addition to biting, however, dogs exhibit a wide range of behaviors which fall under the heading of aggression: stiffening, directly staring, growling, snarling or baring teeth, lunging, snapping and mouthing. Bites may be inhibited, leaving no bruise, or they may puncture and tear the victim. The definition of an aggressive dog may therefore be nebulous: a fearful Shetland Sheepdog bites his veterinarian when restrained for a vaccination; a Dalmatian growls when children approach his empty food bowl; an adult Vizsla growls and snaps at the family's new Welsh Corgi puppy; and a Poodle tugs and bites her owner's pant leg while running together outdoors. Each of these dogs is behaving aggressively, though the owners may differ in their view of the seriousness of each problem.

In order to change or to prevent problem aggression, it is important to understand the behavior. Examining the specific situations in which dogs aggress, we can distinguish between dominance, fear, territoriality, or predation. In addition, physical illness or abnormalities may contribute to aggressive behavior in otherwise tractable pets.

DOMINANCE AGGRESSION

Many people find it hard to believe that an otherwise loving family pet would bare his teeth at, or even bite, members of the family. Yet this is the most common problem for which owners seek professional help. In spite of the aggression and its risks, such dogs are considered by their families to be good pets "99% of the time." That means that the vast majority of the time these dogs show no aggression and are good pets. Dominant-aggressive dogs exhibit growling, snarling, snapping or biting toward their owners and other familiar people in situations which, in many cases, appear to be unprovoked. In fact, this behavior is normal (though very inappropriate); because dogs are pack animals and prefer to live in social groups, they relate to their human family as they would to other dogs. Relationships among dogs in a social group are defined by a dominance hierarchy, in which there is a top, or "alpha," dog and the bottom, or "omega" dog. Most pet dogs naturally accept their role at the bottom of the family's pecking order, but dominant-aggressive dogs prefer to be higher up. While each individual is unique, such dogs tend to act aggressive in the following circumstances:

1. When protecting food (dog food or human food), garbage, and certain objects (toys, stolen objects).
2. If disturbed while sleeping or resting, especially in socially significant areas such as furniture.
3. When a favored family member is approached or touched by other family members.
4. When they feel certain actions dispute this status. This can include postures such as bending over the dog, prolonged staring, punishment, pulling by the leash or collar, or even petting.

Although dogs reach sexual puberty before the age of 1 year, they do not achieve social adulthood until 1 to 3 years of age. Dominant-aggressive behavior may emerge in puppyhood, but dogs more typically begin to exhibit serious aggression when they approach social maturity. Because this behavior appears to be inherited (with components of learning), it cannot be completely "cured." Aggression can often, however, be controlled so that the dog remains a good pet. Several breeds, such as the English Springer Spaniel, Cocker Spaniel, Akita and Dalmatian, have a reputation for such behavior; however, dominant-aggressive dogs can be of any breed or mix. Owners of such dogs should seek behavioral counseling for a treatment plan designed specifically for them, and treatment must continue for the life of the dog.

Severely aggressive dogs are often described by their owners as having "rage syndrome"; the majority of such dogs are exhibiting dominance aggression but are particularly unpredictable and intense in the way they respond to their owners. For example, a severely dominant-aggressive dog may "ask" to be petted, only to suddenly bite the person petting him. In some cases, the biting may continue until the dog is restrained or the owner escapes; hence the term "rage."

Aggression toward children cannot be tolerated. Photo by Dr. Gary Landsberg

At this time the causes of this abnormal type of aggression are poorly understood and may include seizures or other inherited or congenital abnormalities. In any case, when a pet is potentially dangerous to the family, euthanasia may be the safest option. Dogs with a history of biting may always bite again, presenting an unfortunate dilemma, particularly to families with small children.

Many mildly or moderately dominant-aggressive dogs improve significantly with treatment and, for owners able and willing to change the problem, can be good pets. To control dominance-related aggression, owners must first prevent injury to themselves. Situations in which the dog has threatened family members should be avoided. For example, dogs growling when approached while lying down should instead by called over to the owner. The selective use of a basket muzzle allows pets to continue "hanging out" with the family whereas otherwise they may need to be isolated. Family members should not attempt to correct pet transgressions or threats with physical punishment and should retreat rather than confront. Using aggressive corrections on a dominant-aggressive dog often causes the growling to escalate into a bite.

To control dominance-related aggression, owners must first prevent injury to themselves. Situations in which the dog has threatened family members should be avoided. For example, dogs growling when approached while lying down should instead be called over to the owner. The selective use of a basket muzzle allows pets to continue "hanging out" with the family during chaotic times. If the dog threatens anyone when it is not wearing the muzzle, it is most important that nobody gets injured. Punishment must be avoided. Using aggressive corrections on a dominant-aggressive dog often causes the growling to escalate into a bite.

What then can owners do with these dogs intent on running the household? They can remove what most dogs crave yet take for granted: attention. Withheld attention can transform independent dogs into dependent, more compliant ones. Instead of receiving it for nothing, the dog is told to earn it by sitting or lying down first. In addition, such commands are issued before anything even remotely desirable, such as a thrown ball or an opened door. Obedience training alone will not control dominance aggression, but when used in a controlled program of behavior modification, it is essential. Any training should include positive and fun rewards for the dog food, favored toys or praise are safer and more useful than conflict. Head collars or halters, are preferred to conventional training collars for control while on lead, and a lead should be attached to the dog at all times, whether indoors or out. If appropriate, medication may be prescribed by a veterinary behaviorist.

Dominance aggression can be enigmatic for pet owners. If a dog has bitten someone in the family, behavioral counseling will help with decisions about whether the dog should remain in the household, and with guidance for a treatment plan with safety as the primary concern. A veterinarian or veterinary behaviorist should be contacted when such behavior is seen; early intervention offers the best hope for changing dominance-related problems.

TERRITORIAL AGGRESSION

Territorial aggression is distinguished from dominance aggression by the target: while dominant-aggressive dogs direct their threats to familiar people, territorial dogs display barking, growling or biting toward unfamiliar people (or those who come and go daily, such as postal workers).The natural tendency to sound an alarm when someone enters their home and yard, or approaches the family car, is exaggerated in some dogs. Territorial aggression is often a learned behavior, aggravated by long periods of unsupervised time within view of passersby. Dogs left alone in a fenced yard or tied to a dog house commonly become aggressive—behavior easily reinforced as the "intruder" walks by (and therefore away). In addition, it is frustrating for such a social animal to be isolated for many hours, and vices such as barking and digging go hand in hand with territorial barking and aggression. When the gate is accidentally left unlocked or the dog's chain snaps, dog bites are a common problem. Owners of such dogs may seek help when someone is bitten; personal safely and liability concerns compel them to change this behavior.

Territorial aggression is most pronounced in the socially mature dog (1-3 years), after which it tends to plateau. However, more severe aggression can be learned at any time. Some breeds, such as German Shepherds, Rottweilers, and Belgian Malinois were developed for guarding behavior and are predisposed to territorial aggression. However, dogs of any breed or mix can have problem behavior. We have all met (and perhaps owned) dogs which had to be restrained at the door as visitors enter, and were hastily confined to a bedroom during dinner. Aggressive behavior may be a problem in the house or yard, or it may be a problem away from the home when dogs lunge at people walking, jogging or bicycling past.

To control territorial aggression, it is important that the dog no longer make his own decisions about which people pose potential danger and which are "safe"; in fact, most visitors or passersby may be threatened. In spite of the pet owner's fears, controlling territorial aggression should not affect the dog's protective instincts when an intruder arrives through the window at 2 a.m. In most cases, sounding a barking alarm is sufficient. Although many pet owners express satisfaction with their good watchdogs, problems arise when dogs have the freedom to bite.

Breeds that were developed for guarding behavior, such as the Rottweiler, are predisposed to territorial aggression. Photo by Isabelle Francais.

First, it is most important to physically control the dog. She should no longer be free to reinforce her own territorial behavior by running along the fence as people walk past, growling at houseguests entering the room, or bolting out the door towards delivery people. Instead of tying dogs onto cables and chains or allowing free time in the yard, they should be taken for supervised, on-lead walks. If any time is spent unsupervised in the yard, reliable fencing is critical; underground radio-frequency fences are potentially quite dangerous, because the strongly motivated dog will run right through the shock, toward the victim. Another problem with underground fencing is its invisibility to pedestrians, inviting accidental access onto the dog's turf. In the home, territorially aggressive dogs should always be on lead when visitors arrive (and for the duration of the visit). If visitors enter unannounced, the dog should be on lead or otherwise controlled at all times.

Punishment for aggressive behavior is unlikely to truly change the dog's motivation to bite. It must be given 100% of the time and it must be unpleasant enough for the dog to care; these "rules" are difficult to follow on a day-to-day basis. A shouted "NO" may be meaningless to some dogs, for example. In the absence of the owner, such a dog may take his chances and bite while he can. Instead, the dog should be conditioned to tolerate (or even enjoy!) the arrival of houseguests or pedestrians. Again, obedience training emphasizes the SIT-STAY and DOWN-STAY commands, using food, toys or praise. Such positive reinforcement is both powerful and humane. When the dog has been trained reliably and maintains the STAY indoors, owners should practice in more distracting areas, such as the yard, the sidewalk and more crowded places. Finally, desensitization and counterconditioning techniques are used while "targets" approach, pass by, or interact with the owner.

Dogs aggressive within the home must be trained to maintain a STAY away from the door and from guests. They can be released after the initial chaos of arriving visitors, but may require a basket muzzle and indoor lead. If no muzzle is used, a head collar and indoor lead should be used at all times. Arrivals can be positive for dogs if they include food, which can be offered in small pieces as rewards for the SIT or DOWN, from the owner or, better yet, the visitor. Rewards can be tossed onto the floor rather than given directly to the dog. Treats should be available at the door, beside the dog's "station," and in the guest area (living room).

Territorially aggressive dogs can be managed with these techniques. For help with specific problems, or with any dog capable of biting, a veterinarian or veterinary behaviorist should be consulted.

FEAR-RELATED AGGRESSION

Whether being chased by children, held down for a vaccination at the veterinary clinic, or punished harshly, the fearful dog often protects herself by biting. Both family members and unfamiliar people may be the targets of such a bite. How can we distin-

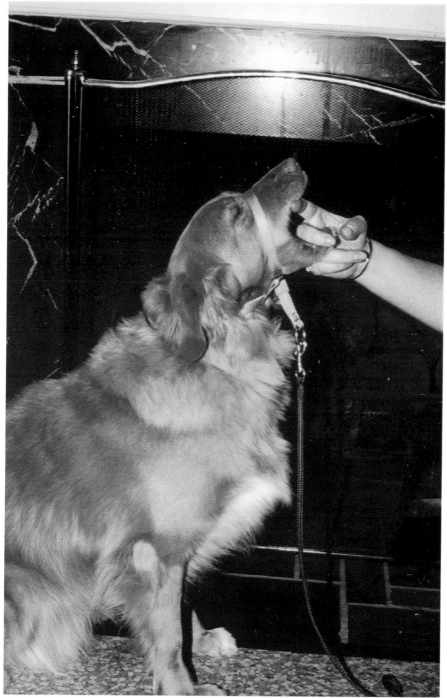

Head collars or halters are preferred to conventional training collars. In this case, Grace, a Nova Scotia Duck Tolling Retriever is fitted with a halter. When properly applied, the halter does not stop dogs from eating, drinking or barking. It is a control device, not a muzzle. Photo by Dr. Gary Landsberg.

guish between fearful and dominant dogs? Either can react aggressively to punishment, restraint, being cornered or even when petted. As with any behavior problem, details are important: what is the dog's general personality profile? Confident personalities are more likely to be dominant, and tend to stand tall, with ears forward, tail held high (or wagging), and direct eye contact. Fearful dogs, on the other hand, appear less secure in many circumstances, with a lowered head, ears flattened, tail held between the legs, and a tendency to avoid confrontation. When avoidance is not possible (for example, if cornered) the dog may bare her teeth and snap or bite.

As with other problems, the causes of such behavior are both innate and learned. Dogs predisposed to wariness, such as German Shepherds and many toy breeds, are more likely to develop fear-related aggression, but all breeds and both sexes may be fearful, and such behavior can be a problem at any age (although it is usually first seen in puppies or adolescents). Inadequate socialization of puppies to different colors and shapes of people may result in fear of children, wheelchairs, beards, hats and even people of skin color different from the owners. Physical abuse, of course, is a predictable cause of fear-biting; many dogs that appear to have been abused, however, are simply inadequately socialized.

Treatment of fear-related aggression must be aimed at desensitization and counterconditioning (described elsewhere in this book) of the dog to accept the source of his fear.

Severely fearful dogs may benefit from temporary anti-anxiety medication during the training program. Medication can lessen stress without sedating or tranquilizing the dog, so that she is more willing to learn. For each situation in which the dog seems afraid, helpers should be recruited. As with other training programs, a lead allows control of the dog. First, the basic "quieting" commands are taught or reinforced: SIT, SIT-STAY, DOWN and DOWN-STAY, using lots of food treats or special toys—whatever turns the dog on. This should be done in a safe, undistracting place (usually in the dog's home). Next, the "stimulus" is introduced. For example, a dog afraid when people approach outdoors should be trained first indoors, then out. When he is reliably and happily obeying the STAY, a person can begin to approach and pass from a distance, while the dog is rewarded. It is important not to reassure any expression of fear—to the dog, this is reinforcement. Instead, it should be ignored. If the approach is too frightening, it has probably come too soon in the program. Soon, anyone approaching will be considered not only a reason to receive rewards from the owner, but a source of treats themselves.

Dogs exhibiting fear-related aggression should not be physically punished. The fear itself, of course, should never be punished, but instead be counterconditioned as described here. Other inappropriate behavior should be corrected verbally only, or by leading the dog away by a lead, and immediately followed with obedience commands for which the dog can be praised.

PREDATORY AGGRESSION

Predatory aggression towards people is rare, but can happen. After all, dogs are predators, regardless of breed or ancestry. Some dog breeds were developed for this behavior and may be more likely to act like predators, stalking and killing small prey (squirrels or cats, for example), such as terriers. When is such aggression a risk to humans? The most common human victim of predatory attacks is the small infant. At this age, babies are less likely to be considered members of the "pack," and more likely to appear prey-like. Contrary to popular impressions, such attacks are not rooted in "jealousy" but in instinct. No small infant should be left alone with a dog; regardless of how friendly and trustworthy the family pet has been, he has the potential to kill a young baby. With this simple fact in mind, it becomes natural for parents to carry the child from room to room, or simply restrain the dog with a lead, in a crate, or behind a barricade when the infant is alone for even a minute.

When bringing a baby home from the hospital, it is helpful to first bring home soiled or used clothing such as a tee shirt or diaper, and to allow the dog opportunities to explore the new baby's room. On the day of arrival, the new mother should greet her dog while someone else holds the baby, and under controlled circumstances the new arrival can then be sniffed and greeted in turn. After the first few days, most dogs summarily dismiss the baby and ignore it; any evidence of anxiety, pacing and circling, or whining in the presence of the baby should be discussed with a veterinarian or veterinary behaviorist.

Yorkshire Terrier puppy being tested for sociability and ease of handling. Photo by Dr. Gary Landsberg.

Predatory instincts may also be aroused toward people running or moving quickly. Dogs are easily stimulated to chase a running deer, for example, and are considerably worse when they are in groups; even a pair of dogs will facilitate predatory behavior in each other. For this reason, packs of dogs are especially dangerous when free to chase bicycle riders or running children. Predatory attacks can be prevented by controlling the freedom of dogs even miles from where children play. If chased by one or more dogs it is wiser to stand or lie still than to run away.

Because predatory aggression is an innate behavior, it is not easily controlled by training. The best treatment for this problem is prevention.

AGGRESSION TO CHILDREN

Children can present a special problem for dog owners and are often the targets of growling, snapping and biting. For understandable reasons, such behavior is very upsetting, regardless of its reasons. Dogs targeting children may be motivated by fear, dominance, territorial behavior or even predation (see above): even dogs normally tractable with adults may express agitation to an infant or toddler. Dominance-aggression in some dogs may be exhibited specifically to children, seen as "puppies," and never to adults. Dogs unfamiliar with children, or those with memories of a painful encounter, may be fearful. Such dogs will tend to avoid a confrontation until cornered. Territorially aggressive dogs are typically not choosy and may threaten any intruder, regardless of age or size. Predatory behavior, as discussed above, is potentially seen in all dogs.

Regardless of motivation for aggression, biting dogs should be leashed (attached to the owner) or actively supervised, muzzled or crated in the presence of small children. Predatory aggression presents a special problem because even nondominant dogs socialized to small children may suddenly attack a small infant. Aggressive behavior, which in some households may be regarded as mild, is potentially more dangerous in a family home. Because of the natural transgressions of children, prevention of problems (as distinct from treatment) should be emphasized.

Dominance Aggression

Dogs exhibiting dominance-related aggression (in the situations described above) to children may or may not exhibit similar aggression toward adults. Unlike fearful dogs, they are less likely to avoid the child before threatening. Such dogs should be treated as described for any dominant-aggressive dog, but with several important limitations. While adults may follow "rules" necessary for safety, toddlers and small children cannot be trusted to be consistent. For this reason, emphasis should be placed on avoidance of aggression-inducing situations. In a home with family or visiting children, a basket muzzle is a necessity. Crating the dog (or confining him to an exercise pen among the family) is an alternative to muzzling; at the very least, dominant-aggressive dogs should be leashed and attached to the adult owner at all times. To prevent problems, the dog must be actively supervised whenever the child is awake.

Children over the age of 3 years can be invited to help with obedience training, offering food rewards for good behavior. In addition, all positive attention to the dog can be limited to times the baby or child is present. If this is consistent, and the dog is ignored when the child is sleeping or out of the home, he will soon learn to enjoy the presence of children. Dogs should never be disturbed by children while resting, sleeping or otherwise being still (unless working with a behaviorist in active desensitization exercises). Similarly, children should be unconditionally asked not to bend to the dog's face. Such "rules" are helpful, but it is most important to understand the risk of injury continues to be greater in homes with small children, and that prevention is the most effective tool. In some cases it may be advisable to find an adult-only home for the dog. Mildly dominant-aggressive dogs often improve as children mature.

Territorial aggression

Treatment of territorial aggression directed toward children is the same as that directed toward adults. In homes where friends of children run through doors and gates, the dog should be closely supervised, muzzled or confined to a crate or exercise pen. Under controlled circumstances, children can be asked to enter, ring a small bell, and toss the dog a food treat or ball so that she learns to associate children (or any visitors) with something fun.

At times aggression to unfamiliar children may actually be dominance-based. Behavioral counseling will help distinguish between different reasons for aggression, allowing a more specific approach to treatment. In addition, many territorially aggressive dogs are quite fearful.

Fear-based or defensive aggression

Dogs can be uncomfortable with children if they are unaccustomed to them, or if they have learned to associate children with pulled ears and poked eyes. A dog previously bored with the family's new baby may run from her as soon as she

Children and dogs must be taught to behave properly toward each other and should always be supervised when together. Photo courtesy of Pete Curley.

learns to crawl. Defensive, or fear-based, aggression can be seen if the dog is trapped under a table, cornered, or simply disturbed at the wrong time, and can be difficult to distinguish from dominance-related aggression.

Any dog that snaps at children should be seen by a veterinarian to rule out pain as a cause of the aggression. Arthritic hips, for example, are a common problem and can be quite painful when the dog is pushed. Ear infections are another frequently seen source of discomfort, perhaps the reason for a bite when hugged or petted.

Fearful dogs should not be reassured or punished for their behavior because neither response will reliably prevent aggression. Instead, a desensitization program should be started, in which the dog is gradually and safely exposed to children both in and out of the home. Praise and food rewards should be generous when the dog displays tolerance or friendliness. As with dominant-aggressive dogs, the presence of children should be associated with happy tones of voice, attention, play and exercise. The dog should be ignored when children are absent or asleep. Appropriate safety measures, such as muzzling, are preferred to isolation of the dog, though the dog should be given a "child-free" space in which to retreat by choice.

When fearful behavior is severe enough to interfere with training, anti-anxiety medication may be prescribed by a veterinarian or veterinary behaviorist.

PREVENTION OF AGGRESSION

Before Adopting A Puppy

The behavior of adult dogs is the synthesis of genes and the environment, or what the dog has learned. Many minor behavior problems can be prevented choosing the right puppy; new owners can therefore increase the odds of having a good pet by choosing carefully. Although impulsively purchased puppies of all pure breeds and mixes often turn out well, matching the personality and needs of owner and dog can cement the attachment between them (prospective owners should be aware, however, that breed characteristics are generalizations). For example, some breeds with a reputation for dominance-aggression are the Chow Chow, English Springer Spaniel, Lhasa Apso and Dalmatian. German Shepherds and Rottweilers are likely to exhibit territorial behavior, while Australian Shepherds and Shetland Sheepdogs seem to be fearful. Terriers and northern breeds such as the Siberian Husky may be more predatory than other dogs. Sporting breeds are likely to need more vigorous exercise than owners have time to provide. Sex differences are also important to consider in the choice of a pet; males tend to be more dominant and more of a challenge to obedience train, for example. Neutering either males or females will reduce such differences. Mixed breed puppies, of course, can be excellent pets, and it may be possible to predict personality characteristics if the pup's ancestry is known. There are resources to help

Before choosing your dog, be aware of each breed's unique characterisitics. For example, the Chow Chow is likely to exhibit territorial behavior. Photo by Isabelle Francais.

with the selection of a puppy by breed and sex.

Once the decision is made to purchase a purebred puppy, where can one be found? In general, breeders can be divided into those who have experience with the breed, along with concern about health and temperament, and those who do not. Prospective owners should avoid hobby breeders unless such concern is well documented.

When a breeder has been selected, and if she agrees to sell a puppy (for the sake of the pups, many breeders will extensively interview each family for suitability), the next step is choosing one puppy out of an irresistible litter. In some cases, a "puppy aptitude test" or temperament test will have been performed at 7 weeks of age. For information about such tests, see *Behavior Problems in Dogs*, by William Campbell. Although future dominance is not always predictable, it is possible to identify behaviors such as (current) dominance, mouthiness, boldness, submissiveness and fearfulness in the individual pups. In general, the "middle of the road" puppy is best; shy, fearful puppies and those who are quickest to leap up and greet (and mouth) the family may not be ideal pets. A healthy, even-tempered puppy will also approach and greet visitors eventually.

Puppy Management

All puppies should be introduced to a crate and taught to accept it quietly. The obvious benefit is to housetraining, but more subtle benefits include "portability" of puppy (leading to better socialization), and control of normal destructive chewing. Crates also condition puppies to relax and to feel safe while owners are away. Plastic airline crates are preferable to the open cage crates because they are more reminiscent of a "den." Wire crates can be covered with a sheet or blanket to better simulate a shelter. The crate should be placed in a relatively busy area in the home (but out of the household's traffic) to avoid isolation.

Feeding time is an excellent opportunity to work with all members of the family. Children can contribute to care by placing the food bowl on the floor. Meals are preferable to free choice feeding for this reason; the puppy is told to SIT-STAY, the food placed down, and periodically a special food item can be placed in the bowl while the puppy is eating. In this way, it will learn to associate approach with a reward.

Dominance exercises condition the puppy to accept physical control by all members of the family; such exercises, although firm, should be done in a positive and gentle way, rewarding the pup at each step with praise, petting or food.

a) Enforced Down. The puppy should be held in a DOWN position by placing one hand on the hips and thighs, and the other on the shoulder, holding the pup on its side. This exercise teaches the puppy to accept arbitrary physical control. Struggling behavior should be corrected with

Practice basic obedience commands regularly. Aggressive or potentially aggressive dogs will benefit from reinforcing obedient behaviors.

a soft growl or "Uh Uh." Once quieted, the puppy may even fall asleep. This position should be held for 15-30 minutes, daily for the first week, then 2 to 3 times weekly up to the age of 4 months. Remember, this is not a punishment, and it should be performed gently.

b) Dominance Lift and Roll. Owners should regularly and nonpunitively lift the puppy and look into its eyes, or roll it onto its back—struggling behavior should be gently corrected, and the puppy released when it is still.

c) Teach Puppy to Accept Touch. Regular petting should include examination and touching of every body part—ears, mouth, paws and individual toes and the inguinal area. Small food rewards and soft praise should be given generously, and all members of the family should repeatedly and gently handle the puppy.

If the pup resists handling, don't give up! These are the exercises to practice with to gain dominance. Gradually and with rewards, they will be successful in the vast majority of cases.

Puppies should be walked on leash regardless of size, and taken to as many different environments as possible. Excursions should be deliberately scheduled, and should include exposure to other animals, to the car and to crowded places. Fearful puppies should not be lifted and coddled; instead, fear should be ignored while any curiosity by the puppy is enthusiastically praised. Food rewards can be handed out to strangers greeting the puppy. To greet a fearful or shy puppy, the person should not make direct eye contact, but instead should bend to the ground (looking away!) and invite the puppy to approach. The puppy should be exposed as much as possible to children and babies, to wheelchairs, umbrellas, and people of different races and sizes. This is particularly important in the first 4 months of life.

Basic obedience exercises for the young puppy are critical and should include the SIT, SIT-STAY, DOWN, DOWN-STAY, COME and controlled walking—formal HEEL exercises are better left for the older puppy (6 months). All training should include small food rewards and an easy, nondemanding pace. Training should be shared by all members of the family, including young children under supervision.

To discourage mouthing and jumping, play should be limited to fetch, exercise, and other games which do not encourage bad behavior, such as hide-and-seek. Rough play and even tug games may blur the distinction between people and dogs, leading to mouthing, growling and lack of control as the puppy matures.

Early Identification of Behavior Problems

The earlier a problem is identified, the easier it is to change. Common behavior problems seen in puppies include mouthiness and jumping. Pushing the puppy away often reinforces the behavior; owners should be advised to control the puppy with a leash (with which to correct the behavior) and to reward for nonaggressive, appropriate behavior. Bending down will discourage jumping. All family members should use the SIT command and be consistent with jumping corrections.

Food-related aggression is common in growing puppies and should immediately be corrected by removal of the food. The owners should then spend time desensitizing the puppy to approaches (by bringing special food to the bowl) and even to hand-feed for a few weeks (followed by random hand-feeding). Although indirect, teaching the SIT-STAY is a valuable part of training for such puppies. If he growls over objects such as toy bones, they should be removed and then hand-held while the puppy chews. All approaches should be accompanied by special rewards. Food aggression may be the earliest sign of future dominance-aggression, and should be addressed as soon as possible.

Puppies exhibiting resistance to discipline (by running in circles or "backbarking") should be restrained on a leash. Dominance exercises should be practiced daily and persistently until the puppy relents. Owners of such "dominant" puppies must practice positive-reinforcement training daily. Some puppies are oversensitive to even verbal discipline and may yelp, attempt to run away, and urinate submissively when restrained. For these dogs, the intensity of corrections should be lessened, and positive reinforcement training stepped up.

Even mild problems can become serious as the puppy matures; owners of growling or biting puppies should seek behavioral counseling for help in training their pup to be a well-behaved adult member of the family.

SUMMARY

All dogs have the potential to bite people, whether familiar or unfamiliar. For example, as dog owners we may tolerate or encourage watchdog behavior—but some dogs cannot distinguish between a burglar and a visiting child. Other dogs may be loving to their owners until their food is touched, and then growl menacingly. Understanding the inherited and learned causes of dominance, territorial, fear-induced and predatory aggression is a first step toward the control of these common problems. In most cases, careful selection and training of puppies can help prevent aggression before it becomes serious.

ADDITIONAL READING

Beaver, BV: Profiles of dogs presented for aggression. Journal of the American Animal Hospital Association, 1993; 29(6): 564-569.

Borchelt, PL; Voith, VL: Aggressive behavior in dogs and cats. Compendium on Continuing Education for the Practicing Veterinarian, 1985; 7(11): 949-957.

Overall, KL: Treating Canine Aggression. Canine Practice, 1993; 18(6): 24-28.

To discourage mouthing and jumping, avoid aggressive games such as tug-of-war. Although tug-of-war is a fun game for dogs, there are times when it can become dangerous or encourage bad behavior. Be certain you can stop the game when you want and avoid using clothes and towels; use only chew toys. Photo by Dr. Gary Landsberg.

Dr. Petra Mertens studied veterinary medicine at the University of Munich in Germany and was employed there at the Institute for Ethology and Animal Welfare from 1992 to 1994. She later received the advanced German degree of Doctor medicinae veterinariae. Dr. Mertens completed her residency in Animal Behavior at the Tufts University School of Veterinary Medicine Behavior Clinic in Grafton, Massachusetts. She is currently at the Institute for Ethology and Animal Welfare, Ludwig Maximilians University, Munich, Germany.

Fighting Between Dogs

By Dr. Petra A. Mertens
Tufts University
School of Veterinary Medicine
200 Westboro Road
North Grafton, MA 01536

INTRODUCTION

Aggression is one of the most common (and potentially the most serious) behavior problem of dogs and presents a challenge for both the owners and the veterinarian. It is a complex and multidimensional problem which is influenced by numerous factors. Although most aggressive behaviors in dogs can be considered normal for the species, they may be incompatible with the expectations of the owners. Aggression towards other dogs is caused by mechanisms similar to those described for aggression directed towards humans, although the treatment may vary. Understanding the dog's motivation to perform a certain behavior is the first and most important step to appreciate the problem, followed by treatment and prevention.

WHEN DO DOGS FIGHT?

Sally, a seven-year-old female Golden Retriever, had been living happily with her owner for several years. Shelby, a Springer Spaniel, was introduced to the household three months ago, and is now almost one year old. The dogs seem to like each other. They play a lot, sleep on their owner's bed together and love to run around in the back yard. However, Shelby sometimes seems to act "strange." She attacks Sally for no obvious reason and initiates fights. Lately the fights seem to be more intense and occurring more frequently. Reprimanding Shelby for her behavior and keeping her in her crate did not improve the situation. The owner was concerned, especially after Sally got seriously hurt during the last episode.

This behavioral problem is called sibling rivalry. It occurs in dogs that live in the same household and are not allowed to establish dominance or a "pecking order" on their own. When the first fight occurs, the owners are shocked and scared. Usually, they feel sorry for the dog that gets attacked or the loser of these fights. They support the "victim" and sometimes punish the aggressor.

Fights occur in competitive situations, such as mealtimes, vigorous play, or passing in narrow or cramped areas. Usually, the dogs live peacefully together when left alone by the owner. They start fighting the moment the owner arrives at home. In an attempt to be fair, the owner naturally will support the dog that seems to be the underdog. By doing so, they misinterpret the relationship between the dogs and reverse their roles, which will cause continuous, intense fighting.

Barney, a 1-year-old German Shepherd Dog, represents another common example of dog-against-dog aggression that is a reason for frequent complaints by dog owners. Barney has always been a very nice and friendly puppy. Two months ago he started to growl at other dogs he met during his daily walks in the neighborhood park. This aggressive behavior increased steadily. His owner had kept him on a short leash ever since Barney initiated a fight with a male Dalmatian. Barney's owner was seeking advice. The dog was pulling on the leash whenever he saw another dog, barked excessively and acted like he almost intended to kill the other dog. This behavior seemed to be even worse when the dog was running loose within the fenced in backyard.

Dogs clearly signal their intentions to one another by body postures. Photo by Petra Mertens.

Regardless of breed tendencies, any two dogs can communicate through common social behaviors. Photo by Petra Mertens.

WHY DO OUR DOGS FIGHT?

Many dog owners have experienced similar kinds of aggressive behavior in their dogs. Fighting is actually part of the natural behavior of dogs, yet rare amongst dogs in a stable group. Treating these problem behaviors requires a detailed understanding of basic dog behavior, body language and social organization of a pack or group.

Dogs were domesticated approximately 12,000 years ago, when the first wolves lived close to human communities. Today, these "wolves in our living-room" (as Desmond Morris, a respected writer, calls dogs) still exhibit behaviors that are similar to those observed in the wild. While basic dog behavior is similar between all canines, there also are important differences that need to be considered; as for example the different needs, habits, and communication abilities of the various breeds. As a result of selective breeding, dogs come in various sizes and shapes and vary greatly in terms of behavior and temperament. Each dog is an individual, yet it is obvious that certain breeds are more likely to exhibit dominant behavior- for example Dalmatians, Cocker Spaniels, Springer Spaniels, Rottweilers, Alaskan Malamutes, Huskies and Bull Terriers. Breeds such as most sheep-herding dogs, German Shepherd Dogs, Bernese Mountain Dogs and Doberman Pinschers tend to be more fearful.

Despite many breed differences, one thing even a Yorkshire Terrier and a Great Dane have in common is their social behavior. The canine social system is a so-called dominance hierarchy. The members of a group will develop a hierarchical organization which guarantees security and stability for each member in order to avoid fights and injuries. Ranking is established through social signaling and aggressive encounters whereby one of the dogs dominates another and establishes a superior position in the rank. The highest ranking individual is a so-called alpha-male or -female. A stable social hierarchy is important during disputes, since the lower-ranking dog often will concede to his superior, thus reducing the likelihood of fighting. A single newcomer (no matter if in a home or park play-group) may cause radical changes in the group structure, and subsequently in each individual dog's behavior.

Both dominance and fear may cause aggressive reactions in dogs and lead to a fight. It is essential to determine the reason for the dog's aggressiveness in order to treat the problem in the appropriate way.

Physical dominance plays a minor role in establishing a hierarchy. Psychological domination determines most relationships and thereby helps to avoid disadvantageous fighting, which could cause injuries. Usually, dogs live in harmony with all group members. Most disputes are solved by the use of threatening body postures and dominant gestures. The dogs will stand parallel, walk slowly and stiff. They try to put their chin on the other dog's back. They may growl and put their hackles up. The sub-ordinate dog will carefully lower its head and tail, avoid eye contact, or even roll on its side and lift a leg. Another submissive gesture is the release of small amounts of urine while exposing the genital region. The dominant dog accepts these submissive signals, walks slowly away and possibly urinates on a nearby tree to mark the territory.

A common misconception is that alpha dogs will initiate fights; this is not the case. The alpha dog seldom performs threatening gestures and rarely fights. Often it is a lower-or middle-ranking dog who is socially uncertain that snaps, threatens, or bites another dog who ranks in a position close to its own. The actual fight is very noisy and the owners are afraid that the dogs might injure or even attempt to kill each other. However, it is the quiet and short fights between high ranking dogs that should concern the owners.

Why are domestic dogs fighting frequently if they can establish dominance in a non-confrontational and peaceful way? One of the major problems with many pets is a lack of socialization. Usually, dogs do not grow up with members of their own species. Most puppies are separated from the litter at the age of eight weeks, before a hierarchy has been completely established. In the new family, the puppy is not exposed to other dogs in the neighborhood until it has received its shots and established immunity levels. In addition, many dog owners unintentionally reinforce inappropriate and antisocial behavior of their dogs by increasing the tension when the dogs meet each other. When confronted with a member of their own species, the puppy may react fearfully. Many dog owners tend to keep their puppies on a leash during those first contacts or even take the puppies in their arms. In this position many dogs start to react aggressively, growl, snap and bark. The owners will pet and praise the puppy in order to calm it down. The attention the puppy receives rewards the dog for its aggressiveness and will reinforce the behavior. A vicious cycle often develops, where the puppy now may be restricted to the leash and the owner avoids contact with other dogs. Being on a leash increases tension, since it does not allow the dog to escape and move freely. The presence of the owner increases the dog's self confidence and causes great likelihood of an aggressive threat. The puppy often becomes progressively antisocial, and may end up completely isolated from other dogs or confined to his yard.

Another reason for canine aggressive behavior is predation. Fearful dogs may run away from some dogs to avoid confrontation and predatory dogs may chase these fearful animals. Predatory behavior seldom leads to an aggressive attack, but will increase the fear of other dogs and therefore should be avoided.

A common problem is the confrontation with other dogs on a dog's private domain. If the same dogs meet on neutral territory, fights usually can be avoided. This is an important fact to remember if a dog owner plans to introduce a new dog to the household.

HOW CAN FIGHTING BE PREVENTED?

Before choosing a new family dog, it is a good idea to contact a local veterinarian or behavior specialist and ask for specific information on the different characteristics of each breed, the advantages of a purebred dog or a mixed breed and the possibilities for adopting a dog from an animal shelter, in order to be able to choose the right dog and avoid problems. Once a puppy has been purchased, intensive socialization is the key for prevention of behavioral problems related to dog-dog aggression. Ideally, this training should start during puppyhood, as soon and as intensive as possible. The puppy should go on frequent walks to get accustomed to meeting strange dogs and be able to play with other dogs. Puppy playgrounds and puppy kindergarten are ideal settings for training. Surrounded by many dogs of different sizes, breeds and ages, the dogs learn various skills for communication and interaction with other dogs. When dogs are allowed to play freely, they spend their time playing games containing elements of fighting. If a puppy is too pushy or bites too harshly the game will be terminated abruptly by the other dog. The owners should not intervene, because it is important for the puppy to learn to inhibit the force of its bites and excitement.

While playing with adult dogs, the puppy will be taught not to overstep its bounds. The adult will give the puppy one single warning before reprimanding it. The puppy will then go overboard in its attempts to signal appeasement and deference. These experiences are very important for the development of a dog. A normal adult dog will rarely injure a puppy. Reprimanding is a natural way of teaching puppies correct manners which enable them to interact with other dogs safely.

Puppies learn surprisingly fast. The dog's experience should be supported by positive reinforcement of appropriate behavior by the owner. After interacting in a friendly manner, the dog should have the clear understanding that the owner is happily praising good behavior.

It is essential that the owners maintain a stable social group and do not give up once they have a friendly and playful puppy. The puppy must have plenty of opportunities to learn how to greet its elders before it reaches puberty and meetings become critical. If the puppy is not given enough opportunities, problems occur by the time the dog reaches adolescence. After a few unfriendly encounters, it may become uneasy about meeting other dogs.

If a dog that has been the only canine family member has to be introduced to a new dog, it is advantageous to plan this first meeting carefully. Taking an unknown dog into the home of another dog may lead to aggressive reactions caused by territoriality. Both dogs should be taken to a neutral fenced-in area. Initially, the dogs can be kept on a leash to allow the owner to control the situa-

tion. The owners should avoid showing any kind of fear or tension because the dogs will sense this and react accordingly. Once the dogs have contacted each other in a friendly manner they can be taken off the leashes and be allowed to play freely. While the dogs meet, the owners should praise the friendly behavior and motivate the dogs to approach. The new dog can now come to its new home with the rest of the family and enter its new territory. If the older dog makes any approaches to react aggressively it should be reprimanded briefly. Challenging situations should be strictly avoided. Favorite toys and food, especially rawhides and bones, should be removed a few days ahead of time. The owners should not pay specific attention to either one of the dogs in order to avoid "jealousy." The new puppy will now explore the environment, carefully monitored by the other dog and the anxious owners. After this first experience, the dogs should be allowed to play. Once they play or lie down to sleep, the most critical period is over and the dogs have a good chance of being friends and enjoying the advantages of a peaceful multi-dog household.

WHAT CAN BE DONE TO TREAT DOG-DOG (INTRASPECIFIC) AGGRESSION?

There is no magic solution or quick fix for treating behavioral problems, especially if they are related to aggression. The first and most important step is to contact a local veterinarian offering behavior counseling. She or he will be able to evaluate the

Given the opportunity, dogs quickly determine their own social order. Photo by Petra Mertens.

specific problem that is underlying the dog's behavior and be able to give further advice concerning treatment of the condition. This is the safest and most efficient way to resolve the problem.

FIGHTS WITH "STRANGE" DOGS

It is essential that the dog learns basic commands, such as "sit," "stay," "down," "come" and "off." If necessary, it may be helpful to seek advice of an experienced dog trainer. Obedience training should be part of the daily routine. For training to be successful it is essential that the owners are dominant and in charge of all dogs in the household. It is important that the training is motivational and fun for both the owner and the dog. It should be easier to avoid fights if the dog can be called back if it gets into a potentially dangerous situation.

Any aggressive encounter must be reprimanded immediately. The dog has to know that the owner sincerely disapproves obnoxious behavior. Further, it is important that the dog understands that it is being reprimanded for acting obnoxiously, not for meeting another dog. Therefore, friendly behavior must be praised. Physical punishment of any kind will not work. It will cause an increase of tension and anxiety, which does not bode well for a friendly encounter.

The "human pack member" has to clearly dominate the dogs. In case one dog is growling, snapping or showing any other sign of dominance towards people living in the household, it is necessary to treat this condition first as explained elsewhere.

The best approach for training appropriate behavior is a method called counterconditioning. The principle is that the dog performs a simple behavior, e.g., obey to a command ("sit" and "stay"), which excludes the undesirable behavior. The owner must determine which alternate behavior they want to train the dog to perform. This can be anything, but the behavior must be incompatible with the fighting.

The owners start training in a quiet environment, take the dog off the leash, and train it to do the alternate behavior on command. An ideal training setting would be a neutral fenced-in area (e.g. a tennis court or a school yard). If the dog follows the command it can be praised for obeying and receive a tiny piece of a special food treat that the dog really likes and only gets during training sessions, e.g., cheese or hot dog. Initially the treat will be given each time the dog obeys. After it has learned the command, the treat should be given intermittently.

Once the dog consistently obeys the command, the owners should present the stimulus (another dog on a leash) at a low intensity (far away). As the dog reacts to the other dog, the owners give the command and immediately reward the dog with a food treat and praise for responding. If the dog obeys the command a few times, the distance between the dogs can be decreased gradually. If the dog fails to obey at one stage, the owners must return to the previous level. Reprimanding and choking on a chain will exaggerate agitation and should there-fore be strictly avoided. If necessary, a so-called "Promise® Halter" should be used in order to achieve better control over the dog. Once the training has started, the dog should never have a chance to perform the unwanted behavior again. This technique works well, but it requires a commitment from the owner to be effective.

FIGHTS OF DOGS LIVING IN THE SAME HOUSEHOLD

It is essential to determine the dominant dog in the "pack." Age, sex, size, health and breed are influencing factors. As mentioned earlier, the breed has an important impact on its behavior. A Cocker Spaniel, Springer Spaniel, Bull Terrier or Jack Russell Terrier may be smaller than a Great Dane or German Shepherd dog, but due to their temperament, they are likely be the leader of their pack.

Young puppies are rarely dominant, but may challenge another dog in the household when they reach puberty. Many owners seeking advice for cases of sibling rivalry report that the first problems occurred after a new puppy turned one or two years of age.

Unneutered male dogs are often dominant over a female dog. It may be harder to keep two or more dogs of the same gender in one household than a mixed group of male and female dogs. Although it is often believed that male dogs are more aggressive than females, we receive more complaints by owners of two or more females than from owners with a multi-male household.

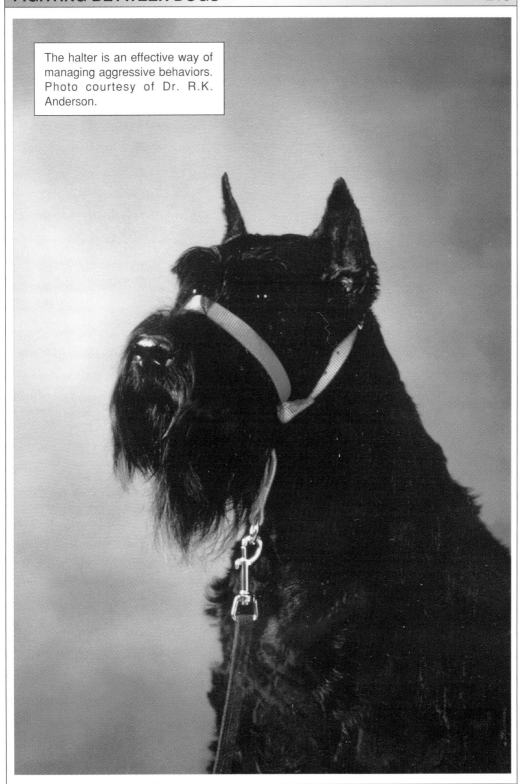

The halter is an effective way of managing aggressive behaviors. Photo courtesy of Dr. R.K. Anderson.

These rules may help to determine which one is the dominant dog. However, it is essential to observe the dog's behavior to be certain. The dog that is attempting to be dominant will commonly initiate the fights. Some dogs will guard certain toys, food or even their favorite person. If the owners make the wrong decision, the fighting will get worse and a dog may be seriously injured. If the owners are not sure about the "pecking order," they should ask a behavior specialist for advice.

Once the owners have determined which dog is attempting to be the dominant dog in the household, they have to avoid showing any preferences for the subordinate. Reassuring the aggressor and reprimanding the subordinate will contribute to the rapid establishment of a stable social structure. Reasons for fights vary. In the eyes of a dog, attention, food, space and toys are valuable things that need to be guarded. To avoid stimulation and competition, it is necessary to remove toys, bones and food. The dogs should not be allowed on the furniture and the owner's lap. The dominant dog will be treated accordingly: it is allowed to eat first, to be close to the owners, it walks through the door first and it will be praised and petted in front of the subordinate dog. This way ranking is supported clearly and the dogs do not have any reason to "argue."

This approach seems to be simple, but owners are usually uneasy to follow the recommendations. It may seem cruel and unfair to punish and neglect a dog that has been attacked for no obvious reason. But it is essential to understand that the owners may cause or perpetuate the fighting until they stop trying to manipulate the ranking in preference of the underdog.

In severe cases, dogs have shown intense aggression over a long period of time and it may be impossible to achieve satisfying results without professional advice. Some veterinarians specialize in treating behavior problems of companion animals. It should certainly be considered to contact these specialists if the approaches described above failed to solve the problem. A behavior modification program, specifically designed for the individual case will improve the situation significantly.

Neutering may have a positive effect on the frequency of inter-male fights if both dogs are neutered, but does not necessarily reduce aggressive behavior in general. A neutered dog will no longer smell like a male to other dogs, which reduces the tension of social encounters between male dogs. At the same time, the castrated dog is less likely to issue threats itself. Spaying a female dog will not reduce aggressiveness unless the aggression is related to the estrus cycle. Sometimes neutering a female dog may even increase its tendency to fight.

In some cases it may be necessary to support the treatment pharmacologically. Depending on the case and the underlying cause for the dog's aggression the use of medication may be indicated. This decision has to be made by a veterinarian after a physical examination of the dog, the evaluation of possible medical conditions and the diagnosis of the problem. In the past the application of a female hormone, progesterone, was quite common in cases of intraspecific aggression in dogs. Due to the large number and severity of side effects, more and more veterinarians prefer to prescribe anxiolytics, beta-blockers and serotonergic drugs, such as BuSpar®, Propanolol®, Elavil® or even Prozac® to treat behavioral problems related to aggression.

WHAT SHOULD YOU DO TO INTERRUPT A FIGHT?

Breaking up fight by hand is a hazardous procedure and owners may get bitten by their own dog. Different techniques have been described to break up a fight, such as throwing a bucket of water on the dogs, hitting them, shouting and pulling them apart by their tails, hind legs or scruffs. Whichever method is used, the owner has to be certain that the dog will not react adversely.

Therefore, it is probably the safest solution if the owners do not physically intervene, but continue to verbally reprimand throughout the fight. Screaming a command like "sit" communicates that the owner is annoyed and that the dog is in trouble. Surprisingly, many dogs obey. As soon as the dog sits, the owners have to firmly instruct it to "stay" until the dogs have calmed down. If this approach does not interrupt the fight, it may become

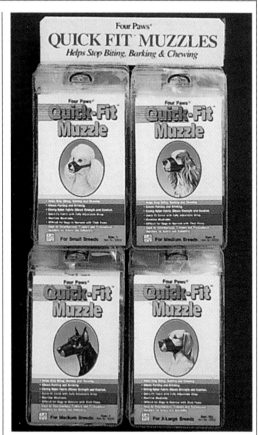

Owners of potentially aggressive dogs should invest wisely in a muzzle. Pet shops offer quality muzzles for sale. Photo courtesy of Four Paws.

obvious that the dogs will not stop fighting until one dog is seriously injured. Usually the owners will not have a bucket of water available to throw at the dogs. Therefore, they may consider pulling the dogs apart. It is very dangerous to touch them anywhere close to their head. If necessary, the handlers should try to grasp the dog's tail or hind legs (at least one strong person per dog) and pull them apart. It is certainly dangerous and ineffective to physically punish dogs while fighting. Punishment is even more senseless after the dogs cease fighting.

Naturally aggressive dogs should not be encouraged to playfight. Close supervision is essential. Photo by Isabelle Francais.

Whatever the owners decide to do, they have to keep in mind that dog bites can be severe and dangerous. Fighting dogs are generally overexcited and aroused. In this situation, dogs are likely to turn against the owner if she/he decides to physically interfere, even if a dog would never bite a person in a normal situation.

SUMMARY

Intraspecific aggression, directed towards dogs living in the same household or dogs in the neighborhood is a common behavioral problem. Respecting the dominance hierarchy the dogs establish, motivational training, and extensive socialization are the best ways to achieve friendly encounters between dogs. The owners need to learn to control the dog efficiently, using supervised obedience training and counterconditioning techniques. Once fights occur, consulting a veterinarian and behavior specialist that provides a careful diagnosis and treatment plan will help the owner to solve the problem successfully.

ADDITIONAL READING

Fogle, B: *The Dog's Mind.* Viking Penguin, Inc., New York, 1990.

Hart, BL; Hart, LA: *The Perfect Puppy.* W.H. Freeman and Co., New York, 1988.

Marder, A: *Your Healthy Pet: A Practical Guide to Choosing and Raising Happier, Healthier Dogs and Cats.* Rodale Press, Emmaus, PA, 1994, 216pp.

Neville, P: *Do Dogs Need Shrinks? What to Do when Man's Best Friend Misbehaves.* A Citadel Press Book. Secaucus, NJ, 1992.

In veterinary practice since 1984 (graduate of the University of Montreal), Dr. Stefanie Schwartz also has an undergraduate degree in psychobiology (McGill University, 1979) and a graduate degree in ethology (University of Montreal, 1988). As a lecturer and consultant in pet behavior problems for over 10 years, she is the author of several texts on animal behavior in veterinary practice and contributes articles on small animal behavior to scientific journals, magazines and newspapers. Based in Newton, Massachusetts, Dr. Schwartz is Clinical Assistant Professor at Tufts University's School of Veterinary Medicine.

Dogs & Kids: The Family Pet in the Family with Children

By Stefanie Schwartz, BSc, DMV, MSc

Veterinarian, Pet Behavior Consultant

163 Lexington Street

Newton, MA 02166-1333

INTRODUCTION

Pet dogs fulfill a variety of conscious and unconscious roles in our lives. A dog may play a simple role as comforting companion but it may also embody more complicated psychological symbols. A dog may represent the ideal parent that generously grants unconditional love. Its playfulness encourages us to abandon adult preoccupations, entertaining us as our own siblings or playmates used to do in childhood. A dog can also become a surrogate child, tapping our parental instincts to nurture and protect. A pet's dependence upon us to attend to its daily needs is made more poignant should it become ill.

Young couples commonly adopt a pet together. This lets them practice parenting styles and experiment with family dynamics. Life-partners are thus able to work toward complementary parental skills and shared responsibilities before beginning a family of real children. It might even allow them to work through some unresolved parental conflicts from their own childhood or adolescence. It is not unusual for veterinarians to hear pet owners refer to their dog as their "first baby." When the real children are due and finally introduced to the family pet owners suddenly re-awaken to view their surrogate 'baby' as a potential threat to their vulnerable infant.

PRELIMINARY TRAINING

The single most important rule guiding the introduction of a new baby to a resident pet is that it must be gradual. In most cases, parents have 9 months to prepare for the arrival of a new family member. Pets should be given advance time to adapt to this change, too. Dogs should have the opportunity to become familiar with anticipated changes that a new baby will make long before it arrives. The introduction of a new family member also has social significance to the family dog. A dog's social status is influenced by the family's dynamics. All this changes when a new child arrives and continues to evolve as the child develops.

An essential first step in the process for dog owners is to review obedience skills. If this basic training was omitted, it is never too late to learn. Ask your veterinarian to recommend a dog trainer that offers group classes. Private training is effective as well but your dog will not be exposed to the same distractions that test its skills nor will it have the opportunity for healthy social interaction with other dogs. Whether you pursue private or group training, do not send your dog away to be trained. You must acquire the skills so that you can work your dog. Pre-existing behavior problems, regardless of their perceived importance, should be evaluated by a veterinarian specializing in pet behavior problems. It is wise to identify and to resolve behavior problems before life is further complicated with caring for a newborn.

Obedience training should be reviewed on a daily basis. Set realistic goals for yourself and your pet. Begin with 2 or 3 practice sessions that last 10 or 15 minutes and make them as enjoyable as possible for both you and your pet. Practice every day, in every room of your home and outside during leash-walks. This way, you can expect your dog to be obedient everywhere and not just in the room where you did the training. Obedience skills provide you, the owner, with vocabulary that allow you to communicate with your dog.

The 5 basic commands are 'sit/down/come/heel/stay'. Call your dog's name first to get its attention. Follow this with the one-word command in a firm tone. Immediately reward your dog's obedience with verbal praise ('good dog!') or petting or even a small food treat. This training can then be applied to controlling your dog in a variety of unfamiliar situations including the introduction of a newborn. The most useful sequences are 'sit/stay' and 'down/stay'. These allow you to direct your pet toward appropriate behavior in any given situation and will be applied in the gradual introduction program to be outlined later.

Even a curious and affectionate pet may unintentionally harm a child at any age. An infant may be accidentally dropped because of an over-zealous jumping dog with the friendliest of intentions. Your pet's nails should be kept well-trimmed to minimize accidental scratching. A pet might lick an infant's face in a friendly gesture to groom the new family member or simply to familiarize itself with the new scents. This may expose an infant to undesirable microbes. A sleeping infant that is unable to shift its position may have difficulty breathing because of an affectionate pet who only seeks to cuddle.

The goal of training should be to teach your pet positive associations

Children must be instructed and supervised properly whenever they are handling dogs.

with elements directly or indirectly related to babies. The dog should be allowed to investigate the baby's body odors on a baby blanket before the infant is brought home from the hospital. During this investigation, reward your pet with praise, petting or a small food treat. Your pet should develop a positive association to the infant before they are ever introduced.

New activities associated with child care may be purposely practiced in front of pets so that they can become familiar with them. For example, prospective parents can carry a doll as an imaginary newborn and go through the motions of changing a diaper, including the use of baby powder. It has been suggested that a pet be encouraged to place its head near a pregnant woman's expanding belly so that it can familiarize itself with the baby's heartbeat. There is no proven merit to this suggestion since it is unlikely that a dog or cat can identify the fetal heart sounds or understand the connection between pregnancy and the arrival of a newborn. Some pets seem to be attracted to investigate body odors of pregnant women. It is not unreasonable to suggest that they are able to detect changes in body chemistry associated with pregnancy without higher understanding of what has caused the changes.

Teach your pet to remain calm and controlled in the presence of a newborn by practicing 'sit/stay' while your spouse holds the surrogate child. When your dog can demonstrate reliable obedience and calmness it can be permitted to gently investigate the 'imaginary baby'. Play tape recordings of a crying infant, recorded at the hospital nursery, at progressively higher volume during training sequences over many days. Lavish your pet with abundant praise for appropriate responses to your commands to 'down/stay'. When the recording reaches peak volume and your dog remains undisturbed, add additional training elements such as pretended diaper changes. This training can be so thorough that your pet will react little to the arrival of the real baby.

INTRODUCING YOUR PET AND INFANT

Regardless of how well you and your dog have prepared for the newborn, it might be best to delay their introduction for the first few days. Make a special effort to spend extra time with your pet by continuing its normal daily routine. Take your dog on leash-walks at consistent times and stick to usual feeding schedules. Spend a bit more time playing with it or, if your pet enjoys it, a quiet moment brushing it. After several weeks, all enjoyable interactions (play, petting, treats) should take place when the baby is in the room. This is intended to make a positive association between the baby's presence and pleasant experiences.

Training techniques should be designed to teach the dog to associate the baby with positive experiences only. Whenever the baby is brought into the room, play, food, treats or affection should be lavished upon the dog and whenever the baby is out of the room, affection, attention and food should be withheld. Negative associations can be avoided by ensuring that the dog is never punished or ignored in the baby's presence.

As the newly expanded household begins to feel normal, the next step toward familiarizing the resident pet and baby can commence. While one adult holds the baby, another adult can control the dog on a leash and in a 'sit/stay' at the other end of the room. The handler's attitude should be relaxed and reassuring to the dog. If the dog is calm and obedient, it can be given lavish rewards of food or attention a bit closer to the baby's position each day. After each successful session, the next session should take place a little closer to the baby. After at least 2 or even 3 weeks of consis-

Some children are naturally fearful of dogs, as is this forsaken tyke.

tently good behavior, the supervised dog can investigate the baby. Eventually, supervised visits can occur without leash restraint. No matter how much confidence you have in your pet's training and temperament, wisdom recommends caution. No one, least of all an infant or child of any age, should be left unattended with an animal or unfamiliar person in a situation they cannot control.

Consider other potential situations of risk. For example, hire experienced baby-sitters that are also comfortable with pets. Leave clear instructions with them regarding how to supervise your child, your pet and the contact restrictions between them. Always be vigilant whenever your child is near other people's pets, even if they belong to your friends. This is equally important when your pet is exposed to other people's children.

Children who grow up with dogs have a natural rapport and affection for them.

WARNING SIGNS AND POTENTIAL PROBLEMS

Most dogs readily adjust to the new baby. The chances of quick and successful socialization can be greatly increased by ensuring that puppies have plenty of exposure to children and infants during their first few months of life when they are most adaptable and impressionable. There are, however, important indications of a pet's potential for problem behaviors towards children. A pet with a history of aggressively guarding food, toys and other valued objects can be predicted to harm a child who innocently approaches or attempts to remove something from the dog. Similarly, uncontrolled and wild behavior toward people or poor cooperation to obedience training could translate into possible problems with a new child. A pet that is known to react anxiously in new situations or with unfamiliar people may not adjust smoothly to a baby. A pet that has demonstrated strong hunting instincts, or that runs away even occasionally to roam free may pose a significant threat to an unattended baby.

A pet that has displayed aggressiveness toward anyone, including you, must be considered a danger to a child. Adult pets that have never been exposed to children as pups or kittens may be fearful of children and could harm them if they feel cornered or pursued by an active child. If your pet fits into any of these categories, you should seriously consider whether it is wise to attempt training. Certainly for extreme cases, the use of a muzzle would be wise during training and introduction trials. A veterinarian specializing in pet behavior should be consulted for additional training tips and evaluation of your pet.

Although some dog breeds have wonderful reputations as gentle and protective family pets, a dog of any breed could injure a child under certain circumstances. Certain breeds are statistically more frequently associated with attacks against children. Your child's safety is a priority. If your pet's history suggests it may be unreliable with children, or if you cannot commit the time and effort to retrain it, it might be best to consider finding your pet a new home with older children or no children at all. Pets that have not been exposed to youngsters during formative phases in the first few months of life or who have had unpleasant experiences with abusive children may not adapt well in families with children.

In times of stress, dogs and cats may void in undesirable locations. Inappropriate elimination of urine or feces can be triggered by the changes instigated by a newborn child. Inappropriate urination or defecation can even occur in the baby's room or on the baby's blanket or clothes. Another favorite target is on or near the owner's bed. Territorial marking with waste deposits is a response to anxiety and in no way should this be viewed as an act of jealousy, malice or revenge.

Keep soiled diapers in a pet-proof container. Investigation of waste products is a normal means of individual identification in many species, in-

Puppies and toddlers becoming acquainted. Photo by Isabelle Francais.

cluding dogs and cats. Dogs have occasionally been known to swallow soiled diapers. This distasteful act may reflect a normal parental function in adult dogs that keeps offspring and the den area clean. This behavior is valuable for the health of the young not only because of basic hygiene but because lingering odors may attract predators.

PET TOLERANCE AND THE TODDLER

The most sensitive time between dogs and babies is associated with the child's toddler phase. Once the baby becomes mobile, first when it crawls and then learns to walk, its dynamics with the family pet is significantly altered. Although a dog may have become accustomed to its owner's new focus of attention and seems to have adjusted well to the presence of an infant, the emergence of an active child and the energy it generates is totally unfamiliar. The critical transition occurs when a dog must learn to recognize that the new, ground-level moving target is the same bundle that until recently had been carried from place to place. While dogs that have already shown an active and eager hunting instinct are obvious high risks, innate tendencies in dogs that have never displayed any predatory predisposition may suddenly be awakened.

Predatory patterns are not the only form of pet aggression that may be provoked during this phase of a child's development. Keep in mind that even the most gentle dog can be pushed beyond reasonable levels of tolerance. Defensive forms of aggressiveness must also be con-

sidered. Many pets are actually fearful of small children. These pets would rather avoid contact with toddlers that may pursue them unmercifully with tiny fists ready to pinch, poke or pull various body parts. If, however, a pet is unable to run away or finds itself cornered by a menacing child, defensive tactics may include aggressiveness.

Another change that occurs as your child grows translates into shifts in the social structure of the family. The social nature of dogs has many parallels to human social behavior. Just as there are hierarchies in human families (and society), dogs establish dominance hierarchies, too. Your dog interacts socially with you much as it would in the company of dogs. One of the ways that positions of social status are achieved is for confronting dogs to test each other's determination to maintain or surpass its dominance rank. Most confrontations are subtle but some may be more violent. In your dog's mind, your child likely has a submissive role in the dynamics of your family 'pack'. When young children affectionately hug a dog or lay on top of it in play, for example, the dog may interpret this as a direct challenge by a subordinate pack member. The dog might retaliate to defend its social rank by threatening its challenger with a warning growl. If the child does not heed the warning and persists, it might get bitten.

Another possible source of problems at the toddler phase is the attraction to explore a pet's waste. Clean any indoor "accidents" immediately. Control a child's access to a cat's litter box (without disrupting the cat's access, of course). Remove your dog's waste from your yard. Make sure that your pet is screened once or even twice a year for intestinal parasites that might be transmitted to children.

Parents should be aware that there is nowhere near the same quality control or safety standards for toys marketed for pets compared to the guide-lines set for children's toys. It is important to inspect pet toys and equipment and to remove those that are of potential danger to your toddler. Conversely, be aware of a curious pet that may swallow a part of or an entire child's toy.

Some dogs are very possessive about favorite toys or food. Children can be unaware of their own jeopardy should they unintentionally disturb or intentionally threaten a dog that is guarding a valued object. Dogs may even consider a child's toy as their own if they take a fancy to it. If you have noticed that your dog is prone to aggressively guard objects it considers of exceptional value prior to your baby's arrival, this behavior should be remedied in earnest. If this is not noticed before or worsens after the

Rottweilers have an inherent desire to protect home and family.

birth of your child, it will be extremely important to concentrate on educating your child and strictly supervising the interactions between your child and the family dog. Although it might be best to feed dogs in a separate room to avoid problems, the best advice is to train puppies from the outset to have their food handled and removed. This can be accomplished by hand feeding. Young puppies can be taught to tolerate being approached and petted during feeding by training them to leave their bowls for tasty food rewards. For re-training a guarding adult dog, introduce new commands such as 'drop it' or 'leave it' to control their use of valued objects. A veterinary behaviorist should be consulted to evaluate this form of aggression in an adult dog.

CHILD EDUCATION AND THE FAMILY PET

When a baby becomes independently mobile, its activity with or nearby family pets should be supervised. Parents should be vigilant. Be aware of where the baby is and where the pet is at any given moment. Their locations relative to each other may be easier to manage by controlling the pet rather than an active child. It might be helpful to keep your dog by your side in a 'sit/stay' while the baby is in motion. Always reward your pet with gentle praise and petting for its obedience. Reassure your pet if it seeks a safe haven by your side as it flees a pursuing child and use this as a warning call to educate your child.

It is more likely that your pet will require protection from your child and not the reverse. Unfortunately, children are not aware of the pain they can inflict on a pet in the process of their normal investigations of the world surrounding them. Young children have been known to bite, pinch, hit, squeeze, chase, twist, kick, pull, toss, drop and generally stomp on pets. It is unfair to test a pet's tolerance by permitting this to occur. Your children's friends and the children of your friends and relatives should also be monitored when your pet is nearby.

From the moment it begins to crawl, a child should be taught exactly how to interact appropriately with your pet. It is not enough to tell it what not to do. A child's undesirable behavior is an opportunity for you to teach it a desirable alternative. Spend a few minutes everyday showing the child which parts of a pet's body that are allowed to be touched and how to gently pet them. Explain to your child that no one, including your pets, likes to be disturbed when they are having a nap, or eating, or playing with a favorite toy. Teach your child that if your pet runs away from them it should be left alone. Inform them that if your pet does not want to play with them that you would be happy to instead.

Children generally do not recognize their own physical strength. It may be helpful in some cases to educate the child by role playing. Ask

This child senses a safe, loving companion while adults might let their prejudice cause them to fear this dog.

your child to pretend to be a dog or cat while you imitate your child's behavior. This could help your child to better understand the limits you set and might even avoid serious injury. If your child fails to cooperate, it may be wise to separate him from your pet until it can exhibit more reliable learning. It may even be necessary, and indeed humane, to place your pet temporarily or permanently in another home. No pet should be allowed to endure unnecessary suffering. Even the kindest, most reliably patient animal has a breaking point.

If you are considering a pet in order to teach toddlers or teenagers how to be responsible people, make sure that your expectations are realistic. In most cases, the responsibility of pet care will be yours alone, no matter how much your child promises to participate. Finally, if the purpose of acquiring a pet is to teach your child about sexual reproduction and the miracle of birth, consider a more appropriate method. Your child can learn about this lesson from many other sources available at school or your local library. Your pet does not need to experience sexual activity or pregnancy to improve its temperament or fulfill its life. The pet overpopulation does not need more contributions. If you truly want to teach your child to be kind and responsible, arrange for your pet to be neutered at an appropriate age as advised by your veterinarian.

If you are already aware of even the smallest problems with your pet before your new baby is due to arrive, make a special effort to resolve them.

Many behavior problems tend to worsen if left unchecked and often appear magnified through the eyes of a sleep-deprived new parent! If you are considering acquiring a new pet after the addition of a new baby, think about the additional investment of time and energy that responsible pet ownership demands. It might be best to wait until your 'real' children are older and more mature.

SUMMARY

Pet dogs and cats can fulfill symbolic roles in our lives, for example, as surrogate children. When real children are introduced to the family, however, their potential harm by family pets may be realized for the first time. With the arrival of each child, family dynamics are altered and directly impact our companion animals. Pets should be gradually prepared and introduced to children under supervised and controlled conditions. Pre-existing pet behavior problems should be dealt with prior to a child's arrival, whenever possible. Preventative measures and the vigilance of parents underlie the basic discussion of potential problems between pets and children in this chapter.

ADDITIONAL READING

Kilcommons, B: *Good Owners, Great Dogs.* Warner Books, NY 1992.

Rafe, S: *Your New Baby and Bowser.* Denlinger Publications, Fairfax, VA, 1990.

Siegal, M; Margolis, M: *Good Dog, Bad Dog.* Henry Holt, New York, 1991.

Dr. Gary Landsberg is a companion animal veterinarian (dogs and cats) at the Doncaster Animal Clinic in Thornhill, Ontario. He is also extremely active in the field of pet behavior. He operates a referral consulting service for pets with behavior problems, and has presented lectures in seminars throughout North America and in Europe. He has written numerous articles, edited a number of behavior texts and videotapes and is a coauthor of a number of books, including a veterinary textbook entitled the Practitioner's Guide to Pet Behavior Problems. Dr. Landsberg is the past president of the American Veterinary Society of Animal Behavior.

Behavior Products

By Gary Landsberg, BSc, DVM
Doncaster Animal Clinic
99 Henderson Avenue
Thornhill, Ontario
L3T 2K9

INTRODUCTION

There are numerous products on the market that have been designed to prevent undesirable behavior in our pets. Leashes, harnesses, collars or head halters are needed to keep most pets under control, especially when outdoors. A cage provides a safe comfortable home for the dog when the owners are not available to supervise. Alternately, child locks and child barricades can be used to keep dogs away from potential problem areas. Dogs also need objects that will safely meet their need for chewing and play. Should problems begin to emerge, there are also products that have been designed to stop undesirable behavior just before or as it happens. This chapter is designed to provide some information as to the types of products that might be helpful for to dog owners.

AN OUNCE OF PREVENTION

Although there may be a great deal of variability depending on the breed, size, and age of your dog, every dog will have some minimum requirements for play, exercise, chewing, feeding, and elimination. (If you do not neuter, your pet will also have some sexual interest and desires).

Although neutering can successfully remove most sexual desires, all of your pet's other needs must be provided for. If you're a novice at dog care or want some additional guidance that this book does not provide, a good starting place is to pick up some of the excellent videos and books available on training and health care. Your veterinarian can provide you with some good suggestions, and you'll find a number of recommendations throughout this book. There are even videos designed for your dog to watch. These "doggy videos" won't train your dog for you, but if your dog likes to watch TV, they might help to keep it occupied when you aren't available.

Since dogs, especially young puppies, need to chew, its important to find a few chew toys and products that the dog enjoys. A good chew toy may also help in maintaining good dental health. Don't choose toys based on manufacturers' claims or because they look like fun. Each dog is an individual. Find a few products that are safe, durable and most important, that your dog enjoys. Nylabone® products are extremely durable and have been designed to appeal to most dogs. If the novelty of a particular toy begins to wear off, it may be necessary to buy new toys on a regular basis. For dogs that continue to chew on everything but their dog toys, it might be helpful to utilize toys where small bits of dog food or treats can be lodged inside. By designing or choosing the right chew toys for your dog, a great deal of expensive damage to the household and personal possessions can often be prevented.

While chewing may satisfy one of your dog's basic needs, exercise and play periods are also required. Play provides much needed attention and interaction with owners and other pets in the household. It is also a great way to use up a little energy. If we do not provide a stimulating enough environment for our dogs, then attention is often directed toward much more undesirable behaviors, such as destructiveness, housesoiling, barking, or self-directed chewing. Choose a game that your pet enjoys. Retrieving, chasing, pull-

ing, tugging or jogging can all be considered.

There are a variety of leash, halter, and harness systems that can be used for walking and control. Although choke or pinch collar systems may be effective for some dogs they often cause undue discomfort and fear. If pulled too hard they may also cause injuries. Some body harnesses will effectively stop pulling, but they do little to provide the owner with additional control. One of the most effective means of controlling unruly, disobedient and "headstrong" dogs are head halters. With the head halter the owner gains control naturally through pressure exerted behind the neck and around the muzzle. Since the halter is attached around the muzzle, it does not choke, and can be used to effectively control barking, chewing, coprophagia, and even some forms of aggression. As soon as the misbehavior ceases the owner merely releases the leash, and rewards the dog for calmness.

For housetraining it may also be helpful to purchase commercial odor eliminators, to ensure that the pet is not attracted back to the spot by the residual odor. The dog's sense of smell is extremely acute, so don't rely on commercial cleansers to do the job. Odor eliminators use bacteria or enzymes to break down the odor entirely. Be certain to purchase a concentrate, or sufficient quantities of the product to saturate the entire area. It might be helpful to ask your veterinarian for recommendations.

Another important part of preventive training is to expose young dogs to as many new sounds, people, and

Veterinarians and dog behaviorists recommend Nylabone® products for their safety as well as their healthful advantages.

Cage training. Note that the cage includes a chew toy and cushion. It is not a detention facility.

situations as possible. Most puppies get used to new sounds and situations very quickly, and should therefore show less fear and anxiety to these sounds and experiences when they grow up. If the home or kennel is somewhat isolated, and the puppy cannot be sufficiently exposed to these new situations, tape-recorded sounds can be purchased or can be prepared by an industrious owner.

PRODUCTS THAT CAN BE USED SHOULD PROBLEMS DEVELOP

Once behavior problems develop there are numerous products that have been designed to interrupt or deter undesirable behavior. Most of these devices provide the owner with a method of discouraging inappropriate behavior without causing fear of the owner. To be successful punishment must be administered during misbehavior, and must be sufficiently noxious to deter the pet. There

is no point in using a device if it is not sufficiently alarming to immediately stop the behavior. On the other hand, it is of no use (and may be harmful) for the device to cause an excessive level of fear or discomfort. The effectiveness of a device will depend on how it is used, where and when it is used, the type of problem, and the pet's motivation to perform the behavior. This is one area where you do not want to rely on "cheap" imitations or "knock-offs." Follow the instructions carefully, and supervise the pet well during the first few applications. If the device is not immediately effective or causes excessive fear, its use should be discontinued.

Finally it should be noted that some behaviors cannot be corrected with a punishment or distraction device. Fearful and overly submissive behaviors often become worse if the pet is made more fearful. For example, the dog that urinates on the floor because of excitement or submission each time the owner approaches, will become more frightened or excited (and the problem will get worse) if punishment is used. If a pet is acting aggressively because he is frightened, punishment may cause the pet to be more frightened, thereby increasing the aggression. If a punishment device is not effective immediately, seek advice from your veterinarian as to what other devices or techniques might be utilized.

OWNER ACTIVATED DEVICES
a) Direct interactive punishment

Direct punishment devices include audible trainers and ultrasonic trainers. These devices must be activated

Using a child barrier to puppy-proof a home.

by the owners as soon as the inappropriate behavior begins, and should be "turned off" as soon as the inappropriate behavior ceases. Direct punishment devices have two important functions. During training applications they can be used to distract the pet so that it can be trained and rewarded for performing an appropriate behavior. Another use would be to teach the pet that the inappropriate behavior (e.g., jumping up, chewing) has immediate undesirable consequences, and that as soon as the pet stops the unpleasant noise will go away. Some training devices also provide an audible "safe" tone which can be used to reinforce good behavior. Pocket rape alarms are also often effective. Since each pet is an individual, it will be necessary to determine which device is the most effective for an individual pet.

b) Remote control punishment

For punishment to be effective, the pet must learn that each time the undesirable behavior is performed it will have unpleasant consequences. If the owner can punish the pet remotely, while remaining out of sight,

the pet will not associate the "punishment" with the owner. On the other hand, if the pet realizes that the owner is administering the punishment, the problem may cease when the owner is watching, but the pet will learn that the behavior is safe (and fun?) when the owner is away. A commonly used remote punishment technique is to wait in hiding, with a water rifle, and to spray the dog as soon as the inappropriate behavior begins. It might be more practical to monitor the pet with a monitoring device (see below). Another method of administering remote punishment is to plug in an alarm, water sprayer, or hair dryer in any area that the pet is likely to misbehave (e.g., housesoiling, chewing, etc.). Then, using a remote control switch, the device can be activated as soon as the inappropriate behavior occurs. Another form of remote punishment is when a long leash is left attached to the dog's halter. As soon as the pet begins to misbehave (digging, jumping up), the leash can be pulled from a distance, while the owner remains out of sight. For more serious problems, or when greater range is required, a remote control shock collar (Tritronics Inc., Innotek Inc.) may be more effective (provided the problem is serious enough to warrant its use).

c) Pet Monitors

Since it is imperative that pet owners use these devices during (not after) misbehavior, a pet monitor is another practical training tool. A small motion detector, The Tattle-Tale® (K-II Enterprises) is capable of picking up the movement of a dog or cat on virtually any surface. The device can be set up in any area where the pet might "misbehave" (scratching, garbage raiding, climbing on counters, furniture etc.). When the alarm sounds it alerts the owner that the inappropriate behavior is occurring. Home security monitors can also be used.

BOOBY-TRAPPING THE ENVIRONMENT

Booby traps are a practical form of punishment since they train the pet to avoid the site of misbehavior even in the owner's absence, provided the deterrent is sufficiently noxious to interrupt the behavior. Another important consideration is whether the device needs to be reset for each new application. Although devices that utilize shock or discomfort might be excessive for most problems, alarms and monitors might not be sufficiently

aversive. Choosing the appropriate device should be based on the application, the pet's level of motivation to perform the behavior, the pet's sensitivity to the product, owner acceptance, cost, and the seriousness of the problem.

With a little planning and ingenuity it is often possible to design a successful booby trap out of everyday items. A few strips of double-sided tape, or an upside down plastic carpet runner may successfully keep pets out of an area. A Rube Goldberg type of apparatus can be designed to stop chewing. For example, take an object that is likely to be chewed and spray it with any type of pet repellent or even some underarm deodorant. Attach a string from the object to a

Pet shops offer a wide array of safe chew products. Nylabone® manufacturers the most reliable and safest of all dog bones, guaranteed to outlast any similar nylon or polyurethane products. Photograph courtesy of Nylabone®.

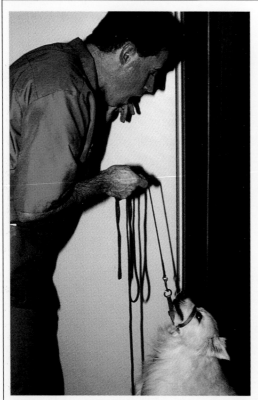 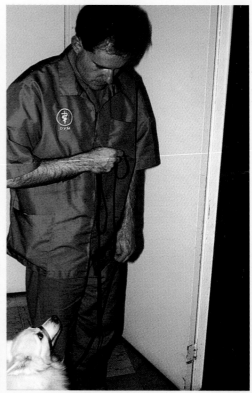

A firm pull on the leash is used to stop undesirable behavior such as barking or play biting.

The leash is immediately released as soon as the dog obeys.

Handheld trainers. From left to right: battery-operated rape alarm; Easy Trainer ultrasonic and safe tone; Dog Stop air-horn; Pet Agree ultrasonic device, and; Barker Breaker battery-operated sonic device.

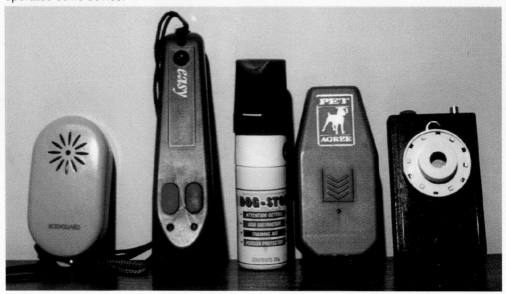

Remote punishment. The object in this case is to punish with a Super Soaker while remaining out of sight.

pets away from selected areas inside the home. The ScatMat® (Contech Electronics) is a "shock mat" that comes in a variety of shapes and sizes. It can be placed in virtually any area from a windowsill to a sofa, and there are even sizes designed to fit around a plant or Christmas tree. The SofaSaver™ (Aris Enterprises) is a sofa-sized mat that emits an audible alarm when any pressure is applied to the mat. It is battery-operated and has a light to indicate whether or not it has been activated in the owner's absence. The Snappy Trainer™ (Innovative Pet Products) is a mousetrap device that can set up in any area that the dog might misbehave. A plastic flap is fitted over the end of the mousetrap to prevent injuries. The Scraminal™ and Critter Gitter™ (Amtek) are motion detectors with built in alarms. The Critter Gitter, with its loud alarm and flash-

flat piece of cardboard, and set it on a nearby table or countertop. Next make a pyramid of empty cans on the cardboard. When the pet begins to chew the cans will topple. This exercise may have to be repeated with a few different objects, but the pet should soon lean to avoid chewing any object that has been sprayed. Most dogs can be kept away from furniture, garbage cans, or other areas where problems might occur, by setting a few mousetraps, upside down in the area.

Invisible Fencing® (Invisible Fence Co.) uses a tone/shock combination to contain dogs on a property or to keep pets away from certain areas without the need for barriers or fences. An indoor unit can be used to keep

A properly-applied halter device.

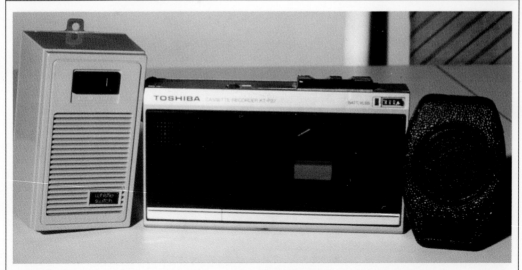

Remote training technique. A whistle switch is attached to a tape recorder. Any aversive sound (e.g., alarm) or firm command (Get off the couch!) can be controlled remotely. The apparatus on the left plugs into an outlet, the recorder (center) attaches to the plug and the transmitter/switch is located on the right.

A Promise™ Halter, with a loose remote leash.

ing light has been designed primarily for outdoor use. A number of commercial products have been developed to deter undesirable chewing. The most effective are extremely bitter, non-toxic and have no taste appeal. Products such as bitter apple and tabasco sauce may occasionally be effective, but some pets actually find them appealing. Some garden centers also stock animal repellents that chase pets away by irritating the nasal passages (sneezing powder).

Because barking is a highly motivated, natural behavior that often occurs in the owner's absence, bark-activated devices are often the only practical solution. Shock collars use variable levels of shock to interrupt undesirable barking. Collars that emit a tone or ultrasonic beep each time the dog barks may occasionally be effective. The Yapper Zapper ™ (Norwego) has been designed to mount on a dog's cage and automatically spray the dog with water each time it barks. A bark-activated alarm, The Super Barker Breaker™ (Amtek) provides a loud shrill signal each time the dog barks. The device must be set up in a room or area where the dog barks, since it is not designed to attach to the dog's collar. The Aboistop™ (Vetoquinol) and the A.B.S. (Immunovet) are collars that emit a small spray of citronella each time the dog barks. It is a humane alternative to shock collars, however not all dogs will be deterred by the spray.

SUMMARY

There are many behavior products available to the public and most have been discussed in this book. This chapter is intended to inform the consumer about these various products and how they can be most effectively used. Always consult your veterinarian about products that are most applicable in your particular situation.

Booby-trapping the home. The Scat Mat shock mat; Critter Gitter motion detector, the Snappy Trainer and the Tattle Tale motion detector.

Booby-trapping for chewing. The slipper which is about to be chewed is booby-trapped with a cord attached to a piece of cardboard on which is piled 14 empty cans. The cans will tumble down when the chewing begins.

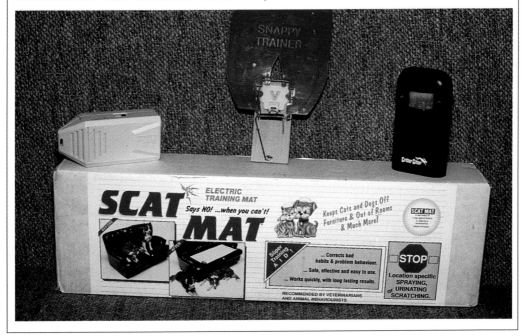

PRODUCT MANUFACTURER INFORMATION

Direct Interactive Punishment
"Barker Breaker"
Amtek Pet Behavior Products,
11025 Sorrento Valley Court, San Diego,
  CA 92121
800-762-7618; 619-597-6681

"Pet Agree" / "Dazzer"
KII Enterprises, P.O. 306, Camillus, NY
  13031
800-262-3963; 315-468-3596

"Easy Trainer"
Austin Innovations
2600 McHale Court, Suite 140, Austin, TX
  78758
800-966-2275; 512-339-6765

Monitoring Devices
"Tattle Tale"
KII Enterprises, P.O. 306, Camillus, NY
  13031
800-262-3963; 315-468-3596

Remote Punishment Devices
"Basic Trainer", "Free Spirit" (Remote shock
  collars)
Innotek Incorporated
9025 Coldwater Rd., Bldg 100A
Fort Wayne, Indiana, 46825
800-826-5527; 219-489-0369

Examples of taste deterrents

100/LR (Remote Shock Collars)
Tritronics Inc.
1650 S. Research Loop,
Tucson, AZ, 85710
800-456-4343

Booby traps (Environmental Punishment Devices)
"Invisible Fencing"
Invisible Fence Co.,
355 Phoenixville Pike, Malvern, PA 19312-
  1197
215-651-0999

"Scraminal" / "Critter Gitter"
Amtek Pet Behavior Products,
11025 Sorrento Valley Ct, San
Diego, CA 92121
800-762-7618; 619-597-6681

"Scat Mat"
Contech Electronics
P.O. Box 115, Saanichton, BC,
V0S1M0, Canada
800-767-8658; 604-652-0755

"Snappy Trainer"
Innovative Pet Products
8601 F5 West Cross Drive, Suite
209
Littleton, CO 80123-2200
800-854-8800; 303-797-0900

Scat Mat in place to protect leather sofa.

Sofa Saver alarm to keep pets off furniture.

"SofaSaver"
Aris Enterprises
10 West 46th Street, 4th Floor,
New York, NY 10036
212-840-2570

Bark Deterrents
"Aboistop" (citronella bark collar)
Vetoquinol Canada
675 St. Pierre South,
Joliette, Quebec, Canada, J6E 3Z1
514-759-0497

A.B.S. (citronella bark collar)
Immunovet
5910-G Breckenridge Parkway
Tampa, FL 33610
800-627-9447

"Bark Eliminator", "Bark Diminisher"
(shock bark collars)
Tritronics Inc.
1650 S. Research Loop,
Tucson, AZ, 85710
800-456-4343

"Bark Inhibitor" (shock bark collar)
Innotek Incorporated
9025 Coldwater Road, Bldg 100A,
Fort Wayne, Indiana, 46825
800-826-5527; 219-489-0369

"Behave" (ultrasonic bark collar)
Elexis

7000 NW 46th St., Miami, FL 33166-5604
305-592-6069

"Silencer Collar"
Austin Innovations
2600 McHale Court, Ste 140, Austin, TX
78758
800-966-2275; 512-339-6765

"Yapper Zapper"
Norwego,
P.O. Box 216,
Highland, Illinois, 62249
618-654-6762

Halters
"Halti"
Company of Animals
P.O. Box 23, Chertsey, Surrey KT16 0PU,
UK
0932-566696

"Promise System" / "Gentle Leader"
Premier Pet Products
2406 Krossridge Rd.
Richmond, VA 23236
800-933-5595

Exercise, Play and Chew Products
Nylabone® Products
TFH Publications
1 TFH Plaza, 3rd and Union Ave,
Neptune, NJ 07753
908-988-8400

Dr. U. A. Luescher graduated with his doctor of veterinary medicine degree from Zurich in 1979. In 1984 he completed his PhD from the University of Guelph and got his professional certification from the Animal Behavior Society in 1992. He is currently an assistant professor of ethology at the Ontario Veterinary College in Guelph, Ontario Canada. Dr. Luescher is a Diplomate of the American College of Veterinary Behaviorists.

Stress and Conflict-Related Behavior Problems

By Dr. U. A. Luescher,
Department of Population Medicine
Ontario Veterinary College,
University of Guelph
Guelph, Ontario, N1G 2W1
Canada

INTRODUCTION

Most of our family pets seem to lead leisurely, carefree lives. They lie in the sun, eat, drink, run about, play and may even obey the occasional command! All the same, many dogs frequently show signs of stress or conflict. In some dogs, stress may cause an almost permanent disturbance of behavior. Of all the dogs which are treated for behavior problems at the Ontario Veterinary College, about 9% are affected by a stress-related condition known as compulsive disorder.

There can be various sources of stress in a pet's life. These generally relate to the dog's environment and social relationships. Their effect on the dog depends on the individual animal's genetic make-up and previous experiences. We will come back to this point later.

CAUSES OF STRESS-RELATED PROBLEMS

Dogs are stressed if they are chained for extensive periods of time away from a secure place and from social contact. A dog which is tied is exposed to strange people and dogs and has no possibility of escaping. This is probably the main reason why dogs that are chained often become aggressive. The chain also prevents the dog from seeking a more comfortable place, and from enjoying social contact with his owner. Chaining also restricts exercise. Confining a dog in an enclosed run has some of the same disadvantages, but at least the fence provides some sense of security for the dog.

For many dogs who are not used to it, being confined to a cage is very stressful, as are other forms of physical restraint. In these instances, stress results mainly from fear and the inability to escape a presumed or real danger. (With proper cage training, however, a cage can be the most secure and comfortable place for a dog.)

Dogs are gregarious creatures by nature and form complex social systems. Under domestic conditions they develop dominance relationships, attachments, and alliances with the human family members. These intricate social relationships are necessary for a dog's psychological well-being, but if disturbed, they can become a significant source of stress. Dogs are very sensitive to unstable relationships or changes in the social group, to unresolved dominance struggles, and to changes of their own social position. If they form strong attachments to the owners to the point

Playing Frisbee may help fulfill your dog's natural prey drive and hunting instinct. Photo by Karen Taylor.

where they feel insecure on their own, they may develop separation anxiety when left alone. If a dog had to continually compete for resources such as food or the owner's attention, be it with another dog or maybe a child, this would be stressful as well.

Other causes of stress relate to the unnatural environment in which we keep dogs. Although dogs have been domesticated for some 12,000 years, longer than any other domestic species, the innate behavioral program which they inherited from their ancestors has not changed very much. All our dogs, from the Chihuahua to the Irish Wolfhound, are still predators, programmed to trot about for long periods of time and to hunt and kill their prey in cooperation with their pack members. They are social animals and depend upon one another for their survival and well-being. They dig and find shelter in dens. They communicate with others by marking their environment with urine. They roll in unsavory items, maybe to mask their own smell.

A family pet may not have the opportunity to express much dog-typical behavior. Exercise is often minimal. The opportunity to hunt can be given by throwing balls or Nylabone Frisbees™, with a bone molded on top, but for some dogs, this may not be enough. If owners work full time, the dog is denied, among other things, the opportunity for normal social behavior during most of the day. Many owners find it offensive when their dog sniffs urine or feces of other dogs, or sniff another dog under the tail. They also may deny social contact to other dogs because they are afraid that a dog fight might ensue. Preventing a dog from living out his innate behavior program, (that is, not giving the dog at least some opportunity to be a dog) is an obvious source of stress.

Many dogs will whine or bark or circle while their food is being prepared. This prefeeding excitement is an expression of conflict because the dog is highly motivated to eat, but cannot get at the food. A dog confined to a kennel may show similar signs when he sees his master, but cannot get to him or her. Although these two examples of frustrated motivations may seem harmless, they may have serious consequences for some dogs. The continuous spinning or barking of some kenneled dogs and separation anxiety are more severe expressions of frustration.

A dog is said to be in a motivational conflict when he experiences two opposing behavioral tendencies at once. For instance, a dog may want to socialize with a stranger and at the same time, he may be afraid of that person. Maybe this dog was well socialized as a puppy and loves people, but had a bad experience with a stranger. He is now in a conflict between making social contact and running away, and this situation causes a great deal of anxiety. A similar situation exists in dogs that are territorial but at the same time fearful. Ferocious barking is often an expression of such a conflict.

Our interaction with dogs is often inconsistent, and this inconsistency can cause a motivational conflict in our dogs. Sometimes we use one command for more than one thing. When we say "down" we may sometimes mean that the dog should lie down, or at other times, that he should get off the furniture. Another common example is the command Come. Usually the dog is rewarded for coming on this command, but sometimes we call the dog because he did something bad, and then punish him when he comes. Next time we call the dog he doesn't know if he will be rewarded or punished for coming, so he is in an approach-withdrawal conflict.

Giving rewards that were not earned, and using punishment more than half a second after the fact, both contribute to uncertainty and stress. Training methods which involve punishment, such as the widespread use of the choke chain, are usually counterproductive because punishment is exceedingly difficult to apply correctly. For example, if timing is not precise, from the dog's point of view, punishment is entirely independent of his behavior and seems to "come out of the blue."

The use of punishment is stress-inducing because it is aversive and because its application is so difficult. Also, it can make some behaviors even worse. Most types of aggression escalate when punished. Any behavior which expresses submission or fear will only intensify in response to punishment. A dog that crouches or goes down on a "sit" command, should never be corrected with punishment. Similarly, a dog that rolls over and urinates when the owner returns home or piddles when greeting a stranger, will get worse if punished for this behavior. This is because these submissive behaviors are the dog's way of saying "don't hurt me. The dog will obviously keep expressing his submission in response to punishment, and become severely stressed because the owner doesn't seem to understand.

Many dogs are fearful of certain things in the environment. This can be due to their genetic makeup or to early experience such as lack of socialization. A common inherited problem is fear of sounds such as thunderstorms. These dogs are frightened but cannot escape from the thunderstorm and thus they can get extremely anxious. Similarly, a dog that was not socialized to children as a puppy may be fearful of children. To such a dog, the presence of a new baby in the same household can be very stressful.

SIGNS OF STRESS

Behavioral signs of stress in a dog may range from very subtle to very obvious. More subtle signs include the refusal of food rewards, licking the lips, and yawning (watch for these signs during your obedience sessions!). More obvious signs are barking, whirling, urine marking or aggression. These acute signs of stress indicate that the situation is aversive for the dog.

The stressful condition may last only for a short time, and the dog will soon resume normal activities. In these cases, the stress has only temporary effects on the dog, and no permanent damage has been done. However, if the stressful situation occurs often, or lasts for a long time, it can result in long lasting, or possibly irreversible disturbances in the dog's behavior. Affected dogs may keep repeating a conflict behavior for many hours a day. Initially, they responded to acute stress, but they now perform the abnormal behavior even when the original cause of the stress is not present. At this stage, any form of excitement will trigger the behavior. In the worst case, a dog may display a conflict behavior whenever he is awake and not eating. At this stage, the condition is called "Compulsive Disorder" and the conflict behavior has developed into a compulsive behavior. This change in the nature of the conflict behavior goes along with changes in chemistry of the dog's brain. Most dogs can be distracted and the behavior can be interrupted, but some dogs respond very little to outside stimuli while performing a compulsive behavior.

Dogs can develop a great variety of compulsive behaviors. Which one(s) they develop depends on their ge-

Acral lick dermatitis in which a dog continually licks at one area on the paw. The result is ulceration and inflammation.

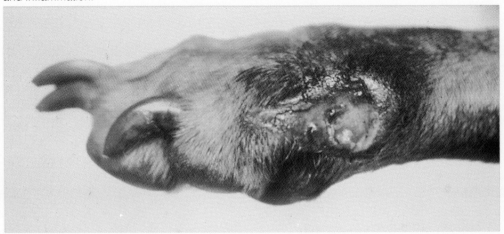

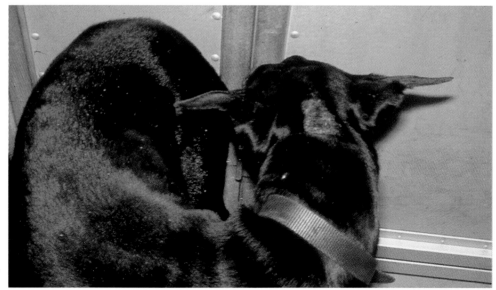

Flank sucking is most common in Doberman Pinschers.

netic background and probably also on the source of stress. A common compulsive behavior is excessive licking of the same body part, most often the wrist, to the point where the skin gets raw and a lick granuloma develops. Other dogs may chew their feet or scratch themselves incessantly. Snapping at imaginary flies is a typical example of a compulsive behavior. Dogs that chew constantly or suck on a blanket all the time are likely to suffer from Compulsive Disorder.

Most people have seen bears or tigers in zoos pacing up and down in their enclosure. Dogs may develop very similar behaviors such as pacing, going in circles, or in figures of eight. Others may chase their tail, sometimes biting and injuring it. Others again may freeze and, in this frozen position, often seem to stare at the ceiling, at a light bulb, or at shadows. Some compulsive behaviors involve vocalization such as rhythmic barking over long periods of time, or growling usually directed towards the dog's own body. This growling is a form of aggression and may escalate to actual attacks on the dog's own body, and to self-injury and self-mutilation. Some dogs will not bite themselves, but instead suck their flank.

PREDISPOSITIONS FOR COMPULSIVE DISORDER

As mentioned above, some dogs are more prone to develop compulsive disorder than others. This may be due to an inherited susceptibility or to previous experiences. A genetic predisposition can determine three things:

- how easily a dog is stressed (e.g. genetically fearful dogs are easily stressed)
- how likely the dog is to develop a compulsive behavior in response to stress, and
- which compulsive behavior he will develop.

Dogs will differ individually, but there are also some strains within breeds that are more readily affected with a particular compulsive behavior. For example, Dobermans are more prone to flank sucking than other breeds. Some lines of Bull Terriers are known to have a tendency to whirl. German Shepherds are most likely to express stress by chasing and snapping at their tail. The most intricate compulsive behavior is performed by some Miniature Schnauzers. When they sit on the floor, they will frequently look at their rear, get up, turn around and sniff and maybe scratch the spot they have been sitting on. This sequence is repeated frequently.

Previous experiences can contribute to the susceptibility for compul-

Although certain breeds may be more prone to compulsive behaviors, not all breed representatives will show signs—most are perfectly happy and normal.

sive disorder in various ways. The early upbringing of a puppy has a profound effect on how well adjusted or how fearful it will be as an adult. Previous experiences that caused fear or uncertainty in the dog will increase the likelihood that he will develop Compulsive Disorder. Also, dogs that developed a compulsive behavior earlier in their life will readily redevelop it when put in a stressful situation again.

PREVENTION AND TREATMENT OF COMPULSIVE DISORDER

A dog that focuses almost his entire life on licking a particular part of his body, or on chasing his own tail, does not make a nice pet. His owners will be distressed not only because they cannot enjoy a normal interaction with their pet, but also because they are worried that there is something physically wrong with him. What is most distressing to the owners is when the dog inflicts injury on himself. What is not obvious to the owner, but constitutes a severe disturbance, is the change in the dog's brain chemistry. For all these reasons, veterinarians are working hard to develop methods of reliably diagnosing, preventing, and treating Compulsive Disorder.

Although the behaviors described above are often signs of Compulsive Disorder, they may sometimes be expressions of disease. It is therefore important to consult a veterinarian before any treatment attempt is made. Your veterinarian is in the best position to differentiate between disease and a behavioral disorder, and to decide what diagnostic tests are necessary in each individual case. After

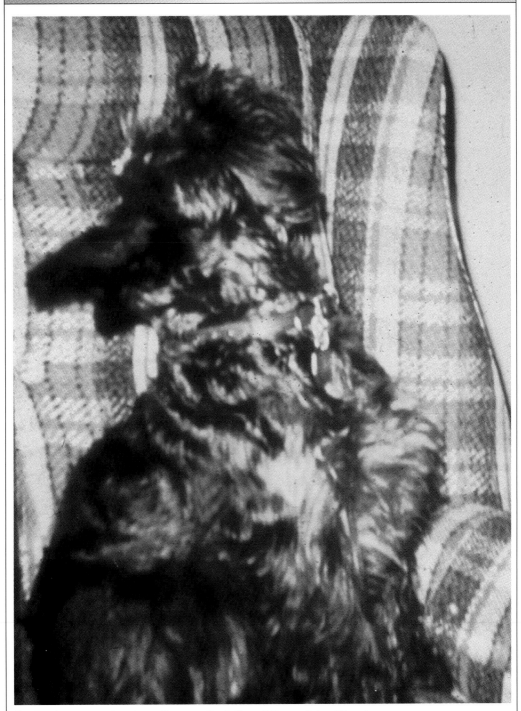

Staring into space is yet another manifestation of Compulsive Disorder.

possible physical problems are ruled out, a diagnosis can usually be made on the basis of a thorough history.

Prevention of compulsive disorder must focus on three things: selective breeding, proper upbringing of the puppy, and a consistent and low stress environment. Since Compulsive Disorder is more common in certain lines or breeds, it is obvious that a predisposition is inherited. Animals which developed a compulsive behavior in spite of proper upbringing and treatment, should not be used for breeding.

The proper upbringing of a puppy is of paramount importance to its later behavior and psychological well-being. Puppies that were not exposed to everyday stimuli (such as different sights and sounds, people, children, other dogs, etc.) before 12 weeks of age, may be fearful for the rest of their lives. Similarly, puppies that had a traumatic experience during the fear period (8-12 weeks of age) may be shy or fearful as adults. Fearful dogs are under almost continuous stress (except perhaps in the security of their own home) and are likely to develop compulsive behaviors. Early socialization with exposure to different stimuli and careful treatment during the fear period, go a long way to prevent Compulsive Disorder.

Since one of the major causes of Compulsive Disorder is an unpredictable environment or inconsistent dog-owner interaction, consistent treatment of the dog is the key to preventing compulsive behavior. A dog forms expectations of what is going to happen throughout the day, or of what the owner's reaction to his

behavior will be. An erratic schedule, such as sometimes skipping the evening walk, can frustrate a dog's expectations and cause stress. A regular schedule for feeding and for exercise (i.e. daily walks with the dog, not just letting the dog out in the yard) will help prevent Compulsive Disorder. If the owner's reaction to the dog's behavior is contrary to the dog's expectations, such as is the case with inconsistent or inappropriate use of commands, rewards, and punishment, the dog is in a state of helplessness and severe stress. Consistency in dog-owner interactions can be achieved with good reward-based obedience training and is probably the most important factor in preventing Compulsive Disorder.

The treatment of Compulsive Disorder has to address the same points. First and foremost, the major source or sources of stress should be identified and corrected. To identify the cause of stress may be difficult, but can often be accomplished when a good history is taken, and once the circumstances under which the compulsive behavior was observed initially, are known.

If the source of stress is a new baby, a thunderstorm, or the owner's daily departure for work, it cannot be removed. In these cases, the dog needs to be desensitized to the cause of the stress (the stressor). This is achieved by gradually exposing the dog to the stressful situation and simultaneously rewarding him for staying relaxed. If the dog is under stress because he is globally fearful (afraid of everything), this method is impractical because the dog would have to be desensitized to everything in the environment. In these cases, the strategic use of an antianxiety drug may achieve the same results.

Since the dog-owner relationship often contributes to the problem, and since owners often inadvertently reward the dog for the compulsive behavior by paying attention to it, it is advisable to temporarily interrupt dog-owner interactions and rebuild a new, consistent relationship. This can be achieved when owners ignore their dog completely for two to four weeks, except for several daily obedience sessions. Obedience training has to be reward-based and must not involve any corrections. Furthermore, the owner is to abstain from any punishment for the rest of the dog's life; if the dog engages in unacceptable behavior, he can be distracted, given a command to perform a different behavior, and then rewarded for performing this acceptable behavior. An increase in exercise and a regular schedule will also help to decrease anxiety and will help in the treatment of Compulsive Disorder.

If the behavior has gone on for a long time, these behavioral methods alone may not be sufficient. In these cases, your veterinarian may prescribe a drug which can help to reverse the biochemical changes which took place in the brain during the development of the Compulsive Disorder.

In very severe cases, a method known as "Counterconditioning" may be employed in addition to the above-mentioned measures. With this technique, the dog is distracted (e.g. by a loud noise) whenever he performs the compulsive behavior. A command for another behavior is then issued (the dog has to be trained first to understand and obey this command). This other behavior has to be incompatible with the compulsive behavior, so that the dog cannot perform both at the same time. For example, a dog that chews its front foot could be trained to lie down on command with the head extended flat on the ground. As soon as he chews his foot, he would be distracted, told to lie down flat, and he would be rewarded immediately upon obeying that command.

SUMMARY

Compulsive Disorder is a quite common and complex behavior problem. If you suspect that your dog is suffering from Compulsive Disorder, we encourage you to seek the help of your veterinarian, since successful treatment is possible. By paying attention to the suggestions made for prevention of this disorder, you will likely be able to avoid the need for treatment.

ADDITIONAL READING

Blackshaw, JK; Sutton, RH; Boyhan, MMA: Tail chasing or circling behavior in dogs. Canine Practice, 1994; 19(3): 7-11.

Luescher, UA: Conflict, stereotypic and compulsive behavior. Presentationn to the American Veterinary Medical Association Annual conference, July, 1994.

Luescher, UA; McKeown, DB; Halip, J: Stereotypic or obsessive-compulsive disorders in dogs and cats. Veterinary Clinics of North America, Small Animal Practice, 1991; 65(2): 401-413.

Caroline B. Schaffer is Director of External Affairs at Tuskegee University's School of Veterinary Medicine in Tuskegee, Alabama. She also serves as advisor to Tuskegee University's Human-Animal Bond/ Animal Behavior Club and supervises the University's volunteer program that prepares veterinary medical students and their pets to work in pet-facilitated therapy programs. Prior to moving to Tuskegee University, Dr. Schaffer worked as a research associate in small animal surgery at Iowa State University's College of Veterinary Medicine and practiced small animal medicine and surgery in group practices in a suburb of Chicago, Illinois, and in Columbus, Ohio. She was honored by the Association of Teachers of Veterinary Public Health and Preventive Medicine with their Michael J. McCulloch, M.D. Memorial Award in 1994 "in recognition of her outstanding contributions in research,

teaching, and service related to the human-animal bond." She earned her Doctor of Veterinary Medicine degree from The Ohio State University College of Veterinary Medicine in 1971. She and her husband raise, breed, and show Pekingese. She wrote, produced, and directed an instructional video, "The Tuskegee Behavior Test for Selecting Therapy Dogs," in 1993.

David D. Schaffer is currently a resident in psychiatry at the University of Alabama at Birmingham. He received his D.V.M. from Tuskegee University's School of Veterinary Medicine in Tuskegee, Alabama, in 1971. After practicing small animal medicine and surgery in Columbus, Ohio, he returned to academia. He earned a PhD in pharmacology from Loyola University of Chicago in 1980 and completed a post-doctoral fellowship in clinical pharmacology at the University of Chicago in 1982. Thereaf-

Dogs Uplifting People's Spirits

By Caroline Brunsman Schaffer, DVM
David D. Schaffer, DVM, PhD, DO
Tuskegee University
School of Veterinary Medicine
Tuskegee, AL 36088

ter, he did research in veterinary pharmacology and taught veterinary pharmacology and physiology at both Iowa State University's College of Veterinary Medicine and Tuskegee University's School of Veterinary Medicine. He helped to establish Tuskegee University's Human-Animal Bond/Animal Behavior Club in 1989-90. He earned the Doctor of Osteopathy degree at the University of Osteopathic Medicine and Health Sciences in Des Moines, Iowa, in 1993. His diverse professional training merges his interest in and respect for the human-animal interdependent relationship. He and his wife share their lives with eight Pekingese, two of whom are active pet-facilitated therapists at the Tuskegee Veterans Affairs Medical Center in Tuskegee, Alabama.

INTRODUCTION

If dogs could talk, would they volunteer to work as therapists in hospitals, nursing homes, and other institutions? Maybe they would. Dogs and other animals throughout the nation and the world are putting sunshine into the hearts of people who are shut off from the rest of the world because of either emotional, physical, or behavioral problems.

On the other hand, maybe they would not volunteer. Just as not all people enjoy visiting with animals, not all dogs want to sit on a stranger's lap or go for a ride on a wheelchair. Not all will lie patiently for a tummy rub or enjoy a rough massage. Not all dogs enjoy entering unfamiliar surroundings with strange sounds, odors, and activities.

After years of being barred from entry into hospitals and nursing homes because of fears of health risks from injuries or zoonotic diseases (i.e., infections shared by people and pets), dogs and other companion animals are now being welcomed with open arms. Having a resident dog (one who lives at the facility) or a visitation dog (one who comes to the facility on scheduled visits with its owner) has become so popular that some institutions even advertise that they offer pet-facilitated therapy when they are recruiting health care providers.

Dogs have gained popularity as therapists in institutions because of a wide range of success stories. It is no longer unusual to hear about the benefits dogs give to the sick, the lonely, and the elderly. Stories abound about people who hadn't talked for months or years until a dog came to visit, about nursing home residents who are happier and more sociable when a dog is sitting beside them, about hospitalized patients who need less pain-relieving medications when a pet is present, about dogs who help with physical therapy sessions by encouraging patients to brush them or to throw a ball for them to fetch, and about care givers who are more attentive to their patient's needs when a dog or other pet comes to visit.

Promoters of animal-assisted activities talk about the enhanced human interactions that occur when owners see how readily their dogs accept people regardless of their

This little fellow does wonders in the spirit-lifting department.

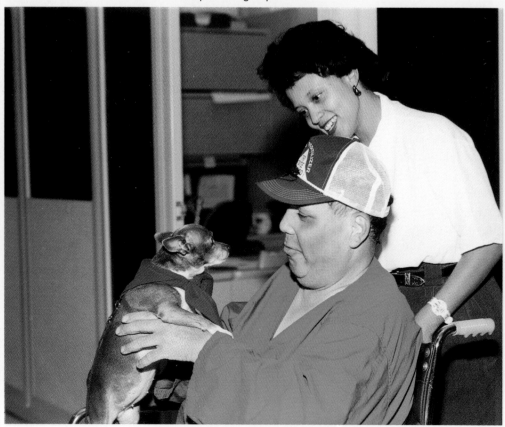

Peek-a-boo with two Pekingese—a delightful afternoon for anyone.

physical appearance or mental state. Some pet owners, previously uncomfortable in institutions, have become very effective and dedicated volunteers simply because of their eagerness to share their pet's love with a stranger.

The stories of dogs serving as therapists for children and adults with physical or emotional problems are heart-rending. Consider the valuable interrelationship between people and therapy dogs exemplified by a Labrador Retriever at a special education class, a Newfoundland at a mental health institution, and a menagerie of dogs at a nursing home:

An occupational therapist in an early childhood special education course hands an autistic, withdrawn five-year-old girl a book and asks her to read to the Labrador Retriever at her side. The child takes the book, plops down next to the school's therapy dog, and reads out loud to the dog with incredible emphasis and clarity. "You're reading!" exclaims her teacher. "I don't know how to read," the girl protests. In fact, no one had taught her to read and, until asked to read to the dog, no one knew she could.

A patient at a mental health institution suffers from bouts of depression and anger. Once a week, he grasps the leather leash of a massive

Newfoundland and lets her pull him and his wheelchair outdoors. There, he lovingly brushes the therapy dog and asks her to play ball. Except for this weekly visit, the man stays in his room and rarely speaks. For one day a week, he forgets to be angry because the dog is willing to be his friend.

Residents of a Veterans Affairs Medical Center nursing home welcome a menagerie of mixed and purebred dogs of all sizes and shapes for a biweekly visit. A small-framed, 80-something woman excitedly gathers her fellow residents and insists they pet each dog. A very dignified resident walks to his bed, sits down, and asks a Golden Retriever to come join him. Soon the therapy dog is fast asleep, relaxed by the marvelous massage of the elderly gentleman. He has forgotten many things, but he still remembers the pleasure that comes from a dog. A Pekingese goes to the bedside of a man crippled with arthritis and rolls over so that his gnarled hand can stroke her belly. A Dalmation-mix wiggles with pleasure as a normally quiet man in a wheelchair becomes extremely animated. He laughs and babbles and laughs some more as the dog nestles close and asks for more hugs. They are in a world of their own, united by a special kind of love.

GROWING ACCEPTANCE OF DOG THERAPY

Recognition of the diverse benefits of people-pet interactions has contributed to growing acceptance of pet-facilitated therapy and other animal-assisted activities by physi-cians and nurses, psychiatrists and psychologists, physical and occupational therapists, social workers and educators, and institutional administrators and trustees throughout the world. After years of being barred from entry into hospitals, nursing homes, and schools because of fears of health risks to people from injuries or zoonotic diseases, dogs and other companion animals are now being welcomed with open arms.

Fears of major health risks have not materialized. In a study of 233 skilled and intermediate care facilities in Illinois, for example, only 24 facilities reported any safety problems over a one-year period. In another 12-month study, 284 Minnesota nursing homes found no incidence of infections spread by pets and only 19 mechanical injuries--only two of which included broken bones--due to pets as compared with many injuries due to falling in the bath or out of bed.

Although it is true that animals appear to be working miracles through pet-facilitated therapy, not all dogs are miracle workers. Contrary to popular belief, not all dogs give unconditional love. In addition, not all people enjoy the companionship of animals. Some may even mistreat the animals who come to visit them.

JOB INTERVIEWS FOR DOGS

So, which dogs can help the sick, the physically or mentally challenged, the lonely, the dying, and the elderly? Just as a person must go through a screening process when applying for a job, so, too, should every potential

Retrievers are among the most outgoing doggy therapists in the field.

canine therapist be selected with care. All dogs should pass a behavior test that simulates the facility they will visit.

If dogs are not selected for their good health and suitable behavior, the prejudice against pets in nursing homes and hospitals could return. The doors could, once again, be slammed shut in the faces of canine therapists. Tragically, many people would be denied the potential benefits that come from interacting with a dog because of the carelessness of those who did not participate in a comprehensive screening program.

The only way to know with certainty how a particular dog will respond to patients/residents at a given institution is to take him into that institution. However, the potential injuries to people and the potential stress on the dog that could occur if he reacted poorly in the novel environment make it safer to first test through simulations. This testing requires commitment, creativity, and time if it is to accurately assess the dog. The test must simulate as nearly as possible the facility where the dog will be working. It should include those sights, sounds, odors, and activities that the dog might encounter on any visit. If, for example, the dog is to visit people in wheelchairs, then he should be tested around wheels. If he is to visit children, then his interactions with children should be observed. If he is to work with other

Few things can put asunder the natural human-animal bond.

animals, then his interactions with each species should also be observed.

People throughout the United States have designed behavior tests to help select animals for special tasks. Some institutions require proof that a pet has passed a specific test; others have no requirements. For example, some permit only registered "Pet Partners," i.e., pets who have passed the behavior and health screening test and handlers who have passed the written examination given by the Delta Society, to interact with patients and residents.

Regardless of the institution's requirements, dog owners would be wise to have their dogs tested before taking them to an unfamiliar setting. Some dogs are too aggressive. Others too fearful. Some may even be too playful. A good behavior test helps an owner determine the suitability of his dog for a particular therapy program. It also gives him a better understanding of his dog's tolerance level. Ultimately, it is the owner's responsibility to be sure that his dog will behave appropriately and will not be unduly stressed by the therapy program.

A few of the behavior tests in use in the United States include the Tuskegee PUPS Test (acronym for Pets Uplifting People's Spirit) of the Tuskegee University School of Veterinary Medicine, Tuskegee, Alabama; the Pet Visitation Screening Test of the San Antonio Delta Society, San Antonio, Texas; the Canine Good Citizen Test of the American Kennel Club, Raleigh, North Carolina; the Pet Partner Test of the Delta Society, Renton, Washington; the PAWS Temperament Test (acronym for Pets Are Working

Saints) of the Frazier Memorial United Methodist Church, Montgomery, Alabama; the Temperament Test of the American Temperament Test Society, Inc.; and the Puppy Behavior Test of William E. Campbell as presented in Behavior Problems in Dogs, 1975.

A MODEL BEHAVIOR TEST

The Tuskegee PUPS Test is described in this chapter as an example of how a dog might be selected. This test was designed so that:

1. People with minimal knowledge of companion animal behavior could easily administer the test and evaluate the responses,
2. Activities at each station would not overwhelm the pet,
3. The test would be safe for the pet, handler, and evaluators,
4. The various situations that could be encountered during a nursing home/hospital visitation would be simulated,
6. Evaluations would be objective--not subjective,
7. The pet's interactions with other animals and with strangers of both sexes would be observed at more than one station, and
8. The behavior exhibited in the test would be a reliable predictor of behavior that would be exhibited in the arena in which the pet would be working.

To meet these eight criteria, the PUPS Test was designed in a grid format that asks the evaluator to describe the pet's body language. The veterinarians and veterinary medical students who created the test deliberately avoided subjective terms such

Classifications of Canine Posture

Depending on conformation and individual idiosyncracies, dogs may exhibit some or all of the characteristics in a given category. It is imperative to observe the entire dog before classifying his posture.

Attentive

Ears up
Eyes moving, not fixed
Lips relaxed
Head up
Hair down
Weight equally distributed
Tail stiff & horizonal
Tail moving slowly as aroused
Non-verbal

Playful

Ears up
Eyes moving
Lips relaxed
Hair down
Leaning back, weight shifted to rear
Front foot may wave at target
Tail wagging high, broad, fast
Animated, exaggerated , bouncing movements
May pant, bark, or whine

Aggressive

Ears forward at first, out & down as escalates,
    back when attacking
Eyes fixed, staring at target
Lips raised, mouth slightly open
Nose wrinkled
Head high
Hair raised over rump & back of neck
Leaning forward, weight shifted to front
Body stiff, tense
Front leg may point at target
Tail stiff & high over back, tip may quiver
May growl, snarl, & bark

Classifications of Canine Posture

Depending on conformation and individual idiosyncracies, dogs may exhibit some or all of the characteristics in a given category. It is imperative to observe the entire dog before classifying his posture.

Submissive

Ears down
Eyes down
Lips down, retracted horizontallly
Head down
Hair down
Leaning back, weight shifted to rear
Tail may wag horizontally, hang down,
   or be tucked close to body
May whine

Passively submissive

Ears down
Eyes down
Lips down
Hair down
Head down
Lying on side or back
Tail tucked close to body
May urinate

Fearful

Ears back & down
Eyes wide open & fixed
Mouth open slightly
Head down
Hair raised over neck
Leaning back, weight shifted to rear
Tail tucked tight under abdomen
May tremble & defecate
Makes fast moves if threatened
Looks for escape route
Whines

©Tuskegee University, 1993

as excited, shy, and happy. Instead, non-judgmental terms such as ears forward, tail stiff and high, and lips raised were used to describe the pet's posture.

The grid format was designed to minimize the amount of writing required by the evaluator. Key aspects of the eyes, ears, mouth, tail, etc. were selected as the elements that would be most expressive and easiest to observe when the test animal encountered another animal or a person. These elements were selected based on reports by animal behaviorists on the body language that animals use to communicate nonverbally with others of the same species. As shown by the six postures (attentiveness, playfulness, submission, aggression, fearfulness, and passive submission) represented in Figure 2, the entire body must be observed before interpreting a dog's reaction at each station. Observing only one feature such as ear carriage could be misleading.

Eight stations (Waiting Room, Examination Room, People Hall, Distractions, Obstacle Course, Noise Hall, Elevator Simulation, and Simulated Day Room) were designed to simulate the conditions of the nursing home/hospital where the pet who passed the PUPS Test would be working. The simulations were selected because, although an animal's behavior may be 99% reliable in its own home, the behavior may be extremely different in a novel environment.

The evaluator who marks the test sheets does not determine the pet's admission into the PUPS Program. A panel of three people reviews the pet's body language as reported at all eight stations and then gives the pet either an unconditional pass, a conditional pass, or a failing evaluation.

Every handler/owner is told what strengths and weaknesses were observed through the pet's body language so that the handler will be sensitive to the pet's needs during the visitation. If the pet received a conditional pass, the handler is instructed accordingly and given suggestions that may later enable the pet to earn an unconditional pass. If the pet fails, the handler/owner may seek behavioral counseling so that the pet can be re-tested later.

If the interactions between the pet and the handler are flawed, the panel advises the handler and gives specific recommendations to remedy this relationship. Trust and affection between the dog and its owner/handler appear to be part of what enables a dog to work its magic in unfamiliar surroundings. An owner/handler who is attentive to his pet's needs can prevent unpleasant or dangerous encounters.

It is important to note that the Tuskegee PUPS Test as presented here was designed as a screening test for nursing home and hospital visitations. If a dog were to be invited to a different institution, then the test would be modified to more closely simulate that setting. If, for example, dogs will be visiting a school for autistic children, then they would need to be handled by children and subjected to the sounds and manipulations that they might encounter in that setting. Only then can the dogs say, through their body language, how they feel about interacting in that environment.

TESTING AND LEARNING NEVER END

Passing a behavior test does not ensure that a dog will react well in the institutional setting. If, in spite of previous screening, he behaves inappropriately at the institution, then he should be removed immediately from the program. It is unkind to the dog and potentially dangerous for those in the institution to force the dog to continue in the program.

Also, just because a dog passed a behavior test does not ensure that he will always be effective. Dogs learn quickly to associate unpleasant experiences with particular sights, sounds, and odors at an institution. To prevent "burn out," the dogs must receive consistent positive reinforcement at the institution (see chapter on Rewards and Punishment). The owner/handler must remain focused on his dog at all times, reward him for appropriate behavior, and be ready to quickly remove him from any uncomfortable or dangerous situations.

For peak performance, the length of each visit should match each dog's energy level and attention span. Most visitation programs report that one hour is the longest the average dog should be asked to work.

The diverse messages conveyed by a dog's tail illustrate how important a knowledge of canine body language and behavior is for those using dogs for therapy. A happy, friendly dog wags his tail, but so might a highly aggressive dog.

For a pet program to be successful, it is necessary that the owner/handler remain with the pet and be responsible for the pet's well-being. It is also advisable for an institutional staff member who understands the patients/residents and who is responsible for their well-being to accompany the pet and the owner/handler.

To continue to be an effective therapist, a dog must rely on his owner/handler to recognize when he is stressed and act quickly to relieve the stress. Typical signs of stress in dogs are those physiological responses associated with stimulation of the autonomic nervous system. Stress may result in overt or subtle behavior changes. These subtleties may range from signs such as dilated pupils, tense muscles or tense facial expression to sweaty paws. Overt signs may include yawning, trembling, aggression, salivation, panting, urination, defecation, expressing anal sacs, barking, whining, and hiding behind or clinging to the owner/handler.

When a dog appears stressed, it is safest to immediately remove him from the eliciting stimulus. Later, the owner/handler should determine whether the dog can learn to accept the stressful stimulus or whether the dog will need to be kept from it. For example, a dog may be fearful of the high-pitched, crackling voice of one particular patient. It may be possible to eliminate the dog's fear or anxiety through a carefully designed counterconditioning and desensitization or habituation program or it may be necessary to stop the visits between the dog and that particular patient.

Sometimes the best decision when a dog is overly stressed is to retire him from the therapy program. Not only will the dog be happier, but the patients/residents may also be happier. Few things are worse emotionally for those being visited by a therapy dog than the perception that the pet dislikes them or is stressed by their presence. Before deciding the appropriate course of action, the owner/handler should consult a veterinarian with training in animal behavior for help with the diagnosis and treatment of the stress-related problem.

PLANNING THE ADOPTION

Anyone hoping to adopt a dog for use in a pet-facilitated therapy program or other animal-assisted therapy program would do well to first study the characteristics of various breeds of dogs (see chapter on Selecting the Perfect Dog), learn more about canine behavior, and determine what pet programs exist in the local community. Although it is impossible to know with certainty which puppies will grow up to be good therapists, anyone looking for a prospective therapy dog should select a dog who exhibits a high tolerance to touch. A puppy who appears shy is unlikely to work well.

It is especially helpful to know what happened during a puppy's sensitive period of socialization between four and twelve weeks of age. If a dog has good experiences with people and other animals throughout this period, he is more likely to react well later. If, for example, he has little or no experience with children or loud noises when he is four to twelve weeks old, he may always be fearful of children and loud noises. Ideally, the prospective therapy dog should have had many positive interactions with many people and animals in many different locations during his socialization period.

Besides being socialized to people and other animals, therapy dogs will need to be trained to walk on a leash and to respond to their owners/handlers' wishes. Even if a dog is to be carried, he should wear a leash for added control in case of an emergency. Small dogs may benefit from learning to travel in a pet carrier. This will give them a safe haven should they need to be removed quickly from the people they are visiting. Dogs also needs to be trained so that they will not soil the facility or the people they are visiting.

Dogs who are trained for competition in conformation shows may be as well suited for therapy work as those who have attended obedience classes. Conformation dogs are trained to tolerate extensive handling by many judges and to move with confidence in a variety of noisy and novel settings.

SHARING RESPONSIBILITIES

Selecting an appropriate dog is only one step in assuring a successful pet-facilitated therapy program. The institutions, the dogs' handlers/owners, and the patients/residents all have their own unique responsibilities if dogs are to work their magic. All have a responsibility to be sure the dog feels comfortable and safe.

The responsibilities of the institution include:

1. Providing a safe environment where the dog and his owner/handler will not be injured or become ill,

2. Informing its staff members about the pet program and its goals,
3. Preventing staff members from deliberately sabotaging the program,
4. Alerting its infectious disease control board that dogs will be coming so that proper protocol will be understood and followed,
5. Keeping the dog away from patients/residents who have diseases (such as scabies caused by a sarcoptic mite) that are known to be contagious to/from dogs,
6. Screening patients and staff for allergies and phobias to dogs so that they are not forced to be near animals they either dislike or fear,
7. Providing a staff member who will escort the owner/handler and dog during the visitation and who will facilitate the interactions of the dog by looking out for the well-being of the patients/residents, and
8. Carrying liability insurance that will cover the dog and his owner/handler during their service at the facility.

The responsibilities of the dog's owner/handler include:

1. Selecting a dog who will behave appropriately,
2. Making certain the dog is healthy and free of zoonotic diseases,
3. Keeping the dog on a good preventive health program that includes
   a. regular vaccinations for rabies, canine distemper, hepatitis, leptospirosis, parainfluenza, and parvo virus,
   b. tests for internal and external parasites, and
   c. yearly physical examinations,
4. Cancelling the visit if his dog is not feeling well on the day of a scheduled visit,
5. Bathing and brushing the dog within 48 hours of each visit and being sure the dog's nails are short and blunt,
6. Refraining from applying any perfumes or powders that might cause an allergic reaction in the patients/residents,
7. Protecting the dog and reassuring him throughout each visit,
8. Staying focused on the dog and, preferably, keeping a hand on the dog so that he can be removed quickly if an emergency arises,
9. Knowing the dog's behavior well enough to detect when he is getting tired, feeling excessively stressed, or becoming agitated,
10. Knowing how the dog behaves with dogs and other animals whom the dog might encounter during a visit,
11. Providing the dog with an easily accessible escape route,
12. Helping the dog to get comfortable if he is to sit on a person's lap or lie on a bed,
13. Providing the dog with access to fresh, clean water,
14. Taking the dog to a previously approved area to urinate and defecate,
15. Reporting bites and scratches or suspected bites or scratches to the appropriate staff member in the institution and following the predetermined protocol for handling injuries,
16. Notifying housekeeping if the dog urinates, defecates, or vomits and

cleaning up after the dog as directed by the institution's guidelines,

17. Keeping the dog away from anyone who is eating or who has open food nearby,

18. Prohibiting anyone from feeding his dog during the visit,

19. Keeping the dog from ingesting any medications or chemicals at the institution,

20. Not offering food to the patients/residents,

21. Treating the patients/residents with kindness and respect,

22. Following the rules of the institution,

23. Being prompt, dependable, and appropriately dressed so that his clothing does not get in the dog's way or distract the patient/resident,

24. Accepting the institution for what it is—not trying to change policies, criticize housekeeping, or provide patient care beyond that described under the institution's pet therapy program, and

25. Maintaining confidentiality and respecting the patient/resident's right to privacy.

The responsibilities of the patient/resident include:

1. Being kind to the dog,

2. Accepting that he cannot have a visit if he is abusive towards the dog,

3. Never putting the dog in a potentially dangerous situation,

4. Not monopolizing the dog or prohibiting others from visiting with the dog,

5. Never feeding the dog unless the institution and the owner/handler approve, and

6. Asserting his right to not visit with or handle a dog whom he is fearful of, allergic to, or uncomfortable with.

STOPPING NEEDLESS SEPARATIONS

Significant strides have been made in enabling people in various stages of life to benefit from the human-animal interdependent relationship. Much has changed since Florence Nightingale, the pioneer of modern nursing, mentioned the psychological benefits of pets in her 1893 "Notes on Nursing," and Boris Levinson, child psychologist and father of modern pet psychotherapy, stirred up the psychiatric community with his controversial paper, "The Dog as a 'Co-therapist'," in 1962. Despite the progress, some segments of society are still needlessly separated from animals. More can be done to enable the elderly, the hospitalized, and the immunosuppressed including those infected with the Human Immunodeficiency Virus (HIV) to interact with pets of their own.

Federal laws require that the elderly and handicapped living in federally subsidized housing be allowed to own pets, but, ironically, the elderly who are financially independent and who rent apartments or purchase condominiums in "modern" retirement villages are often prohibited from owning a dog or other pet. How tragic that, while they may have enough money to buy virtually anything they want, they cannot buy a dog! The tragedy is that the dog or another suitable pet would keep them active, add joy to their lonely days and long nights, and provide companionship after their friends and loved ones have died.

The physical and emotional benefits of pet ownership have been proven scientifically to the satisfaction of the U.S. government. Research data on the health benefits of pets for the elderly is convincing. It is time for landlords to change their perception of dog ownership and to welcome tenants who can adequately care for their dogs. A few model programs, such as the ones in Massachusetts and New Jersey, have proven that guidelines can be established that will protect the landlord's property and provide for beneficial people-dog interactions.

More hospitals would do well to adopt policies that will allow for patients to have visits from their own dogs, not just those who are in pet-therapy programs. Some hospitals have, for example, dedicated one or two rooms for pet visits. Patients can reserve a room and make arrangements for their pet to meet them there for brief visits at assigned times. Actress Elizabeth Taylor and comedienne Joan Rivers talk openly about smuggling their dogs into the hospital with them. Clearly, visits with a person's own pet have proven to be even more beneficial than visits from pets belonging to volunteers.

The companionship of dogs is being denied to many people in another segment of society at a time when they can help the most. Healthy dogs with an appropriate temperament can provide physical and psychological benefits to their owners who are im-munosuppressed. These benefits usually far outweigh any risk of the owners' getting sick or injured from their pets; nevertheless, well meaning friends and health care providers frequently recommend that people whose resistance to infection is low due to diseases such as Acquired Immune Deficiency Syndrome (AIDS) or medications such as chemotherapy or corticosteroids get rid of their pets.

Tragically, many people with HIV are losing their pets at the same time they are being shunned by their friends and family. The only time they are touched is when they are poked and prodded in the doctor's office or hospital. For them, a dog may be the only one they can hug and cuddle without fear of rejection. In addition, they may feel that their dog is the only friend who is genuinely happy to see them. Unlike a human friend or volunteer who can visit only a short while, a dog will be absolutely delighted to spend the entire day and night with his owner.

Although it is true that several agents known to infect both people and dogs have been found in HIV-infected people, medical scientists believe that people infected with HIV rarely get these agents directly from a pet. More often, they are acquired from contaminated soil, food, water, wild birds, or infected people.

An immunosuppressed person can care for his dog in such a way that will minimize his risk of contracting a zoonotic infection. Veterinarians can provide an expanded preventive health care program designed to match the client's level of immuno-suppression. The client can also follow the guidelines described in "HIV/AIDS and Pet Ownership," a brochure available through the Tuskegee University School of Veterinary Medicine, Tuskegee, Alabama 36088, to ensure a safe and healthy relationship with his dog. As has been shown in other areas of pet-facilitated therapy and animal-assisted activities, the risk of transmission of diseases between animals and people can be minimized by having the proper information.

SUMMARY

Dogs and other companion animals throughout the nation and the world are putting sunshine into the hearts of people who are isolated because of either emotional, physical, or behavioral problems. Undoubtedly more dogs will be allowed to work their magic as more veterinarians, physicians, other health care providers, and animal lovers show that not all dogs are independent, wild, and unpredictable. By passing comprehensive behavior tests and health examinations and by being paired with owners/handlers they can trust, dogs are proving to be invaluable members of today's health care team.

Dogs and cats working their magic on an accepting cast of patients and caregivers.

ADDITIONAL READING

Between Pets and People, the Importance of Animal Companionship by Alan Beck and Aaron Katcher, Pedigree Books, Putnam Publishing Group, New York, 1983.

Guidelines for Animal-Facilitated Therapy Programs, American Veterinary Medical Association Directory, American Veterinary Medical Association, Schaumburg, IL, 1994.

HABIT (Human-Animal Bond) in Tennessee: An Overview, a video by University of Tennessee, distributed by University of Tennessee, Knoxville, TN, and by The Delta Society, Renton, WA, 1989.

"HIV/AIDS and Pet Ownership," brochure by Gloria Dorsey, Caroline Schaffer, James A. Ferguson, Tuskegee University School of Veterinary Medicine, Tuskegee, AL 36088, July 1994.

Know Your Dog—An Owner's Guide to Dog Behavior by Bruce Fogle, Dorling Kindersley, Inc. New York, 1992.

Man and Dog: The Psychology of a Relationship, by Reinhold Bergler, Blackwell Scientific Publications, Oxford, 1989.

PAT at Huntington, A Volunteer Program of Pet-Assisted Therapy, Training Manual by Holli Rfau, Huntington Memorial Hospital, Pasadena, CA, 1990.

Pet Partners Volunteer Training Manual, The Delta Society, Renton, WA, 1993.

Pet Therapy: A Study and Resource Guide for the Use of Companion Animals in Selected Therapies by Phil Arkow. The Humane Society of the Pikes Peak Region, Colorado Springs, CO, 7th Edition, January 1992.

Pets and Mental Health by Odean Cusack, The Haworth Press, New York, 1988.

Pets in People Places: Responsible Pet Ownership in Multi-Unit Housing by Cynthia L. Anderson, Massachusetts Society for the Prevention of Cruelty to Animals, Boston, MA, 1994.

The Tuskegee PUPS Test for Selecting Therapy Dogs, a video by Caroline Schaffer and John Phillips, distributed by Tuskegee University School of Veterinary Medicine, Tuskegee, AL, 1993.

Therapy Dogs: Training Your Dog to Reach Others by Kathy Diamond Davis, Howell Book House, New York, 1992.

Understanding Your Dog by Michael Fox, Coward, McCann, and Geoghegan, Inc., New York, 1972.

Dr. Ernest Rogers obtained his Bachelor of Arts in psychology with emphasis on physiological psychology. He also obtained a Bachelor of Science in biology. Both baccalaureate degrees were obtained at Guelph University, Guelph, Ontario, Canada. In 1991, he graduated with a Doctor of Veterinary Medicine from Tuskegee University, Tuskegee, Alabama. Currently, Dr. Rogers is obtaining his Doctor of Philosophy, with an emphasis in veterinary pharmacology, from Virginia Polytechnical Institute and State University, Blacksburg, Virginia.

The Brain, Biology and Behavior

By Ernest Rogers, BA, Bsc, DVM
Virginia-Maryland Regional College
   of Veterinary Medicine
Virginia Polytechnical Institute
Duckpond Road
Blacksburg, VA 24062-0442

INTRODUCTION

Many individuals, including veterinarians, view behavior solely as a manifestation of learning, socialization and psychology. However, behavior is a final common output of many body systems in concert with previous learning and the environment. Body systems, including the endocrine, cardiovascular and neurological systems (and others) influence the type, display and intensity of behavior. This chapter elucidates the need for a comprehensive view of the brain and body systems as well as for learning and the environment.

Veterinary clinical behavior counseling often deals with the aspects of psychology that have a direct impact on information acquisition-learning! In many instances, behavior is most easily modified, problems are corrected or avoided, and training to a goal most easily accomplished by using learning principles. In fact, most of this book is dedicated to this premise. Although learning principles are very successfully used in most instances, other problems appear to be more resistant to a purely behavioral modification approach. There are a number of reasons for this. First, the principles applied may be incorrect or inappropriate for the situation, the patient or the environment. Second, the problem may be dynamic, complex or deep-seated. This may require medical or drug therapy in addition to behavior modification. Third, the problem may be based on a physiological condition or disease that has little to do with behavior modification. For example, a dog with epilepsy is unlikely to respond to training exercises. This chapter is intended to serve as an introduction to the complex organization and interaction between the biology of the brain and behavior. Some areas, though covered in more detail in other chapters, will be addressed here to demonstrate the role of brain physiology in the expression of behavior.

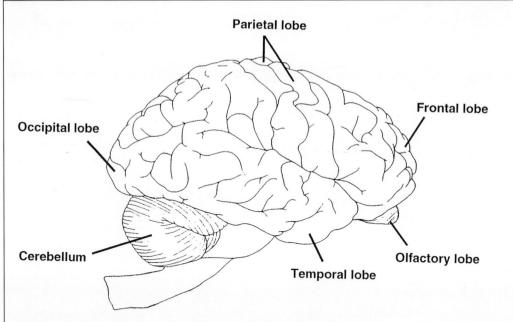

A view of the entire brain from the lateral (side) surface. The lobes described in the text are defined by anatomical landmarks on the surface of the brain. See text for a description of the functions associated with each area.

THE BRAIN

The brain is located within the protective bones of the skull. This organ is of a "jelly like" consistency. The surface of the brain varies in complexity depending on the species.

The brain is organized, grossly, by surface anatomical features. In general, distinct lobes can be visualized from an overall surface view. These features allow some distinction as to functional areas as they relate to the whole brain. The main organizational and "thinking" area of the brain is centered in the frontal lobe. The temporal lobe is associated with the emotional and auditory (hearing) functions. The occipital area is considered the seat of the ability to interpret visual images (sight). The cerebellum acts in concert with the parietal lobe to activate and coordinate movement. The pituitary lobe is the link between the brain and the endocrine system (hormones). The pituitary is found at the base of the brain. This lobe has two distinct parts, the anterior (front) area and the adjacent posterior (back) pituitary area. Both areas are responsible for the release of separate unique hormones that influence other endocrine organs (i.e. pancreas, adrenals and sex organs). This ultimately causes increases or decreases in hormonal levels.

The brain is organized internally into four functionally distinct but interactive levels. The first level of organization is that of the cell unit. The basic cell of the neurological system (brain, spinal cord and peripheral nerves) is called the neuron.

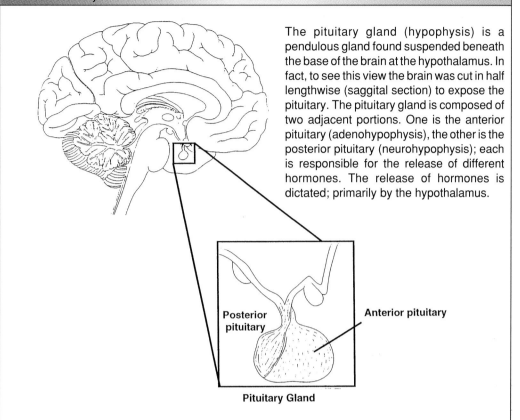

The pituitary gland (hypophysis) is a pendulous gland found suspended beneath the base of the brain at the hypothalamus. In fact, to see this view the brain was cut in half lengthwise (saggital section) to expose the pituitary. The pituitary gland is composed of two adjacent portions. One is the anterior pituitary (adenohypophysis), the other is the posterior pituitary (neurohypophysis); each is responsible for the release of different hormones. The release of hormones is dictated; primarily by the hypothalamus.

Posterior pituitary

Anterior pituitary

Pituitary Gland

Neurons consist of a cell body with two distinct ends, one of which forms a long "wire like" process (the axon). This cell, at its most primitive level, is a communication cell, carrying information from one location to another. The neuron accepts bio-electrical information at one end (dendrite) and transfers this information across its cell body and delivers the information to the next cell through its axon. The distribution of information is therefore from the axon of one cell to the dendrite of the next cell. Information is transferred across a minuscule space (synapse or synaptic gap) between cells by chemicals released by the end of the axon. It is the amount and timing of the chemicals released that conveys information to the dendrite. The chemicals which convey the information by crossing the synapse between cells are termed neurotransmitters. Examples of neurotransmitters that are of particular interest to behaviorists are: serotonin, gamma-amino-butyric-acid (GABA) and dopamine, to name a few.

The second level of organization within the brain is the grouping of "information carrying neurons" into complexes of cables or groups of cell bodies. White matter of the brain is an accumulation of neuronal axons traveling together from their cell bodies to another location. The gray matter of the brain consists of groups of cell bodies located in one common area. Groups of neuronal cell

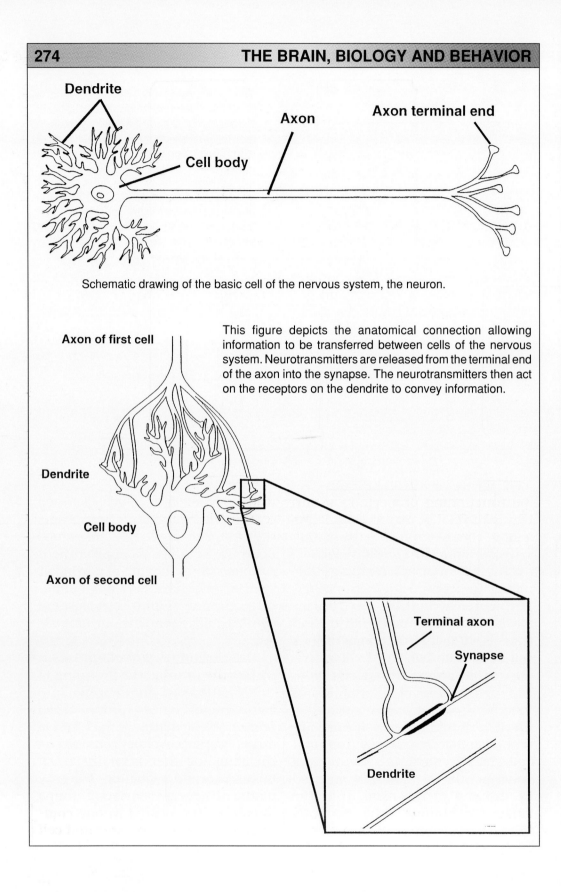

Schematic drawing of the basic cell of the nervous system, the neuron.

This figure depicts the anatomical connection allowing information to be transferred between cells of the nervous system. Neurotransmitters are released from the terminal end of the axon into the synapse. The neurotransmitters then act on the receptors on the dendrite to convey information.

bodies form a nucleus which is a discrete area with specific functions and unique inputs and outputs.

The third level of organization is that of combinations and interactions between larger groupings of nuclei which tend to coordinate and orchestrate specific behaviors. Often, both the second and third levels of organization are redundant, with mirror images of similarly functioning groups of nuclei on both the right and left side of the brain. Examples of grouping of nuclei include the amygdala, hypothalamus or the hippocampus.

A fourth level of organization relates to the complex interactions of the various groupings of areas of the brain that result in a coordinated directed pattern of behavior. This serves the behavioral and survival needs of the animal. The preceding three levels of the brain must be functioning properly to assure that the final common output, behavior, is appropriate and of the correct intensity for the situation. An example of this level of organization is the limbic system, an important area for emotional behavior in both man and animal.

The brain may become dysfunctional at any level of organization. The disturbance may result in bizarre, inappropriate or inconsistent behavior. Hormones can alter the biology and chemistry of the body (and brain) and therefore the expression of behavior. Further, alterations in body chemistry tend to result in behavioral changes. In part, this may explain some strange behaviors (such as pacing and weaving) seen in captive and highly stressed animals. Let's look at some specific behavior problems and how they may be related to brain function or dysfunction.

AGGRESSION

Though aggression may be learned or instinctual, there is a wealth of scientific information indicating that the expression of aggression, the intensity of the aggressive behavior and the initiating events that lead to aggression are associated with discrete areas of the brain.

The part of the brain most commonly thought to be responsible for emotional behaviors (including aggression) in animals is called the limbic system. The limbic system is buried deep in the temporal lobe of both sides of the brain. This system consists of several nuclei that, experimentally, have been associated with aggression.

Damage to the septum (a part of the limbic system) increases the likelihood and severity of attack behavior in animals. This has been termed "septal rage syndrome" and usually consists of biting and scratching attacks directed at some objects. Induced damage to another part ot the limbic system (the ventral nucleus of the hypothalamus) can result in a similar increase in attack behavior. In contrast, another area in the limbic system, the amygdala, is associated with decreased aggression.

Aggression may also be modified by arousal (a function of the part of the brain called the "reticular activating system") and hormonal lev-

If the brain is cut in half widthwise (coronal section) then rotated to see the internal surface, it is possible to see the various groupings of nuclei. At this level of the brain we can see the hippocampus (1), the amygdala (2), and the hypothalamus (3). Note that all of the structures are present on both the left and the right sides of the brain!

els. These can indirectly lead to increased or decreased aggression. Intact males, in general, tend to be more aggressive and more protective (or territorial) than their neutered counterparts. The hormone which appears to modulate this aggression is testosterone. It is for this reason that some practitioners suggest castration as a solution to an aggressive unneutered male. Similarly some female animals have demonstrated increased aggression during periods of estrus (heat) when compared to those in non-estrous periods. Though these hormones predominantly originate from the reproductive organs, the brain modifies the behaviors with respect to the environment, the species involved and the specific situation.

Thus, brain behavior must be considered whenever dealing with an aggressive animal. Behavior modification alone may not be sufficient to correct the situation.

FEEDING BEHAVIOR

Feeding behavior, in part, is controlled by specific regions in the hypothalamus. A "satiation center" can be stimulated to reduce hunger and decrease appetite in an otherwise hungry animal. In a similar fashion, some nuclei of the lateral nucleus of the hypothalamus (hunger center) may be stimulated to increase hunger and feeding behaviors. Hormones also play a role. Insulin and glucagon as well as the nutrient glucose can cause fluctuations in hunger. This can be, to some extent, independent of brain activity.

Pica is a term used to describe the consumption of non-nutritive, non-beneficial, non-food items. For example, the animal that eats sticks or stones receives no benefits for this action. This abnormal behavior may be mediated by a neurologically-related need for oral gratification. If so, successful treatment would require more than just behavioral modification and training.

SEXUAL BEHAVIOR

Sexual behavior has several ties to brain function. Experimental evidence exists to show that lesions in the pre-optic region or anterior hypothalamus results in a decrease in male sexual behavior. In contrast, removal of areas within the temporal lobes (primarily the amygdala) has been associated with significantly increased libido in both males and females.

Pheromones are specific odor-related chemicals given off by animals at specific times during their reproductive cycle. These pheromones communicate information about the receptivity of the female (readiness for mating) or the proximity of a male. These chemicals may act to increase the libido and sexual behavior in both males and females. Olfactory lobes, which are the part of the brain responsible for the sense of smell, are much larger in dogs and cats than the comparative structures in humans. Pheromones, and smell in general, are of significantly more importance to animals than to humans.

Hormones are released and act within the body in response to light cycle, pheromones and ambient temperature, all monitored by the brain.

Hormones are known to change the sexual drive and the associated behaviors. The hormone affecting the sexual drive in males is testosterone, while in females leutinizing hormone, estrogen and progesterone appear to play an active role.

By using drugs (i.e. female hormones in a sexually active male) some behaviors associated with sexual maturity may be reduced. We may also modify sexual development and associated behaviors by castration and ovariohysterectomy (removal of the ovaries and uterus).

Maternal behavior is related to changes in the brain as a result of hormonal fluctuations. Maternal interactions are a result of a combination of changes in brain chemistry (brain environment and neurotransmitters) and body chemistry (hormones). The hormones most notably associated with this behavior are progesterone, estrogen and prolactin. Once prepared by hormones, the individual animal becomes more nurturing. Some typical maternal behaviors include nesting, nursing and increased attentiveness. In the case of pseudopregnancy, all typical maternal behaviors may be seen in the presence of hormonal influences without an actual pregnancy. This demonstrates the powerful influence hormones may have on an animal's behavior.

Though no single aspect of sexual behavior is more important than any other, drug therapy using sex hormones can be useful in modifying some inappropriate behaviors.

COMMUNICATION, OLFACTION AND URINATION AND DEFECATION

Urination, in some circumstances, can be a form of communication in both dogs and cats! This type of communication may tell of one animal's territory or the fact that a female is in heat. As mentioned previously, the olfactory lobes of animals are much larger and more active than those of the human.

The importance of urination or defecation as a form of communication for dogs and cats cannot be overlooked. In most cases, urination and defecation are simply natural body functions. In some cases however, body position, location and quantity of urine or feces can be a form of communication. Inappropriate defecation or urination must therefore be examined as either an inappropriate communication, as a break in house training or possibly as a medical problem.

Hormones may decrease sexual communication and territoriality by their actions on the hypothalamus. Sedatives may decrease arousal associated with marking behavior. Surgically altering an animal's sense of smell (surgical olfactory agnosia) may alleviate problems (such as feline urine spraying) that is unresponsive to other therapies.

OBSESSIVE-COMPULSIVE BEHAVIOR (STEREOTYPY) IN ANIMALS

Obsessive-compulsive (OC) behaviors are those behaviors that are disruptive to the animal's normal ability to function. These behaviors may fall into two general categories.

Some are repetitive, unvarying behaviors that fail to have an apparent function for the animal. Examples include jaw champing (fly snapping) and tail chasing in dogs, and self mutilation (i.e. excessive licking or chewing) in both dogs and cats.

A second category of obsessive-compulsive behaviors are not associated with a repetition of movements. Examples include flank sucking in dogs, standing motionless (freezing) in cats, or staring into space in both dogs and cats.

The signs of OC behavior are as varied as the behaviors themselves. It is likely that multiple brain systems are involved in the development and establishment of these behaviors. Visual hallucinations, as in staring behavior, may be related to dysfunctioning in the visual cortex (occipital brain).

Experimental evidence has been accumulated to indicate that some compulsive behaviors are associated with a disturbance in neurotransmitters scattered throughout the brain. The neurotransmitters most often suggested are serotonin and dopamine. Though much work is yet to be done in this area, there is thus an exciting potential for drug therapy to effectively manage these problems. OC behaviors demonstrate our limited understanding of the brain and its functions as they relate to behavior.

SUMMARY

The examples given above are only a few of the many that demonstrate the complexity of interactions between the brain, biology, learning and behavior. This illustrates the need for a medical and scientific approach to behavioral diagnosis and treatment.

The understanding of the discrete areas of the brain and their effects on behavior is a good beginning but it must must be tempered by the fact that multiple areas of the brain may perform the same functions. One must be aware, that even armed with the most current knowledge, some treatments will fail due to our inability to fully understand the brain, biology, behavior interaction. Further research and clinical experimentation will lead to a better understanding of the brain and associated biology. This is the key to successful diagnosis and treatment.

ADDITIONAL READING

Carlson, N.R., *Physiology of Behavior,* Allyn and Bacon, Inc. Boston, MA, 1977, 650 pp

Hart, B.L. Feline behavior, Veterinary Practice Publishing Company, Culver City, CA, 1978, 110 pp.

Kandel, E.R. ; Schwartz, J.H.; Jessell, T.M.- *Principles of Neural science* (3rd Edition), Appleton and Lange, East Norwalk, CT, 1991, 1135 pp.

Marder, A.R., Voith, V (editors)- *The Veterinary Clinics of North America* (Small Animal Practice), "Advances in small animal behavior," W.B. Saunders Philadelphia, PA, 1991, pp 203-420.

Walker, E.L., *Conditioning and Instrumental Learning,* Brooks / Cole Publishing Company, Belmont CA, 1969, 161 pp.

Index

Dog Books from T.F.H.

The following books are all published by T.F.H. Publications and are recommended to you for additional information:

The Mini-Atlas of Dog Breeds, (H-1106) written by Andrew De Prisco and James B. Johnson. Contains over 400 breeds illustrated with over 700 color photos. This compact but comprehensive book has been praised and recommended by most national dog publications for its utility and reader-friendliness. The true field guide for dog lovers.

Canine Lexicon by Andrew De Prisco and James Johnson, (TS-175) is an up-to-date encyclopedic dictionary for the dog person. It is the most complete single volume on the dog every published covering more breeds than any other book as well as other relevant topics, including health, showing, training, breeding, anatomy, veterinary terms, and much more. No dog book before has ever offered this many stunning color photographs of all breeds, dog sports, and topics (over 1300 in full color).

The Atlas of Dog Breeds of the World (H-1091) by Bonnie Wilcox, DVM, and Chris Walkowicz traces the history and highlights the characteristics, appearance and function of every recognized dog breed in the world. 409 different breeds receive full-color treatment and individual study. Hundreds of breeds in addition to those recognized by the American Kennel Club and the Kennel Club of Great Britain are included—the dogs of the world complete! The ultimate reference work, comprehensive coverage, intelligent and delightful discussions. The perfect gift book. Over 1100 photos in color.

PS-872, 240 pp
178 color illustrations

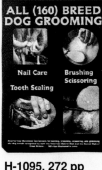

H-1095, 272 pp
over 160 color illustrations

KW-227, 96 pp
100 color photos

H-1016, 224 pp
135 photos

TW-113, 256 pp
200 color photos

H-962, 255 pp
over 200 photos

PS-607, 254 pp
136 B & W photos

TW-102, 256 pp
over 200 color photos

SK-044, 64 pp
over 50 color photos

TS-130, 160 pp
50 color illustrations

H-1061, 608 pp
100 B & W photos

H-969, 224 pp
62 color photos

TS-204, 160 pp
over 50 line drawings

TS-205, 156 pp
over 130 color photos

TS-212. 256 pp
over 140 color photos

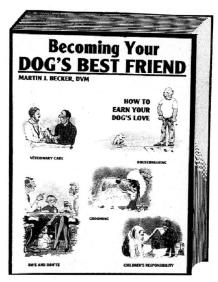

TS-220, 64 pp
over 50 color illustrations

Health and Behavior Books from T.F.H.

Dr. Lowell Ackerman and his team of the nation's leading veterinary specialists offer these excellent titles to assist dog and cat owners in handling medical and behaviorial problems.

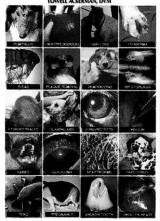

TS-214, 432 pp
over 300 color photos

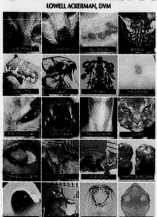

TS-251, 320 pp
over 300 color photos

TS-249, 224 pp
over 200 color
photos